Bury my Heart at Fratton Park

Supporting Portsmouth 1947- 2008

Geoffrey K Fry

COPYRIGHT

GEOFFREY K FRY

2012

PREFACE AND INTRODUCTION

'It was the best of times, it was the worst of times.' These are, of course, the famous opening sentences of *A Tale of Two Cities* by Charles Dickens. The subject was the French Revolution of 1789, and what the Portsmouth born Dickens was saying was that people tended to have two diametrically opposed views of that dramatic event. In terms of 'the best of times,' there could never be a comparable debate about the history of Portsmouth Football Club, since the answer has to be those 'times' when three of the four major honours that Pompey have to their name were won. Despite appearances, I was too young at the time to have any personal knowledge of Portsmouth winning the F. A. Cup in 1939. That said, though, this achievement took place in my lifetime. When Portsmouth won back to back titles in 1949 and 1950, this massive achievement took place in my presence. *I was there*. When Portsmouth won the F. A. Cup in 2008, *I was there too*. Few of us can resist flattery, and over the years many people have urged me to write about Portsmouth on the basis that, though there were still survivors among the ranks of the Pompey supporters from the Golden Age just after the War, nobody could match my memory. Though vain, I resisted the flattery for years because I had too much work to do as a University Professor. Among other duties, this involved writing nine academic books and many research papers, all of which remain unread by millions. What I did learn from that experience was that there is no such thing as an easy book. The problem with writing a book about being a Portsmouth supporter between 1947 - when I started - and 2008 - when Pompey won the F. A. Cup - is one of structure. The past may be another country, but writing up the Golden Age was a straightforward matter for me, and the same could be said of the period down to 1956 when Portsmouth still ranked as a major club. The period between 2002 and 2008 witnessed a minor revival in Pompey's fortunes, which is fresh in the memory, and which had its moment of glory. What, though, do we do with the period 1956-2002? Within that often wretched near half century, there is a choice about what constituted 'the worst of times.' So, the structure that I have adopted is to concentrate on the Golden Age and then the years down to 1956. I then follow this with a broad survey of the period down to 2002, and then I turn in more detail to the seasons down to 2008, when Portsmouth won the F.A. Cup for the second time in the Club's history. It seemed, and seems, a good place to stop. What happened to Portsmouth subsequently would be better dealt with in another book or a second edition of this one, always assuming the author overcomes the problem of getting readers to believe that many of the events took place and that some of the characters involved actually did exist outside of, say, a movie.

In writing this present book, I have been helped and encouraged over the years by many people whom I will now list in alphabetical order: Chris Beckett, David Bell, Terry Clark, Richard Dickason, the Fry Family, Bill Gerrard, Jon Holmes, Zigger Holmes, Zigger Holmes the Second, Roger Holmes, Peter Jeffs, Chris Johnson, Alan Kerby, Derek Kilburn, Jim Riordan, Kevin Ryan, Derek Seymour, Yvonne Seymour, Rick Sweetnam, Marlene Thomas, Paddy Thomas, Barry Thompson. Not all of these people are Portsmouth supporters, and none of them are in any way responsible for the content of this book. This book is dedicated to football widows, especially my wife, and to Pompey fans everywhere, and, especially to the memory of Jim Riordan, a wonderful friend, and a loyal Portsmouth man.

GEOFFREY K FRY

You blocks, you stones, you worse than senseless things!
O you hard hearts, you cruel men of Rome,
Knew you not Pompey?

Julius Caesar

CONTENTS

PART 1 SUPPORTING A MAJOR CLUB: PORTSMOUTH 1947-1956

CHAPTER 1: ZIGGER HOLMES, THE TINN MAN, AND FORTY THOUSAND HUMPHREY BOGARTS

THE ROAD FROM RYDE PIER

'The pub, football, and the family' was what the working class male was interested in, George Orwell reported in *The Road to Wigan Pier*, taking a pleasure, so it seemed, in informing his fellow socially privileged socialists that there was not going to be a proletarian revolution. Orwell was writing in the late 1930s, and as a kind of visitor from another social world. It may well be that the Deep South of England in the 1940s and the first half of the 1950s would have left a different impression on that social observer. Certainly, to judge from the level of attendances, the importance of the cinema could not have been ignored with regard to the War and the years immediately afterwards. French intellectuals later wrote about *film noir* when they analysed the famous movies of that era, and one can see that there were common themes and values in the Bogart classics. That said, though, and without wishing in any way to understate the high quality of the leading films of that era (notably, to cite a superb example, *The Third Man*), 'going to the pictures' was primarily a way of enhancing a life characterised by rationing and austerity. Black and white films for a black and white era. Films, football, fish and chips, and family would be how I would describe what life was like for my working class parents, my sister, and for me in my very happy youth.   My father was one of the few men we knew who was indifferent to the attractions of alcohol; but, like almost every other male at the time he was addicted to cigarettes, which eventually gave him lung cancer and killed him. Outside the family, the love of his life was Portsmouth Football Club. The first season after the Second World War was a good

8

time to fall in love with Pompey, though this was not a matter of calculation. My father had become surrounded at work by Portsmouth supporters, and decided to find out what it was all about, given that few had seemed to care about football when he had lived and worked in Bristol. Whatever the virtues of Bristol, it was not what Brian Clough was later to call a football town. Portsmouth certainly merited that accolade, and Clough praised the Pompey supporters for their intense loyalty, and such fans were numerous also in what could be called the Greater Portsmouth area, and in the Isle of Wight, to which location my father had been sent under the wartime provisions for direction of labour. There was no direction of labour in the opposite direction after the War, and in terms of employment my father always missed Bristol, where a carpenter and joiner could make good money even in the 1930s. There was certainly little in the way of well paid work in the Isle of Wight. So, my father ended up working for the Southern Railway, which company owned the ferry to and from Ryde, where we lived, to Portsmouth Harbour, and cut price fares for my father and his family were among the benefits of being employed by them, and, as it turned out, its successor organisation, British Railways.

So, my father and I could afford to travel regularly to Portsmouth and the home games played at Fratton Park and eventually to the away games in London. Evening games enforced their own timetable, but we tended to set off early for Saturday games anyway, not least in the Golden Age to avoid getting locked out and also to make sure of our favourite perches in the Fratton End, the Portsmouth supporter's idea of Valhalla. Many people now say that there were always Saturday 3 o'clock kick offs, but this was not the case once the clocks changed in the autumn. There were no floodlights before the early 1950s anyway, and until 1956 they were only used for what were literally called floodlight friendlies. By the early 1950s too, newer and larger ships were used as ferries on the Portsmouth run, but, shortly after the War the ferries were paddle steamers which had been among the 'little ships' at Dunkirk. So, we would set off from Ryde Pier, the second longest in England, and once the ferry arrived at Portsmouth Harbour, it was off down the gangplank and on to the jetty and into the railway station, which, in the early days, bore evidence of the wartime bombing raids. It was then two stops along the line to Fratton. As the train approached Fratton Station, if you glanced upwards high to the right you could see the bobbing heads of the people, who, having crossed Fratton Bridge, were making their way to the ground along Goldsmith Avenue. Once we had got off the train and over the railway bridge, we joined them, together with those who had come into Platform 3 on the Brighton train. So many people came off that train that I wondered if there was anybody left to support Brighton's own football team, and years later when I went to see Portsmouth play at the Goldstone Ground the reception that Pompey got as the visiting team was extraordinary. It was not that far along Goldsmith Avenue past the Fratton Goods Yard on one side and the huge pub and then the Danish Bacon Factory on the other before we reached Frogmore Road, and those of us destined for the Fratton End would join the queue to get in. Down the end of Frogmore Road was the main entrance with the words Fratton Park 1898 prominently displayed on the arch. Only one member of the police force was to be seen anywhere, and he was an Inspector stood by a large police car with a microphone, who always told us that the South Stand was full. The orderly nature of the crowd seems remarkable in retrospect, and I have no memory of any of the immature behaviour that is commonplace today. Of course, those seasons just after the War were a good time to be a Pompey supporter, and for me, in particular, football was eventually to be a welcome distraction from life at the grammar school, which I disliked despite the presence of many attractive and intelligent girls.

Football then was by no means the entertainment industry that it is today. There was, of course, no television coverage until the 1950s, and before that snippets on the cinema newsreels were the only pieces of film of the games that were available. The radio had the place that television now has in society, with a commentary on the second half of a Football League game supposed to be the highlight of a Saturday afternoon for people whom we always dismissed as armchair critics. Otherwise, the attention given to football by the B.B.C. monopoly was initially not much more than a reading of the results, and, if you missed that reading, hard luck. The first ever report on what eventually became Sports Report was said to have been of the Portsmouth home game with Huddersfield on 3 January 1948, with John Arlott dashing from Fratton Park down to the Guildhall, or such of it that was left after the wartime bombing raids, to tell the nation how Pompey had won 3-2. The B.B.C.'s West Region eventually covered Portsmouth's away games too, but we were more often dependent on the printed word. Throughout the week, the Portsmouth *Evening News* kept us in touch with what was officially supposed to be happening at the football club, and there were also accounts of midweek games published the next day. Football results were also printed in the stop press section as they came in, even half time scores. Interest in half time scores was such that there was a *Football Mail* scoreboard at the Milton End of Fratton Park, and, when these scores came in, a bloke laboriously filled in the spaces in the same manner as was done at cricket matches. On Saturday, the *Football Mail* sold in the evening would have a blow by blow report of Pompey's game, accompanied by a cartoon of a sailor with thumbs up smiling manically if Portsmouth had won, looking neutral with thumbs level if they had drawn, and the picture of misery with thumbs down if they had lost. On the inside page, the author of the report would write once more about the Club's doings, and how things were. This journalist was called Ranger when we first started going, and he was later replaced by Nimrod, and later still by somebody who styled himself Linesman. Eventually Linesman wrote under his real name, which disappointingly turned out to be Reg Betts. Hollywood would surely have called him something more glamourous. I recall one character played by Bob Mitchum in a Western being called nothing less than Clint Tollinger. Whoever he was, Ranger had the best of things, giving us plenty of good news in the Golden Age. Paper rationing ensured that both the local newspapers and the national ones were thin by the standards of today, though whether they contained less actual information has to be doubted. We learnt to distrust the national newspapers anyway because they favoured the London teams - especially in those days Arsenal - and not surprisingly so since that was where so many potential buyers of the papers lived. One of the Pompey fans that we knew was consumed with hatred of a football writer called Roy Peskett who wrote in *The Daily Mail*, who never seemed to praise Portsmouth, and who, he believed, delighted in their setbacks. My father's solution was for the man to read another newspaper, but the man concerned felt unable to do this because he voted Conservative. Though the voting statistics make it clear that interest in politics was at record levels in the immediate post war period, there was relatively little discussion of the subject on the Isle of Wight ferry that I can recall. An exception occurred when, for no obvious reason, somebody criticised Neville Chamberlain and the Munich Agreement of 1938. One of the many war veterans present responded with the argument that most people at the time had no guts for a fight, and not surprisingly so since nobody in their right mind would want to fight the Wermacht twice. That we knew that the man himself had done just that said a lot for his bravery, though not, given his argument, for his sanity. Some have argued to me that people were less sophisticated and more deferential then than they are now, but many had a wealth of usually unwanted military experience which gets rid of the sophistication argument, and as for deference, throwing out Winston Churchill, the successful wartime leader, at the General Election of 1945 surely was its antithesis. Then again, when Field Marshal Bernard Montgomery made his appearance at Fratton Park as the President of Portsmouth Football Club to say that he was not welcomed would be to put the matter mildly. Some thought this was because he was an Army man in a citadel of the Royal Navy, and others because he was believed to be mad like Churchill, but this distaste seemed to mainly result from the belief that his visits rarely seemed to coincide with Pompey winning. So, on that basis, it seemed to be a case of forget about victory at El Alamein, what about that home draw with Arsenal? The Board of Directors of Portsmouth Football Club did attract respect, and at the time we started to support Pompey there were good reasons for this, given the progress the Club had made during its short history, and obviously because Portsmouth had won the F. A. Cup in 1939. When, though, Harry Wain, one of the Directors, was later found as part of his business activities to have sold dud meat to the Royal Navy, the gaol sentence was widely thought to be wrong. What the Portsmouth fans that we knew wanted was for Wain to be hanged for treason.

When the Club celebrated its Golden Jubilee in 1948, a brief historical booklet was issued to mark the event, though by then we knew quite a bit about Portsmouth's history. Some years later, there were those who believed that Arthur Conan Doyle, the author of the Sherlock Holmes novels, had been a Pompey goalkeeper in the Club's early days, but this does not seem to have been the case. Anyway, my father and I did not need Sherlock Holmes because we had Zigger Holmes, a man from Sandown whom we were told, rightly or not, had never missed a Pompey home game this side of Portsmouth entering the Football League in 1920. Thus, we learnt from him that it took Pompey just four seasons to get themselves promoted from the Third Division (South) as Champions. In the 1923-24 season, Portsmouth scored 87 goals, 28 of them credited to Billy 'Farmer' Haines. Zigger was second to none in his admiration for 'Farmer' or, for that matter, in his regard for the Manager, John McCartney. What mattered most, though, was that Pompey only let in 30 goals that season. Zigger's line was that the popular preference was for goal scoring centre forwards, and the more the merrier, but he himself gave priority to having a sound defence. His reasoning was that football was a low scoring game, and the fewer goals conceded meant the fewer needed for victory or simply to avoid defeat. Only three seasons later, Portsmouth were runners up in the Second Division, and, thus promoted to the First Division, as the top flight of English football was then called. Pompey had the best defensive record in the top two Divisions, which bore out the validity of Zigger's Law of Defence. When it came to scoring, once more 'Farmer' Haines was the star of the show. In the vital match on the final day of the season, namely 7 May 1927, Pompey kicked off a quarter of an hour after their rivals, Manchester City, who duly defeated Bradford City 8-0. The Fratton Park crowd learnt this with Pompey leading

Preston 4-1. 'One more, Farmer' was the cry. Haines, who had already scored a hat trick, added a fourth to take his total to 40 from 42 games. Zigger told us that the 27,000 Portmouth fans present sang 'To be a Farmer's Boy.' Pompey had been promoted because the team had a better goal average than Manchester City, the margin being .005 of a goal. When ill health forced McCartney to retire, his successor as Manager was Jack Tinn, who also ran the finances with the aid of his daughter, and the pair of them were said to never waste a penny. According to Zigger, Portsmouth only survived early on in the top flight by tiring out the opposition by organising trips around the Dockyard for the visitors to see the Royal Navy, then the biggest navy in the world. Pompey finished a distant fourth in the 1930-31 season, but, after the early struggles, it was mostly a tale of mid table anonymity, aside from the 1937-38 season, when Portsmouth did not win a match until November, but then rallied to finish nineteenth. Where Portsmouth did shine was in the F. A. Cup, reaching the Final three times in the inter war period. In 1929, Bolton beat Pompey 2-0, with the losers being handicapped by an injury to left back Tommy Bell. Then in 1934, Pompey were leading Manchester City 1-0 when Jimmy Allen, the England international centre half was injured. He had previously marked Tilson out of the game, but in his absence Tilson got the equaliser, and then the winner for City, with the returning Allen still concussed. Allen was subsequently transferred to Aston Villa for a record fee, and the money spent on the North Stand. In 1939, Pompey reached the Cup Final once more. According to the Captain, Jimmy Guthrie, they were confident that it would be third time lucky. They certainly took no chances, more or less presenting Chelsea with vital points to avoid relegation in the league game a week before the Final. It was so obvious what was happening, according to Guthrie, that the Chelsea crowd sang 'Dear old pals,' and Jack Tinn was worried about a Football League inquiry into the match plainly being thrown, but nothing happened. Wolves were red hot favourites to win the 1939 Cup Final, and understandably so, given that Pompey had finished seventeenth in the League. The Portsmouth team was Walker, Morgan, Rochford, Guthrie, Rowe, Wharton, Worrall, McAlinden,

Anderson, Barlow, and Parker. Much was made later of Jack Tinn wearing his lucky spats, but then he was said to have also worn them in 1929 and 1934. Rather more important seems to have been that this time Pompey were able to keep a full complement of players on the field. Whatever the reasons, which may well have included complacency on the part of Wolves, Portsmouth won 4-1, with Parker (2), Barlow, and Anderson scoring the goals. The Second World War began the following September, and English professional football was suspended for the duration of the War, and the F. A. Cup was not competed for again until the 1945-46 season. Hence the familiar quiz question: which club were the holders of the F. A. Cup for the longest period of time? The answer was Portsmouth.

GETTING STARTED WITH POMPEY

'Give me the child until he is seven, and we will give you the man.' So runs the Jesuit boast, and it could have been that of my parents too, who rammed the values of the 'respectable' skilled working class down my throat from birth. Devotion to Portsmouth Football Club came a little later, given that I was nine by the time that I saw my first match. As far as the 1946-47 season was concerned, down to and including the Christmas fixtures, it looked as if Portsmouth were heading for relegation, which I became very worried about once I found out what it was. A run of seven games without defeat eventually turned things around. The winter of 1947 was a terrible one even in the Deep South of England, and postponements meant that Pompey played no less than six games in May to finally complete their fixtures. On 3 May 1947, I saw my first Portsmouth game at Fratton Park. Pompey drew 1-1 with Wolves. Duggie Reid scored for Pompey, and Denis Wescott equalized for the visitors. The attendance was 37, 711, and most present were outraged by the violence displayed by Stan Cullis, the Wolves centre half and captain, in his dealings with the local hero, and soon to be mine too, Reid. Cullis was at the end of his career, and, it seemed, determined to seek revenge for having been denied a Cup winners medal by Pompey's victory in the 1939 Final, as well as ensuring that Wolves won the title. Wolves were to fall one point short of their

15

target. The noise level emanating from the Fratton End in which we were located was deafening, and I was caught up in the atmosphere, caring passionately that Portsmouth held out, which they did. That one of Pompey's players, Jimmy Scoular, had more than matched Cullis in combativeness did not seem to matter to the Portsmouth supporters, and to my amazement Cullis was later supposed to have shed tears of contrition. When learning of this, the Pompey fans were proud to insist that Scoular would never do the same. Portsmouth had only reached the Fourth Round of the F. A. Cup, but the league position was in the end respectable. Of the 42 First Division games played, Pompey won 16, drew 9, and lost 17, thus obtaining 41 points, and finishing in twelfth place. Pompey had scored 66 goals, and conceded 60. Reid had scored no less than 29 of Pompey's goals, thus equalling Jimmy Easson's record for a top flight season established in that of 1930-31. Nobody has done as well as this for Portsmouth at this level since. To most people's surprise, Jack Tinn resigned as Pompey's Manager at the end of the 1946-47 season. Zigger Holmes told us that Tinn had chosen to go of his own volition rather than being forced out once the Football League authorities discovered that the inducements given to Jimmy McAlinden to persuade him to return to Portsmouth from Northern Ireland after the War had breached the prevailing rules. Tinn was replaced by 'Bow Tie' Bob Jackson, the Chief Scout.

Like its predecessor, the first and second halves of the 1947-48 season were different in character, with the threat of relegation hovering over Portsmouth all the way down to and including the Christmas games. The season before had witnessed two defeats by Arsenal in the relevant fixtures, and this time the two Christmas matches with Manchester United were lost. That meant that Pompey had eleven defeats to their name already. The first of these defeats came on the opening day of the season when Harry Potts scored in the first minute for Burnley, who then, with their defence marshalled by a large central defender called Alan Brown, contained Pompey with some comfort. I still have this mental picture of a forlorn last minute cross from Reid which the relentless Burnley defence snuffed out to ensure their 1-0 victory. Things then picked up at home, with Stoke beaten

16

3-0, and the reigning Champions, Liverpool defeated 1-0 (Reid scoring), and Sheffield United thrashed 6-0 (Jack Froggatt scoring a hat trick), and Charlton were also beaten 3-1. Pompey won away at Huddersfield by 2-0, which mattered because they were relegation rivals, and also recorded a 2-1 win at Middlesbrough, but, aside from a surprising 0-0 away draw at Arsenal, who were to be Champions, the away games tended to be lost. There was also a spectacular home defeat to be endured at the hands of Aston Villa on 8 November 1947, with Trevor Ford scoring all of Villa's four goals in a remarkable display of what it meant to be a traditional centre forward. The Manchester United defeat by 3-1 on 27 December 1947 was to be the last time that Pompey lost at home in a First Division match for exactly twenty one months, but at the time, of course, nobody knew this, and a welcome six game unbeaten run starting with a 2-1 win at Sheffield United on New Year's Day 1948 banished relegation fears. Peter Harris, one of the scorers, was later to say of the Sheffield away game that, once Pompey took the lead, every time he got the ball he ran as hard as he could into the Sheffield half to try and relieve the pressure. Pompey did the double over Liverpool for the second and last time in the twentieth century as a consequence of their 3-0 away win at Anfield on 31 January 1948. It seems worth noting that in the home game with Liverpool, Pompey attracted an attendance of 33,000, but that recorded in the Anfield return game was only 23,097. Though Pompey did not last beyond the Fourth Round of the F. A. Cup once more, everybody seemed pleased that Portsmouth finished eighth in the First Division, winning 19 games, drawing 7, and losing 16 times, thus securing 45 points. Pompey scored 68 goals and conceded only 50. Portsmouth were on the brink of greatness, but I have no memory of anybody predicting this.

I had now seen a complete season of top class football, and I had got used to the atmosphere of Fratton Park. I was a spectator in every sense. I was very young, and I never said anything, watching the games carefully, and listening to what people said about them, remembering what they said afterwards. The games were discussed on the ferry back home, with everybody chipping in, apart from me, of course, and I remember no serious disputes. We were literally in the same boat. Everybody I knew in my home area supported Portsmouth, apart from people who came from other parts of the country and whose allegiance to their original clubs precluded taking up with Pompey. On this basis, we got to know a couple of Manchester United supporters. In those days, there was almost none of this modern behaviour of people supposedly supporting clubs they had no local or family connection with, although I recall one character who contrived to support the London club of the moment. He was written off as a fool, with people deliberately asking him about the fortunes of the clubs he had discarded, and asking him who would be the favoured club next week or possibly even tomorrow. The ranks of the Portsmouth supporters inevitably had a fool or two among them too, and I recall one man who once risked criticising Duggie Reid on the basis that when he himself had played for Sandown in the Isle of Wight his own shot had been harder than that of Reid. 'Sign him up' went the cry, and the clown concerned did not know how to handle the amused contempt that greeted him for years afterwards. The banter usually tended to be good natured and I recall no violence either on the ferry or at the ground or even the threat of it, with the exception of the Cullis incident, and, as I record later, there was a demonstration at a Christmas 1951 game. What I must not do is to overpraise the people I knew, though so many were admirable. In the classic film, *Build My Gallows High*, it was suggested to Bob Mitchum that 'Nobody's all evil.' Of the murderous female concerned, Mitchum commented: 'She gets close.' On the same basis, 'Nobody's all good.' The Portsmouth fans of this time had their virtues, but as I will show some of them were to come to show another side to their face.

Like the movies, football lit up the immediate post war world. To borrow book titles from Portsmouth's very own Charles Dickens, if these were *Hard Times* many had seen harder ones, and they had learnt not to have *Great Expectations*. The experience of the War hung over everything, and not surprisingly so given the state that Portsmouth was in after the bombing raids and the lengthy roll calls of death on the war memorials in Guildhall Square, and the rows of war disabled given special

18

viewing areas just inside the main entrance to Fratton Park. Two World Wars and a Depression in between were written all over the faces of the Pompey crowd, with their hats and caps and dark clothing and mackintoshes, and, above all, their faces lined with experience. In this context, while nobody would pretend that whether Pompey won or lost did not matter to men for whom Portsmouth Football Club was in many respects at the centre of their lives, too many of them had learnt the hard way that Bill Shankly could only have been joking when he said that 'football isn't a matter of life and death: it's more important than that.' It was not just that I was young, but everybody seemed so old even in retrospect, with the exception of some of the sailors, whose white topped caps, sometimes in clusters, were easily picked out among the crowd. In later life, I never discussed the Good Old Days, unless asked to do so by younger fans, and then I kept it brief. That said though, nobody who was there the Fratton Park of those years immediately after the War could ever forget the experience, with the swaying crowds and the huge wall of sound as the Pompey Chimes boomed out from the throats of as often as not 40,000 people, the vast majority of whom looked like Humphrey Bogart, as if they had lived too much, and too soon.

CHAPTER 2: KINGS OF ENGLAND: PORTSMOUTH IN THE 1948-49 AND 1949-50 SEASONS

PROGRAMME NOTES

One of the first things that we always did when we got to Frogmore Road was to buy the official programme. This had a print of H.M.S. Victory on the cover, and, because of paper rationing, it was a very thin affair, mostly consisting of adverts, and with little information in it. The visiting team was always welcomed, and the Board of Directors were always listed. They were just names to us, though we all knew that Vernon Stokes was the Chairman, and the eventually notorious Harry Wain was on the list too, until at the end of the 1949-50 season when they were suspended for a year because of being involved in the McAlinden affair. They were eventually restored to the Board, thus rejoining the likes of Stephen Cribb, John Privett, H. J. Hiley Jones, and my favourite character, Sid Leverett, whom we learnt had been a deep sea diver. The modern cult of the Manager did not exist in those days, and we saw little of Bob Jackson, who held the job from 1947 to 1952. He would talk to Ranger fairly regularly about the way things were going, but there was nothing comparable with the present day news conferences, and Jackson never paced up and down the touchline during the game in the modern manner. My recollection is that 'Bow Tie Bob' used to sit with the Directors during the game. There were no technical areas and no substitutes, and there was just a trainer to run on with the magic sponge in case of injury. There was no fourth official. The linesmen were simply called that, and the referee usually had a relatively easy time of it in controlling the game as this was still a disciplined society, and the rules treated as legitimate behaviour what was often not far short of unarmed combat. I would also guess that the football itself was slower than now, not least because of the playing conditions, though the Fratton Park pitch was of a much better quality than those of the

London grounds we visited. The best referee of that time was generally thought to be Mervyn Griffiths, and the worst somebody we always referred to as Vickery of Bristol, who always wore a pained smile as if perennially suffering from piles.

The players were subject to wage restrictions, known as the maximum wage, which not all clubs paid fully, though Portsmouth did do so. The pathetic nature of the rewards even several years later were summed up for me by a remark by Reg Flewin to Derek Dougan that living in a place with such a pleasant climate as Portsmouth was worth a couple of quid a week to you. Players were also tied to the Club under the retain and transfer system, and, further than this, they tended to live in rented accomodation owned by the Club. Some players lived close to Fratton Park, notably in Milton Road, and others would travel in on public transport. Len Phillips, for instance, would come in on the bus from Copnor, and then walk down the road to the ground with his boots around his neck. My father disapproved of the maximum wage because being a footballer was a short career and he thought that people should be paid what they were worth on the basis that 'the labourer is worthy of his hire,' which was a quote from The Bible that you never hear these days. My father was also against the retain and transfer system on the basis that you should be free to work for who you chose. Nobody else that we knew shared his opinion. One reason for this was that the Players Union was led at the time by Jimmy Guthrie. Though his Pompey link would normally have overidden any other consideration, Guthrie was correctly believed to be a Communist, and, so, he was distrusted. A second reason was that there was no sense of a shortage of talent at that time, and if the conditions of service were that bad why did so many sign up? These rules were not a secret. A third reason was jealousy of the fame of the players on the part of some supporters, who seemed to dislike them being somebodies when they remained nobodies. A fourth reason was that if it was a free for all then the best supported clubs would monopolise the talent and win everything. Since Portsmouth were one of the dozen best supported clubs in English football at the time, my father was not worried about this, pointing out that clubs like Arsenal seemed to do well enough even under the present system, and what did outfits like Brighton contribute anyway? With football booming in terms of attendances, though, nothing seemed likely to change in the near future.

In the middle of the programme, the teams were listed in the 2-3-5 formation that had actually been abandoned in the 1920s, with a goalkeeper, two full backs, three half backs, and five forwards. In principle, this led to individual battles between, say, the centre half on one team who was designated to mark the other team's centre forward, and the right half would deal with the inside left, and the left half would mark the inside right, and the full backs would be responsible for cutting out and often cutting down the wingers, who were styled outside right and outside left.

With the centre half having long since been translated into a third back, the formation later came to be portrayed in terms of a W or WM, and as being unimaginative and rigidly adhered to. If it was that universal a formation, though, how was it that some clubs had a deserved reputation for fielding defensive teams? We have already mentioned Burnley in this respect, and, of course, it was always supposed to be 'Lucky Arsenal' who relied on defence and counter punching their way to victory even at home. Bolton were formidable too. With the Cold War becoming ever more threatening, I remember somebody asking how the hell we would stop the Red Army if it came to it, and one wit suggested the Bolton defence. So, the conventional format placing emphasis on attack was not always observed, and players like Wilf Mannion, Len Shackleton, and Manchester United's Jimmy Delaney were likely to appear anywhere, sometimes causing havoc, and not always to the advantage of their own team. As far as Pompey were concerned, in their title winning seasons I would describe them as playing winning football rather than entertaining football, and Portsmouth played more entertaining stuff at times in the later 1951-52 and 1954-55 seasons when, of course, nothing was won. As for the formation in the title winning years, I would say that Pompey commonly used four defensive outfield players: namely the full backs, the redoubtable Flewin, and

Dickinson. Scoular and Phillips ran what would now be called the midfield, along with Barlow when used, as indeed he often was in the 1948-49 season. In both title winning seasons, Reid was absent much more often than many later remembered, and he was a more sophisticated player anyway than his traditional centre forward reputation suggested. Clarke was not a conventional number 9 either, being a subtle footballer and not remotely the battering ram type, and, alongside Reid especially, would often play in a withdrawn role. Harris and Froggatt were so much more than conventional wingers. I would not wish to suggest that Portsmouth operated 4-2-4 or 4-3-3 formations years before they became the fashion, but it was nearer to 4-3-3 than WM much of the time, and with the emphasis on a sound and uncompromising defence.

If asked to name the Portsmouth team in the 1948-49 and 1949-50 seasons, most people would list them in the conventional format and the team sheet would read Butler; Rookes, Ferrier; Scoular, Flewin, Dickinson; Harris, Reid, Clarke, Phillips, Froggatt. They would be mostly right, but the details were different in important ways, and the best way to deal with the subject would seem to be to copy the notes about the players of the kind that were in the programmes of the time, only adding much more information than space permitted in those days, and, of course, with the advantage of knowing how it all ended. It had better be emphasised that as far as the 1948-49 season was concerned, none of the Portsmouth players were full internationals, and even by the end of the 1949-50 season only three (Dickinson, Harris, Froggatt) had been so honoured when playing for Pompey. Though, as might be expected with Portsmouth being a citadel of the Royal Navy, the Pompey supporters were patriotic, most of them were ambivalent about international calls for our players, and for two reasons. One was that the club and international fixtures often clashed, and you could be left without your best players. The second reason was that the selection was made by the International Committee of the Football Association, the members of which were widely regarded, with every justification, as fools. Until the task of running the England team was handed over from these clowns to

23

Alf Ramsey, the selection process was so amateurish that England's results were no guide to the overall state of English football.

As far as Pompey were concerned, the international selectors tended to leave Bob Jackson in peace to select the team of his choice, and the main players available were as follows.

Butler. Ernie Butler was the only Pompey player who was ever present in the title winning seasons in all of Portsmouth's League and F. A. Cup games.   In his career, Butler, originally signed from Bath City, played 222 League games for Pompey, all of them in the top flight, plus 18 Cup games. He was a very tall goalkeeper, authoritative in the air, and an assured shot stopper. His kicking and distribution were both excellent. Nobody thought that Butler was brilliant, but he was a safe keeper, very reliable on a week to week basis.   Butler conceded less than a goal a game in the League in the two title winning seasons, and the only reason why he was not later as revered by Pompey fans as I consider he should have been was that he gave his poorest performance for Portsmouth in the defeat in the F. A. Cup semi final of 1949, and, unlike me, many never forgave him for that.

Rookes. Phil Rookes was signed originally from Bradford City and he was to play 113 League games for Portsmouth, plus 7 F. A. Cup games.   In the 1948-49 season he played 25 League games, and in the following season just 3.   He could play as either a right back or left back, but all of these particular appearances were at right back.   He broke an ankle in the Stockport Cup game in January 1949 and that was more or less the end of his first team career.   Rookes was a sound, steady, reliable, unruffled back, with good distribution of the ball from defence.

Hindmarsh. Contrary to legend, Bill Hindmarsh played right back more times than anybody else in the two title winning seasons. Hindmarsh only played 55 League and 5 Cup games for Portsmouth, but 44 of those League appearances were in the 1948-49 and 1949-50 seasons. The wonderfully named Jasper Yuell was the original replacement for Rookes, but his poor display in the Highbury semi final in 1949 meant that he was little used again, and in came the ultra reliable Hindmarsh, whom I never saw bettered by any winger, and he was also Rookes's equal when it came to distribution.

Ferrier. Harry Ferrier was originally signed from Barnsley and he was to play 241 League games and 16 Cup games for Portsmouth. Ferrier was at left back for all but 2 of Pompey's League games in the 1948-49 season and an ever present in the second title winning season. He also played in all the Cup games. Ferrier was another player who played extremely badly in the 1949 semi final. This was very much out of character, because he was normally the soul of consistency. In former times, football writers used to describe players like Ferrier as having an educated left foot, contrasting, presumably, with an ignorant rignt foot. Ferrier's ball control and distribution with that left foot was immaculate, and so was his positional sense. He was an adept penalty taker, sending curling lobs in the manner of Johnnie Giles just under the crossbar. Unlike Giles, Ferrier never missed a penalty in a competitive match.

Scoular. Jimmy Scoular was originally signed from Gosport, where he was in the Royal Navy. At first, Scoular only played for Portsmouth by permission of the Navy because he was in prison for various disciplinary offences. If you believed some people, Scoular committed so many offences against naval discipline that his service contrived to link together the Second World War and the Korean War, but, sadly, this tale was an exaggeration. Nonetheless, Scoular's war service proved to be more extensive than it needed to be, which was surprising in some ways given that those who knew Scoular told me that off the field he was a quiet man, and, unusually for a Scot, he drank very little. When it came to football, though, his behaviour was combative, and I remember being told that when Scoular was later at Bradford he would get himself into the mood for a game by savagely kicking the wall of the dressing room. Scoular played 247 League games for Portsmouth, plus 21 Cup games. Scoular played in every Pompey game in the 1948-49 season, though he was to miss 6 games in the 1949-50 season, including vital ones because of disciplinary offences. As a player, Scoular combined the talents of a rugged ball winner with the gifts of a world class passer of the ball, with the accuracy of his long passing being as good or better than I have ever seen, even now. If I had to find a comparable player from more recent times, it would be his fellow Scot, Graeme Souness. Scoular relished his reputation of being a hard case. Duncan Edwards famously said that Scoular was the hardest and best tackler he ever played against. According to Jackie Milburn, who plainly did not enjoy later playing with him in the same team at Newcastle, Scoular always said that he did not start any trouble but he always finished it. Scoular was talking nonsense. He would not stay on the field for five minutes these days.

Flewin. Reg Flewin was a Portsmouth man who played for his home town club in 152 League games and 21 Cup ties. In the 1948-49 season, he only missed 3 games, but in the second title winning season he was absent for 18 games, at one time for illness, and latterly because of injury. Flewin was the centre half and captain in the title winning seasons, and in my opinion the most important player that Pompey had at that time. Flewin was a tall, powerfully built man, who had been a boxing champion when serving in the Royal Marines. Flewin was the toughest man in the team, though it was Scoular who had the reputation. As a central defender, he was domineering in the air, and I retain this picture in my mind of his large red neck thrusting forward as he headed the ball clear. His distribution of the ball was excellent, and so was his reading of the game. Flewin was a commanding figure. That Flewin never played for England aside from wartime games was explained by the talents of his main rival, Neil Franklin. To be fair, at the time that mattered most, the gifted Leon Leuty of Derby also remained uncapped because of Franklin's consistency.

Dickinson. Jimmy Dickinson was a Hampshire man and played for Portsmouth in 764 League games (a club record) and in 64 Cup games. Dickinson missed only one game in the 1948-49 season and only two in the second title winning season. Dickinson remains the most famous player ever to have played for Pompey, winning no less than 48 England caps. Dickinson was later commonly referred to as Gentleman Jim because he was never booked as a player, and many later treated him as symbolising Pompey's title winning team. This was misleading because no team of Dickinsons ever won anything that mattered. Jimmy's defensive abilities were excellent, and the timing of his tackling was exemplary, and, as far as distribution was concerned, he was very skilled at keeping possession. The sweeper did not exist in football at this time, but Jimmy would have been ideal to play that role. As it was, normally playing in a withdrawn role anyway, Dickinson was the ideal man to have at the left side of the commanding Flewin. Jimmy was a vital member of the team, and served as Flewin's ideal lieutenant.

Harris. Peter Harris was a Portsmouth man and fan who played for Pompey in 479 League games (194 goals) and in 35 Cup ties (17 goals). This goal scoring record for a winger was extraordinary, and that Harris only played for England twice was largely explained by the fact that he had to compete with Matthews and Finney for the right wing position. Harris was two footed, and, even now, I have never seen a faster football player than him. Harris played 40 games in each of the title winning seasons.

Reid. Duggie Reid was a huge Scot whom Portsmouth signed from Stockport immediately after the War. Near the end of Reid's life, with the great man gravely ill, the Supporters Club resolved to ease his discomfort by buying a chair large enough to comfortably accommodate him. This search took a long time. In his prime, Reid often looked like he had been carved out of rock, and, of course, he needed to be given the treatment routinely handed out to him. Reid had a good temperament, though I did see him once try to punch one tormentor. He missed. Reid played 309 League games for Portsmouth, as well as 14 Cup ties. In the 1948-49 season, he played 29 times, and 27 times in the second title winning season. Reid was a magnificent header of the ball, and he had a ferocious shot in either foot, only matched in my experience by Peter Lorimer of Leeds.

Barlow. Bert Barlow was the only man in Portsmouth's history to win both a title winner's medal and a F. A. Cup medal with Pompey. Barlow was signed from Wolves in 1939, and, all told, he played 105 League games for Pompey and 11 Cup ties. Few remember that he played 29 times in the 1948-49 season, before being transferred early the next season. Barlow was a very skilled and resilient inside forward, but he was another who had a poor game in the Highbury semi final.

Clarke. Ike Clarke was signed from West Brom in 1947 as a centre forward after Portsmouth had failed to persuade Tommy Lawton to come to Fratton Park. Clarke was to play 116 League games for Pompey and 13 Cup ties. Clarke played 24 times in the 1948-49 season, and 37 times in that of 1949-50. Clarke made full use of his excellent ball control, not least in distribution. Clarke was a very good finisher, and I never saw him miss in a one to one confrontation with a goalkeeper, always being able to better his adversary.

Phillips.   Len Phillips was a one club man who played 243 League games for Portsmouth as well as 18 Cup ties. He made 40 appearances in the 1948-49 season and 34 in the second title winning season. Phillips was the most technically gifted player that I have ever seen play for Portsmouth, and he was outstanding in this respect even in the context of the title winning team. Phillips was a player of vision, and he possessed all of the creative talents. Phillips was what in those days was called a schemer and who these days would be termed a playmaker; a ball holding player who could open up defences from midfield. Besides considerable skill, he was two footed, and he had pace and possessed a very hard shot. Phillips only played for England 3 times.

Froggatt.   Jack Froggatt played 280 League games for Portsmouth as well as 24 Cup ties. In the 1948-49 season, Froggatt made 41 appearances and 39 in the next season. Jack played for England 13 times, mostly later in his career at centre half, but in the immediate post war years, being two footed, he was to be found in any of the forward positions, eventually making the outside left position his own. He had pace, power,

28

and considerable heading ability as well, and some thought that he could match the legendary Cliff Parker in the accuracy of his crosses. Froggatt was physically formidable, and more than able to deal with the violence dealt out to him by the full backs of those days. I recall that in one game against Blackpool, tired of the ankle tapping antics of Eddie Shimwell, Froggatt suddenly turned round and, to the delight of the Pompey supporters, kicked Shimwell, who went down in agony. The referee did nothing, presumably either because he did not see the incident, or because he thought Shimwell had asked for it.

Pickett. Reg Pickett played 123 League games for Portsmouth plus 5 Cup ties. He made his debut in the 1949-50 season, playing 14 times and getting a title winning medal. Pickett was a versatile player and a vital one that season in covering for injured and absent players, usually in midfield.

Spence. Like Pickett, Bill Spence played an important supporting role in the 1949-50 title winning season, in his case covering impressively for Flewin. Spence only played 19 times for Pompey altogether, all of them in the League, but 14 of those were in the second title winning season. He was a very reliable defensive player.

Thompson. Bill Thompson only played 40 times for Portsmouth in the League, and in a couple of Cup ties. He played 3 games in the 1948-49 season and 9 in that of 1949-50. He mostly played in central defence and on the left side of defence. As we shall see, Thompson had his day of glory as a goalscorer. Thompson was the only player of Pompey's Golden Age that I ever met. One thing that he did tell me was that having played against Matthews and Finney, he could anticipate what they were going to do even though he could do nothing about it. Thompson said of Len Phillips that he had no idea what he was going to do, *and* he could do nothing about it.

These days there are many black and foreign players in English football, but this was not the case just after the War. A West Indian forward with pace and skill called Lindy Delaphena played twice in the first title winning season, and five times in that of 1949-50, and also scored in his only F. A. Cup appearance. A Swedish attacking player called Dan Ekner played five games for Pompey in the 1949-50 season, without scoring. Many people still associate the Scottish international full back Jimmy Stephen with the title winning team, but in fact he only made one appearance, and that was in the 1949-50 season.

CHAMPIONS OF ENGLAND: THE 1948-49 SEASON

In August 1948, at the outset of the best season that Portsmouth were ever to have in their history, I have no memory of anybody saying that Pompey were going to be English Champions. After what came to be known thereafter as the Jubilee Match at Fratton Park against Arsenal in late November, everybody thought that we would be Champions, but not before that. An opening day draw at Preston 2-2 (Reid and Barlow scoring) seemed no more than a reasonable start, especially when Zigger Holmes informed us that we had not lost at Deepdale since 1925, and that we usually drew there. I seemed to remember that we had won at Preston the previous season, with Froggatt getting one of the goals, but I did not press the matter. The Preston away draw proved to be the first of thirteen opening games without defeat, a run which established the base from which Portsmouth advanced to take the title. In that early run, Pompey won all seven of their home games. I will now list the thirteen games in date order.

21 Aug 1948	Preston [A]	2-2
25 Aug 1948	Everton [H]	4-0
28 Aug 1948	Burnley [H]	1-0
1 Sept 1948	Everton [A]	5-0
4 Sept 1948	Stoke [A]	1-0
8 Sept 1948	Middlesbrough [H]	1-0
11 Sept 1948	Charlton [H]	3-1
15 Sept 1948	Middlesbrough [A]	1-1

18 Sept 1948   Man City [A] 1-1

25 Sept 1948   Sheffield Utd [H] 3-0

2 Oct 1948   Newcastle [H] 1-0

9 Oct 1948   Aston Villa [A] 1-1

16 Oct 1948   Sunderland [H] 3-0

The Newcastle game was the hardest fought of the seven home matches. Beforehand, we were concerned about whether or not we would get into the ground, despite, as usual, setting off early: but, as it turned out, we got into the Fratton End as part of the 44,000 crowd. Phillips got the winning goal. Flewin was in commanding form, and, indeed, needed to be to subdue his direct opponent, Jackie Milburn, whom I saw play for the first time. Reid got a hat trick against Charlton, one of the goals coming from a penalty. The visiting goalkeeper, Sam Bartram seemed to brace himself for a Reid thunderbolt, but Duggie just slipped the ball into the net. Each visiting team tended to have at least one outstanding player. In the case of Sheffield United, it was Jimmy Hagan, and Middlesbrough had two such stars in Wilf Mannion and George Hardwick. Mannion was commonly recognised as a genius in terms of ball control and insightful play. Hardwick had been England's left back and captain. It was always said of him that he was 'a ladies man' with the accent on the plural. I had no idea what this meant at this time, but in later life I learnt that he had been one of the lovers of Ava Gardner, the Hollywood actress. Hardwick went on record as later saying that at 35 footballers were washed up and might as well be shot, but plainly he had other marketable skills. I also noted that however well or badly some clubs were doing they were treated with respect. This was especially true of Aston Villa, though I knew they had not won a major honour since 1920. Whether or not Pompey would themselves go on to win more silverware then came into question when the run of thirteen games without defeat came to a halt not merely with a 3-0 setback at Wolves, and four further games without another victory. Obdurate Bolton got a 0-0 draw at Fratton Park, the only time that Pompey did not score at home that season, and classy

31

Blackpool got a draw, this time 1-1, while away Portsmouth lost 3-1 at Liverpool and then by the only goal at Derby. Only Harris scored in this lean spell, and Clarke was introduced into the forward line, initially at the expense of Reid, only missing a couple of games during the rest of the season.

It had become clear that the season turned on the visit of Arsenal, the reigning Champions, on 27 November 1948. This game was singled out as marking the Golden Jubilee of Portsmouth Football Club, and the celebrations were elaborate by the standards of the time. Past Pompey players all the way back to the original team of 1898 came on to the field to be presented to the Club's President, Field Marshal Montgomery, and they were given a rapturous reception by the 42,500 crowd. My recollection remains that before the game few Pompey supporters expected a home win. The thinking was that Pompey's recent form had failed to live up to the expectations generated by the excellent start to the season. Further than this, Arsenal had a good record at Fratton Park, with Pompey only having beaten them three times in fourteen visits. In the current campaign, Arsenal had not conceded more than one goal in any League game. Well, they did this time. In the conventional line up of those days, the Portsmouth team was Butler, Rookes, Ferrier, Scoular, Flewin, Dickinson, Harris, Barlow, Clarke, Phillips, and Froggatt. Pompey overwhelmed Arsenal. In his match report published on 29 November 1948, even the skilled football writer, Geoffrey Green, nearly ran out of superlatives. Green wrote that 'inside the first quarter of an hour Swindin [the Arsenal goalkeeper] had twice been beaten and the design of the afternoon was already clear. It was Froggatt who began it all. The hands of the clock had moved forward only nine minutes when the left winger seized upon a loose ball at the edge of the penalty area to slash a low shot home, and gallantly though Swindin played afterwards it did seem that he was late in his dive at this first and vital thrust. It was the tonic that Portsmouth needed. They had hardly stopped congratulating themselves when Barlow sent Harris away on his right with a clever pass. The winger dribbled brilliantly onwards at top speed past three defenders and Clarke, taking a square pass, hit the ball first time on the rise past an astonished defence.'

So, Pompey were in the lead by 2-0. Green continued: 'Portsmouth, carried along by their enthusiasm, were a yard quicker on the ball; they won nearly every tackle; they kept moving forward at top speed, very cleverly at times, in direct, attacking moves. At the base of these attacking moves were Dickinson - he had a splendid match - and Scoular, while on top of this Arsenal never found the answer to Harris on Portsmouth's right wing. Harris, indeed, had something of a field day against [left back] Smith, and the freedom he gained for himself and his colleagues gave the Arsenal defence a strange look. Gone was that sense of security, the smooth positional covering, and its completeness. Mercer, it is true, played well, and [Leslie] Compton afforded Swindin a measure of cover, but for the most part the Arsenal defenders were broken up into single units who groped and scrambled themselves out of awkward corners. Arsenal, to be sure, attacked in spasms, with Lewis and Logie showing clever footwork now and then. McPherson once shot over the Portsmouth bar and Lewis followed suit, but before half time came Portsmouth might well have added to their lead. First, Swindin dived superbly at a shot by Clarke after a quick attack from right to left, and then Barlow hit an Arsenal goalpost with the goalkeeper helpless.' Arsenal tried regrouping in a van attempt to stay in the game, but it made no difference to the way that the second half went. As Green wrote: 'After ten minutes Phillips shot home a corner kick by Harris to give Portsmouth their third goal and so preclude any recovery by their opponents. Some twenty minutes from the end, however, Arsenal received the consolation of a penalty kick - shot by Lewis - for a foul on Roper, but most of the movement was taking place at the other end. Swindin saved finely in turn from Phillips, Harris, and Barlow, and once Harris inexplicably missed a wide open target after another quick attack. Yet Portsmouth were not done with and at the end Clarke, retrieving a long clearance by Rookes, gave Barlow a square pass he accepted with the utmost relish. It was certainly a strange experience for Swindin to pick the ball four times out of his net in an afternoon. As for Portsmouth, they will long remember this happy victory at so appropriate a moment.'

'The wonder of it was that Arsenal escaped a slightly as they did,' was Green's verdict, 'Four goals against a defence such as theirs … was indeed an unusual event. It was as if one of the laws of nature had suddenly changed; that black all at once had become white. Yet there it was. The Arsenal machine lay broken and twisted, and but for Swindin and the framework of his goal Portsmouth might have scored six, seven, or even eight times. Such a total would not have flattered them, for they came out to shape events from the beginning and it was Arsenal who had to conform to the pattern.' Football has attracted many skilled writers, but Geoffrey Green was the most stylish of his time and his contemporary report seems well worth quoting at length rather than relying on my youthful prejudice that Pompey's display in the Jubilee match was perfection. Arsenal supporters whom I knew later who had seen the game thought that they had never seen an English team play better than Pompey had done that day, and one of them said that it was as if Arsenal had been swept aside by a tidal wave. Of the people whom we used to go to the games with who had seen the 1939 Cup Final they all thought that Pompey had played better this time than in winning that major honour, and we were certain afterwards that we would take the title. In my mind's eye, I can still see Froggatt's savage shot for the opening goal tearing past George Swindin, and hear the exultation of that great crowd.

The famous victory over Arsenal was followed by draws, 0-0 at Huddersfield and then 2-2 at home to Manchester United, in which Clarke and Froggatt scored. At the halfway stage of the season, Pompey had 28 points, and three straight wins followed, with Preston being beaten at Fratton Park 3-1 (Harris, Barlow and Phillips) followed by a Christmas double over Chelsea. Pompey won 2-1 at Stamford Bridge (Harris 2) after trailing at half time, and on Boxing Day 1948 a larger crowd at Fratton Park witnessed a 5-2 victory (Harris 2, Barlow, Clarke, plus an own goal). One of Harris's goals was spectacular, when he sprung Chelsea's offside trap and I retained for ever this picture in my mind of him racing

34

half the length of the field to score, always staying ahead of his desperate pursuers. A 2-1 defeat at Burnley on New Year's Day 1949 was a setback, with Pompey only managing an own goal, but three League wins soon followed. Stoke were beaten 1-0 at Fratton Park, Froggatt scoring. Pompey then defeated Charlton 1-0 at The Valley, Clarke scoring. The final 3-1 score line of the game against Manchester City on 5 February 1949 made this victory seem easier than it was. City were leading 1-0 until the last quarter of an hour or so, but then Harris cut loose and gave the legendary Frank Swift and his fellow defenders a torrid time with a display of electric pace. Clarke scored twice and Harris once in what in the end was a thrilling victory. Harris scored in the next game at Sheffield United too, but Pompey lost that match 3-1. Pompey responded to this setback by three straight League victories, starting off with a 3-0 home win over Aston Villa (Phillips 2 and Froggatt). With Clarke ill with pleurisy, Reid returned to the team, scoring twice in a 4-1 win at Sunderland on 12 March 1949, with Froggatt and Phillips getting the other goals. It was Phillips that got the winning goal in the home game against Derby the following Saturday. All seemed set for a straightforward run in for the title, and then came what most Portsmouth fans treated as a hammer blow in the form of an F. A. Cup defeat.

Whether Pompey would have had a Cup run at all but for being drawn four times in a row at home has to be doubted. Nobody was going to beat Portsmouth at Fratton Park that season no matter how badly we played, and it has to be said that the progress that Pompey made to the semi-final had lacked authority, except in the case of the Third Round game with Stockport. On 8 January 1949, Stockport were thrashed 7-0 (Harris 3, Phillips 2, and Clarke 2). The visiting goalkeeper, Bowles, could have been forgiven for being a nervous wreck at the end of the game, but he seemed to arrive at the game in this state, waving his arms around in a frantic manner even when the ball was up the other end. In many respects, it was not Pompey who dominated the game, but the antics of Bowles. Anyway, the 33,590 present seemed pleased enough, and on 29 January 1949, a crowd of 47,188 turned up for the Fourth Round game with Sheffield Wednesday. The Second Division team acquitted themselves rather too well for our comfort, but goals from Harris and Phillips gave Pompey a 2-1 win. The Fifth Round game on 12 February 1949 was against Newport County from the Third Division (South). This time the crowd was 48,581, and many of them had come from South Wales, to judge from the coaches all over Portsmouth city centre and from the people around us in the Fratton End. Some of them invaded the pitch to tie leeks to the net of the goal in front of us. The visiting fans were convinced that they were going to win, and that their player- manager, Eddie Carr, formerly of Arsenal they informed us, would get the goals. This prediction was received with a sunny complacency by the Pompey fans. At half time, Newport were 2-1 up and Carr had scored twice. Was the best team in the country going to be humiliated by this rabble? Not if Barlow had anything to do with it. Barlow took hold of the game by the scruff of the neck, and ran it. Pompey eventually won 3-2, with Phillips scoring twice, and Froggatt getting the decisive goal in extra time. In those days if the Cup tie was level at full time, extra time then followed, the idea being to cut down on the number of football matches for the sake of industrial production. So, after that unconvincing win, it was on to the Sixth Round of the Cup on 26 February 1949, with Derby as our opponents. Derby were to finish third in the League, and they were formidable opponents. The crowd was 51,385, a record still for Fratton Park, and not surprisingly so since I have absolutely no idea how that many were squeezed into the ground that day. We were like sardines. The game was a wonderful occasion, and a draw would have been a fair result. That Pompey won 2-1 was primarily the result of the opportunism of Clarke, who got both of our goals. The winner, scored at the Fratton End, was a brilliantly executed right foot shot out of nothing that flew past Townsend, and nobody privileged enough to be present could possibly forget this wonder goal.

The next step was the Semi-Final on 26 March 1949, which was against Leicester City of the Second Division. That Pompey had avoided Wolves and Manchester United initially pleased us, but from the outset my father had his reservations.

36

He was always 'the cup is half empty' type - so why should the F. A. Cup be any different? It all looked too good to be true to that perennial pessimist. Why should it not be 1939 in reverse? It was conventional wisdom that the Cup and League Double was impossible in modern conditions, so why should the Pompey team of 1948-49 be an exception, especially when we had made a meal of getting to the Semi-Final anyway? We could end up with nothing. If we had played Wolves or Manchester United, then if we lost it would be with honour. They were top flight teams. But Leicester? They were an unknown quantity. As it turned out, though they had done well in the Cup, Leicester were not only Second Division relegation candidates, but, as has been well documented, they would actually have been relegated to the Third Division if it had not been the case that their last match of the season with Cardiff City at Ninian Park was fixed. Ken Chisholm, who was not playing for Leicester that day because of injury, found out about the fix, and won money on a bet. As the possessor now of a vast amount of unwanted knowledge about the second level of English football, I would say that it would be close to impossible to conceive of a modern equivalent relegation zone team at that level having players like Don Revie in their ranks, or, for that matter, Jack Lee, the centre forward, whose career was later cut short by injury but not before he had been capped by England when with Derby, and despite the competition in relation to that role at that time. The wingers, Griffiths and Adam, were impressive, and Chisholm, whose League career included 132 goals, was no slouch when on song. Leicester's problems were in defence, but it seemed to me that on 26 March 1949 that God and, most probably the Devil too, was on the side of the Leicester defence, especially that of their goalkeeper, McGraw. The Portsmouth team that day was Butler, Yuell, Ferrier, Scoular, Flewin, Dickinson, Harris, Barlow, Clarke, Phillips, Froggatt. The general pattern of this game, the first away from home that I had ever seen, remains imprinted on my mind, but the details have been confirmed by reference to the report in *The Times* for 28 March 1949. In the eighth minute, Griffiths, the Leicester right winger, took a square pass from Lee, rounded Ferrier, our normally ultra reliable left back, centred perfectly, and, according to *The Times*, 'Revie's shot would have left any goalkeeper helpless.' Possibly, but what was indisputable was that Butler never got near it. Pompey then piled forward, as they did for most of the match, and we should have scored twice before, at last, we did. In the twenty eighth minute, Harris latched on to a through pass from Yuell, and, outpacing the Leicester defence, beat McGraw. Quite how Leicester were on level terms at half time defied analysis, but in the forty seventh minute worse was to come. Chisholm slammed the ball past Butler to make it 2-1 for the underdogs. Almost immediately, Pompey had a golden scoring opportunity. McGraw was at last caught out of position. Only one defender guarded the goal. The ball fell to Harris in the goal area. The ball bobbled at the last second and Peter screwed the ball past the post. As I was behind that goal and near the front, I can still see the look on his face as the ball went wide. I think that we knew then that the game was lost. If we had equalized, then we would have at least drawn, but the reality was that Leicester not only rode out the siege, but, in the fifty fourth minute, a handling error by Butler gave Revie an easy opportunity. Revie made no mistake. Pompey stormed forward once more. Froggatt went to centre forward, but we never looked like scoring again, let alone pulling back two goals. At the final whistle, the Leicester supporters we spoke to were apologetic. They talked a lot about 'lucky City,' but the hard facts were that Leicester had been granted three chances and they had taken them all. Nobody at the game pretended as some did later when he became famous that Revie ran the match, because Pompey dominated the game territorially, carving out a dozen chances and only taking one. So, in that sense, we deserved to lose. Some writers later maintained that Leicester's backroom staff plotted Pompey's downfall, but it seems strange that their skills were so unsuccessful when applied to Leicester's league campaign. The observation in *The Times* report that 'Portsmouth helped to beat themselves' got it about right. As there had been a clash of club colours, Pompey wore red, and, after the match, or so a Leicester supporter - who was in the stands and made no effort to leave early - told me years later, the Highbury terraces were a sea of discarded red rosettes.

Though we took the time to wish the City supporters the best of luck in the Cup Final, the group of Pompey fans that I went with left Highbury as soon as we could to get down to Waterloo to get home. In those days, and for many years afterwards, there was a road down the middle of Waterloo Station which seemed to be mainly used by the Post Office vans. That evening, it was full of Pompey fans waiting for the special trains and looking as if they had been to their own funeral, and for years afterwards when passing that road I would sometimes think of that unhappy scene. Much of the journey was passed in silence, but in such discussion as there was the general opinion was that the crucial mistake was that made by Bob Jackson in playing Barlow instead of Reid, and Barlow did have a poor game, but then he was not the only one. In conversation with one of my friends years later, Jack Froggatt thought that the whole team, including himself, had played poorly, taking victory over a team like Leicester for granted, as, of course, you probably could ninety per cent of the time these days, but not then. It came to be my belief that on any particular day any professional team can beat any other professional team, as Revie himself found out when he was the Manager at Leeds United, when his gifted and widely hated team were beaten at Colchester in the F.A. Cup in 1971. The Leicester team of 1949 were much more formidable opposition than that Colchester team, but in both cases it was their day. Our little group seemed to take the Leicester defeat better than most on the journey back. The line taken was that, after all, there was no guarantee that Pompey would have repeated the 1939 victory over Wolves in the Cup Final, and the Club already had the F.A. Cup in its trophy cabinet anyway (which is more than Leicester or, for that matter, Colchester can say even now). Moreover, the general opinion was that without the distraction of the F.A. Cup Final, Portsmouth would make certain of winning the title, which the Club had never done before.

When Portsmouth returned to their League programme on 3 April 1949 against Liverpool at Fratton Park, the team got a reception fit for heroes. The noise was deafening and the support accorded to Pompey that afternoon was the most intense and sustained that I can recall many years later, even with experience of much larger crowds at other grounds. Manager Jackson made minimal changes, restoring Reid to the team, and installing Hindmarsh at right back. Liverpool were beaten 3-2 (Harris, Phillips, Clarke), which left nine games to play, six of them away. Indeed, the next away game at Newcastle was generally thought to be the one that would settle the title, given that the Tynesiders were closing on us at the top. So, not surprisingly, on the evening of 6 April 1949, there were no less than 60,611 spectators crammed into St James's Park to watch the match. Pompey crushed Newcastle 5-0, with the wingers getting all the goals, Harris scoring twice and Froggatt recording a hat trick. All the goals were headers. Some years later, the Squadron Leader in charge of me in the R. A. F., told me that he had seen the match, and that Portsmouth had given the greatest exhibition of football that he had ever seen in his life, and that all his fellow Newcastle supporters around him thought the same. Whether this was the case or not, Pompey lost 1-0 at Blackpool on the Saturday, which meant that they needed three more wins to clinch the title. One of them came on Good Friday 1949, though Birmingham had the better of this game at first, and some of the visiting fans celebrated wildly, but Pompey prevailed eventually 3-1 (Reid 2, Clarke). On Easter Saturday, Wolves were beaten 5-0 (Reid 2, Clarke 2, Phillips), and, though defeat followed at Birmingham, where there was some crowd trouble, victory at Bolton on 23 April 1949 would mean that the title would be won. The difficulty was that Portsmouth had never yet won at Burnden Park. Goals from Harris and Clarke meant that Pompey did so this time, by 2-1. When the news reached the Deep South we were absolutely delighted, of course, and the celebrations were not affected in the slightest by the reality that few of us knew where Bolton actually was. Arm in arm, there was dancing in the street in my home town of Ryde when the *Football Mail* came, confirming in print that the title had been won, and the Pompey Chimes were sung with gusto. On the following Saturday, 30 April 1949, Huddersfield were beaten 2-0 (Reid and Clarke), and, afterwards, there were celebrations in Guildhall Square, with the parading of the trophy and speeches from the players all of them rendered incoherent by defective sound equipment. Nobody seemed to mind very much about this, or, for that matter, that the final two away games at Arsenal and Manchester United were both lost. Clarke scored twice at Highbury but Arsenal won 3-2 to finish third. Reid missed a penalty at Manchester United, Crompton saving his shot, and, though both Harris and Reid did score, United won 3-2, and finished runners up, five points behind. Of the 42 games played during this memorable season, Portsmouth won 25, drew 8, and lost 9, thus obtaining 58 points. Pompey scored 84 goals (52 at home), with five players reaching double figures (Harris 17, Reid 17, Froggatt 15, Clarke 14, and Phillips 11). Only 42 goals were conceded, and only 12 at home. Portsmouth's home record during the 1948-49 season of 18 wins, 3 draws, and no defeats has only been bettered once since in a 21 game format at this level.

CHAMPIONS OF ENGLAND: THE 1949-50 SEASON

The consensus among the Pompey supporters that I knew was that Portsmouth would retain the title in the 1949-50 season, though it would be a lot harder this time, because we would be the team to beat. In retrospect, it could be also said that if Flewin had not been absent so many times Pompey might well have won the title again by much the same margin as before instead of doing it on the basis of a better goal average than that of Wolves. Anyway, I recall that the news that Pompey had won the opening game of the season at Newcastle 3-1 (Harris, Clarke, Phillips) was treated as an expected victory. The first midweek game, at home to Manchester City on 24 August 1949 was, however, only a 1-1 draw (Reid scoring), and worst was to come on the following Saturday when Blackpool won 3-2 at Fratton Park. Clarke and Phillips scored, and the general opinion was that the officials had been playing for the visitors. Whether this was so or not, the harsh reality still was that Pompey's proud record of 32 league home games without defeat was over. Nobody could come up with any excuses for Pompey's 1-0 defeat at Manchester City on 31 August 1949, and we badly needed a win at Middlesbrough four days later. Sure enough, Pompey won 5-1, with Harris getting a hat trick, and Clarke and Froggatt also scoring. Then Pompey lost 1-0 at Aston Villa. Just to add to the confusion, on 10 September 1949, Everton were crushed 7-0 at Fratton Park. Reid scored three (including a free kick of savage power executed at the Milton End), and Harris, Clarke, Phillips, and Froggatt scored once. This victory proved to be the first of six games without defeat. Huddersfield were beaten 1-0 on their own ground, Clarke scoring. Pompey then drew at home with Bolton 1-1, Clarke scoring again. On 1 October 1949, Pompey drew 1-1 with Wolves (Reid scoring) before a record crowd for a League game at Fratton Park of 50,248. A week later, Pompey won 3-0 at Birmingham (Clarke 2 and Reid), and at home on 15 October 1949 Derby were beaten 3-1 (Reid, Clarke, and Froggatt scoring). Pompey had now played twelve games, winning 6, drawing 3, and losing 3. This seemed to me to be about the minimum that Pompey could have done to have much hope of retaining the title, and, much more importantly, this opinion was endorsed by Zigger Holmes and his mates when I diffidently put my views to them. Sadly, for all of us, Pompey then won just one of their next seven games, though that was a 4-1 away win at Chelsea on Guy Fawkes Day 1949, with Clarke and Froggatt both scoring twice. The results of the other games were less promising, given that they comprised a 3-0 defeat at West Bromwich; a 0-0 home draw with Manchester United; a 0-0 home draw with Stoke: a 2-1 defeat at Burnley; a 2-2 home draw with Sunderland (despite having been 2-0 ahead at half time); and a 2-2 away draw at then unbeaten Liverpool. Pompey now had two home games against Arsenal on 10 December 1949 and Newcastle a week later, which would take the season to the halfway stage. These games had to be won for Pompey to stay in the race. Goals from Clarke and Froggatt eventually meant the defeat of Arsenal 2-1, and Clarke scored again to give Pompey a 1-0 win over Newcastle.

The second half of the season began badly with yet another defeat at Blackpool, but Pompey won 2-1 at Charlton (Phillips and Froggatt) and won 1-0 in the return match the next day. On New Year's Eve 1949, Froggatt got an equalizer to give Pompey a 1-1 home draw with Middlesbrough. Pompey then took two games to get past Norwich City from the Third Division (South) in the F. A. Cup Third Round. The game at Fratton Park was a 1-1 draw with the Norwich fans convinced that Lindy Delaphena handled when scoring Pompey's goal. I was very well placed to judge this, and it was a legitimate goal. The replay at Norwich attracted a record crowd to Carrow Road to witness Pompey do their stuff this time and win by two Reid goals. Returning to their League programme, Pompey won 2-1 at Everton (Harris and Phillips) and then beat lowly Huddersfield 4-0 at Fratton Park (Froggatt 2, Reid, plus an own goal) before crushing Grimsby 5-0 in the Fourth Round of the Cup. Many people gave up hope of Pompey winning the title again when on 4 February 1950 we lost 1-0 at Bolton. The news that Reid had missed a penalty came as a hammer blow. A week later, it was the Fifth Round of the Cup, and Pompey drew 3-3 at Manchester United. Ferrier scored for both sides, conceding an own goal and the scoring from a penalty kick. Making a rare appearance, Cliff Parker scored, and so did Reid. United won the replay at Fratton Park 3-1, with Harris scoring for Pompey. This game was the only home game in League or Cup that I missed in the two title winning years. For those of us who had not written Pompey off after the defeat at Burnden Park, we reckoned that nine or ten wins from the fourteen League games remaining would be enough. Things looked bleak when Pompey lost the first two away games of this sequence, 1-0 at Wolves, and 2-1 at Derby. Scoular was sent off during the game at the Baseball Ground, which meant suspension later, which added to the problems caused by a run of injuries. Two goals from Harris ensured a 2-0 home win over Birmingham, and following the Derby setback, Pompey at last hit a patch of consistent form, all the more remarkable for the absence of Flewin from half a dozen of the vital games though injury. As at times earlier in the season, Spence proved to be an able deputy. Burnley were beaten 2-1, and a 1-1 draw was chipped out at Sunderland, followed by a 4-0 home win against Chelsea (a Reid hat trick), a 1-0 win at Stoke (Harris), and a comfortable Good Friday home win over Fulham 3-0 (Harris 2 and Froggatt). The weather had changed dramatically by the Easter Saturday, and a high wind wrecked the home game with West Bromwich as a spectacle. That the wind ensured that a speculative shot from Ryan sailed over even the tall Butler at the Milton End to give the lowly placed visitors an entirely unexpected 1-0 win stunned all of us. There were five games left, though, and we guessed that four wins would be enough. We were right - just. A Clarke goal ensured a 1-0 Easter Monday victory at Fulham. It was essential that Pompey won at Manchester United the following Saturday, not least to finish off United's challenge for the title. Two second half goals from Reid and Froggatt won this match. The next game was at home to Liverpool, the early season pacemakers but now destined to finish seventh. The wonderfully named Albert Stubbins put Liverpool ahead, his shot going in off a post at the Fratton End. Pompey raised their game magnificently and Reid and Froggatt (with a stunning header) got the winning goals to the delight of the 47,507 crowd. Then, the F. A. announced that Scoular would be suspended for the rest of the season. Without him, Pompey lost 2-0 at Highbury to Arsenal, whom I remember being described in one of the football annuals I collected in those days as exceeding even their success in winning the F. A. Cup Final by beating Portsmouth.

So, with both Portsmouth and Wolves having the same number of points, though with Pompey having a superior goal average, all turned on the last match of the season to be played on 6 May 1950 against Aston Villa at Fratton Park. Portsmouth had to win. The Pompey team was Butler, Hindmarsh, Ferrier, Spence, Flewin, Dickinson, Harris, Reid, Thompson, Phillips and Froggatt. As had been the case with the Arsenal away game, injury had ruled out Clarke, and with Pickett having not been a success when deputising for him at Highbury, Bob Jackson decided to experiment with Thompson up front. 'A football season that has given excitement and pleasure to many millions ended ... with a flurry of goals ... in key matches and with a series of mathematical calculations,' wrote Geoffrey Green in *The Times*, 'Wolves five goals up at half time and at full steam in an effort to close the mathematical gap with Portsmouth were ... thwarted in their effort by the reigning Champions who were also in no mood to let slip even the most fleeting chance. Portsmouth, indeed, scored straight from the kick off against Aston Villa, a goal in 20 seconds - and from that moment they made certain of their position.' As the game started, the sailor standing next to my father said to him, 'I wonder how Thompson will get on at centre forward,' and then made the mistake of giving his attention to the ritual of lighting a cigarette. 'Not bad,' replied my father, 'He's just scored.' Indeed, racing towards the Milton End in the opening minute, Thompson had hammered a ferocious left foot drive into the net. Reid added a second goal before half time. By that stage, Wolves were trouncing relegated Birmingham City, and we knew this from the details given on *The Football Mail* scoreboard at the top of the Milton End. Wolves went on to win 6-1. We also knew that this made no difference, given a Pompey victory. Reid went on to get a hat trick, and the goal he got from a free kick at the Fratton End was the hardest shot that I have ever seen in my life. It hit the top corner of the net like a rocket. Green was in full flow: 'Long before the end, with two goals already scored by Thompson, normally a half back, and three more goals added by Reid, the new Championship flags … were already flying at each end of the [South] Stand.' Still clear in my memory is the sight of those flags being raised as Pompey coasted to victory.

THE ACHIEVEMENT

Portsmouth did not go to match Huddersfield (1923-24, 1924-25, and 1925-26) and Arsenal (1932-33, 1933-34, and 1934-35) who won the title three times in a row. What Pompey did do was to win back to back titles, and thus equal the achievements of Preston (1888-89 and 1989-90), Aston Villa (1895-96 and 1896-97; and also 1898-99 and 1899-1900), Sheffield Wednesday (1902-03 and 1903-04; and also 1928-29 and 1929-30), and Liverpool (1921-22 and 1922-23). What needs to be emphasised is that Portsmouth won those back to back titles at a time when English professional football was at its popular peak. The period between the 1947-48 season and that of 1951-52 was the Golden Age for attendances, with the highest figures being recorded for the 1948-49 (41,271,414) and 1949-50 (40,517,865) seasons. On 27 December 1949, despite a rail strike in London and many being locked out at some grounds, no less than 1,272,185 people attended Football League games.

These figures were remarkable, especially when one remembers that the numbers of adult males, and, thus the the main market, had been affected by the reality that there were as many as 300,000 war dead, and, inevitably, many more injured. Full employment made a difference, of course, certainly compared with the 1930s, and I recall Raich Carter confessing to having wept when he thought about how in those days the Sunderland supporters had to scrape the money together to watch their team play. Those who were later to be dismissive about the boom years argued that football in the second half of the 1940s offered affordable entertainment at a time when there were few alternatives, but much the same could be said about the deadly dull 1950s when attendances declined. Indeed, in the period between the end of the boom and the formation of the Premier League in 1992 this decline at times became almost embarrassing. In the period 1982-83 to 1991-92, for example, less than ten million people per season watched First Division football as the top flight was then called, and in some seasons the figure was less than half of that attained in the post war peak. The eventual revival of attendances with the Premier League leading the way knocked on the head the notion of any inevitable decline in football crowds because there were so many other things to do. Indeed, it encouraged the thesis that, as entertainment, the football served up in the decades in between had been deemed too boring by its prospective market, and it seemed to me that a contributory factor which eventually encouraged violent crowd behaviour was boredom and the seeking of entertainment by other means. Whether the football served up in the Golden Age of Portsmouth and also of attendances was that wonderful nobody can prove one way or the other, but in a spectator sport the number of fans in relation to the prospective fan base indicates that they thought so at that time. To lavish exclusive praise on the old timers or, for that matter, current players seems as unwise as pretending that the gifted of the past would not adapt to changed tactics and formations, and many would surely welcome the better equipment and pitches and, above all, the rules which limit the use of brutality, though the purveyors of violence of the past

46

might well have loved meeting up with some of the protected species among the modern players. Others may differ, but my own line has always been that, irrespective of the era, the best teams and the best players have tended to be much the same in quality.

Though now only of interest to Pompey supporters and football historians, the Golden Age of football and that of Portsmouth coincided, and, while I have taken care not to overrate Pompey's double title winning team, on the basis of a wide experience of watching top class football all my life I would rank that Portsmouth team as one of the twenty best English club teams that I have ever seen. I would also respectfully suggest that their achievements were attained when the spread of competition did not permit the large number of easy fixtures that the best teams face now. In the 1948-49 season, for example, Sheffield United were relegated despite having Jimmy Hagan in their ranks, and so were Preston with Tom Finney, though it should be added in fairness that Finney missed several games through injuries, no doubt deliberately inflicted. Bill Shankly, who played with him, thought Finney to be the best footballer the world had ever seen, bar none. Less importantly, and more cautiously, I would say that Finney was the most gifted English or British player that I have ever seen. Nowadays, most of the better Premiership clubs have two teams within their squads, and since there is only so much talent to go round it seems in short supply among the lower orders of the Premiership, as this paying customer can testify. Whether this is the case or not, whatever the era only great teams win back to back titles, and all those years ago we were very proud of Portsmouth Football Club and its achievements as we strode like kings down Frogmore Road on 6 May 1950, belting out the Pompey Chimes. If somebody had said that Pompey would win nothing that mattered for nearly sixty more years, we would have laughed long and hard. Yet, this is what happened, and it is to that story that we now turn.

47

CHAPTER 3: THE ERA OF BENIGN NEGLECT: PORTSMOUTH 1950-1956

Nobody would seriously suggest that from 1950 onwards Portsmouth should have dominated English football in the manner of Liverpool did in the 1970s and 1980s or Manchester United did once the Premiership was formed. To think in this manner would be to act like the fans in modern phone- ins who cannot comprehend why their Ordinary Joe club is not taking the football world apart. Portsmouth had been an Ordinary Joe club which had translated itself into being a major club in double quick time. On one view, from 1950 onwards, the only way was down. Why should Pompey have won the F.A. Cup more than a quarter of a century before Liverpool had managed this feat? Why should Pompey have won three major honours, the third of which was secured five years before Chelsea had won anything at all? Why should Pompey have won back to back titles when, at that time, to take just a couple of examples, Tottenham had not won the title at all, and Manchester City had just one title to their name? One justly famous football writer later patronisingly observed that Portsmouth had overreached themselves, but it seemed and seems admirable to me that Portsmouth had made their mark rather than simply knowing their place. Then again, nobody would seriously suggest that Portsmouth should have emulated, say, Aston Villa and Sheffield Wednesday and gone on and won further back to back titles, or, for that matter, kept on filling up the trophy cabinet on an annual basis. So, nobody was suggesting that Pompey should have established a dynasty, but what was remarkable about what happened to Portsmouth after 1950 was that the position of authority that the Club had established was simply thrown away.

In a matter of half a dozen years, Pompey went into reverse, and translated themselves from a major club into being an Ordinary Joe club once more. This was not, of course, a deliberate act of policy, but what the Directors effectively did was to step back and admire Portsmouth's very real achievements and keep on stepping back until the Club collapsed backwords into an abyss of mediocrity. The contrast with the shrewd manner in which Portsmouth Football Club had been built up was stark. That shrewdness had been needed because Portsmouth was primarily a Royal Navy garrison town. Despite its appearance as, say, Leeds with sunshine, Portsmouth didn't have much in the way of an industrial or commercial base. There was no real money there. There seemed to be nobody in or around Portsmouth who could do for the football club what, say, Harry Reynolds and Manny Cussins were later to do in translating Leeds United from nonentities into a major club. Now this did not matter so much in 1950 because Portsmouth Football Club had immense prestige, and because they were very well supported the Club did not need the protection afforded by the maximum wage that so many other clubs did. Though nobody said so except in the ease of retrospect, it would have been in Portsmouth's interest if the maximum wage had been abolished in, say, 1951, when Pompey still ranked as a major club and one with impressive support, rather than 1961, by which time Portsmouth's status in English football had been undermined from within. If the men constituting the Board of Directors at the time deserved the credit for building the Club up over the period 1920-1950 in particular, which they did, then the Board of Directors as a collectivity who presided over Pompey's subsequent decline and fall deserved condemnation for the complacency and ineptitude that they displayed, not least in the managerial appointments that were made after Bob Jackson's departure. At the end of the 1951-52 season, Jackson resigned to take up a similar post at Hull City, where he achieved nothing. At the time, few Portsmouth fans seemed very concerned about Jackson going, partly because Pompey supporters were used to having gifted Managers, and, as if to show that complacency was not the monopoly of the Directors, it seemed to be assumed that another one would simply be hired. For whatever reasons, it was also the case that Jackson was never loved in the way that Jack Tinn was, and certainly in later years the general opinion of him was that he saw the writing on the wall and got out in time. I remember Zigger Holmes saying to me: 'Look at the state he left Pompey in compared with that he inherited from Tinn.' This was true, and Jackson may well have been a better Chief Scout than he was a Manager, and the inability to replace him properly in the scouting role may well have contributed to Pompey's decline. Yet, in Jackson's defence it could be said that Portsmouth finished eighth, first, first, seventh, and fourth in the top flight of English football in the five seasons that he was the Manager, a record that has never been matched in Pompey's history. At a time when Portmouth were important in English football, and when it seems reasonable to believe that men of real ability would have wished to be considered for the role of being Jackson's successor, the Board of Directors opted for another internal appointment as Manager. Eddie Lever's sole qualification for the job was that he had discovered Jimmy Dickinson, and 'recommended him to Pompey. As a Manager, Lever was to prove the truth of the bitter Americanism that 'nice guys finish last.

ANTI - CLIMAX: THE 1950-51 SEASON

At the outset of the 1950-51 season, I knew no Portsmouth supporter who thought that Pompey were going to emulate the feats of Huddersfield in the 1920s and Arsenal in the 1930s and win a third title in a row. Unlike today, players guarded their ages rather better than the contemporary British Government guarded its State secrets from Soviet agents, but there was sufficient information around to work out that most of the players had been at their peak during the title winning years and the team needed reconstruction. Clarke was very much at the veteran stage, and needed replacing, and Reid was thought to be only a couple of years younger. Unlike Hindmarsh and Ferrier, Flewin was still under thirty, but whether or not the injuries he had sustained would allow him ever again be the force that he had been was a subject of discussion. Those who thought that it would be a good idea to sign a better deputy for Butler were proved right. It would also have been a statement of ambitious intent if Pompey had signed Alan Brown, widely considered at the time to be the best young player in Scotland, to bring new blood into the forward line as a replacement for Clarke. Brown was said to be concerned about how he would get into the Portsmouth team, but that consideration also applied in the case

50

of Blackpool, his eventual destination. More vigour and enterprise should have been shown by those running Portsmouth to clinch Brown's transfer in 1950. As it turned out, way past his best, Brown was recruited by Pompey eleven years later.

In their 42 First Division games in the 1950-51 season, Portsmouth won 16, drew 15, and lost 11, scoring 71 goals, and conceding 68. Pompey thus secured 47 points and finished eighth. That Portsmouth looked for most of the season to be destined to end up halfway down the league table owed a great deal to defensive failings. A broken finger sustained during the close season ensured that Butler missed the opening seven games, only one of which (a 4-1 home victory over Sheffield Wednesday on 30 August 1950) was won. Portsmouth's form was inconsistent. A 5-0 defeat at West Brom on 9 September 1950 was followed by three straight wins, with Stoke being beaten 5-1 at Fratton Park, Everton being beaten 5-1 away, and then a 1-0 home victory was recorded over Fulham. A 4-0 defeat at Bolton followed. The two defeats that finished off what few hopes were left that Pompey would be even outside challengers for the title occurred when Pompey lost 4-1 at home to Wolves on 28 October 1950, and a week later lost 5-1 at White Hart Lane to Arthur Rowe's excellent push and run team. Butler the goalkeeper did not take the blame for Pompey's comprehensive defeat on that occasion, but the following week he lost his place after a 3-3 home draw with Charlton in which he and the famous Charlton goalkeeper Sam Bartram both played very badly, and both were dropped as a consequence. The general opinion was that Ron Humpston had proved to be a poor deputy for Butler earlier in the season, but local product Maurice Leather proved to be even worse, keeping just one clean sheet in thirteen appearances, and not surprisingly so, given his ineptitude in the air. It was not just Leather's fault that Pompey's results were all over the place. A 3-1 Christmas Day defeat at home to Chelsea was followed by a 4-1 victory at Stamford Bridge. The next game proved to be a 2-0 F. A. Cup Third Round away defeat at Second Division Luton. There was bitterness about the manner of this defeat among those unfortunate enough to have made the journey.

The Pompey faithful were used to a rich diet of success, and the 1950-51 season never lost its air of anti-climax, though, as we will see, it certainly ended on a high note. To put the matter mildly, I had other concerns that followed from being very ill at one stage. Local rumour had it that I was going to die. There was no doubt that what should have been a straightforward operation had been botched, and a hospital Registrar told me years later that the relevant scar suggested that a knife and fork had been used to do the deed. Anyway, I recovered to a chorus of 'I thought you were dead' from those who had already assigned me to Binstead Cemetery, many of whom had some difficulty in hiding their disappointment. Eventually, I returned to the Portsmouth fold to learn that, far from the 1950-51 season drifting towards mid-table mediocrity, Bob Jackson had transformed Pompey's prospects by what many believed was a stroke of genius. Flewin was only to make 20 appearances all season, with Bill Thompson already having had to deputize for him several times. With seventeen games to go, Jackson switched Froggatt to centre half in place of Flewin. At first, to judge from a 6-3 home victory over Everton, which helped that famous club on its way to relegation, the main benefit of this change seemed likely to be greater entertainment, but Pompey were unbeaten in their last twelve games with less than a goal a game being conceded. Much was made at the time of Froggatt having restored the idea of the attacking centre half, as if Arsenal's Herbie Roberts in the 1920s and his many successors in the role of stopper centre half had taken English football down the wrong road. In reality, Froggatt played much more like the conventional centre half most of the time, as, indeed, he had to, given the formations he faced, and it was his pace that caught the eye, and, indeed, even the attention of that very sad bunch, the F. A. International Committee. After only twelve appearances at centre half, Froggatt played there for England. Of Froggatt, Geoffrey Green wrote that '[his] sense of adventure, speed into the tackle, and quick recovery brings a breath of fresh air to the prosaic position of centre half.' The general opinion among the Pompey faithful had come to be that Froggatt's emergence in this role had transformed Portsmouth's prospects and that we would make a serious challenge for major honours in the 1951-52 season. They were right.

FADING POWER: THE 1951-52 SEASON

During the 1951-52 season, of the 42 First Division games played, Portsmouth won 20, drew 8, and lost 14, scoring 68 goals, and conceding 58. Thus, Pompey secured 48 points and finished fourth. In the F. A. Cup, Portsmouth reached the Sixth Round. All the way down to mid-March, the newspapers were taking seriously the prospect of Portsmouth becoming the first club in the twentieth century to do the Cup and League Double. If the very impressive Tottenham team that had won the title the previous season could not bring off this feat, then it seemed to me and those around me that Pompey were unlikely to do better, though we all expected Portsmouth to win the F.A. Cup. We were wrong.

Pompey were never again to win an away game of any description at Liverpool in the twentieth century, but none of us were very surprised when, on the opening day of the 1951-52 season, Portsmouth won 2-0 at Anfield. Since Pompey have never won any title or any form of promotion without winning at least half of their opening twelve games, it was as well that Portsmouth won no less than eight of them this time. What was worrying was that two of the three defeats were at home, with Blackpool winning 3-1 and Wolves (who did not have a good season) winning 3-2. The Blackpool defeat was later attributed by some Pompey fans to the acting captain, Jimmy Stephen, winning the toss and foolishly electing to play into the sun. There seemed to me to be more obvious reasons and ones of merit why Blackpool- who had a good record at Fratton Park since the War- were three goals to the good by half time. The return game was a 0-0 draw, and Butler managed six clean sheets in the first seven games. An away win at Fulham on 6 October 1951 enthused Geoffrey Green so much that he described the home team as being left 'chasing autumn leaves blown before the wind.' Less imaginatively, I thought Pompey made hard work of a 3-2 win. A week later, Pompey beat Middlesbrough 5-4 in a compelling match. Wilf Mannion played majestically for the visitors, and, combined with the former Pompey player, Lindy Delaphena, to embarrass the home defence at times. I can still recall Delaphena scoring calmly from a penalty in the face of savage abuse from the crowd. International calls, including a first England cap for Phillips, partially explained what was already threatening to become an annual away defeat at West Brom, this time by 5-0. There then followed the best spell of results that Pompey recorded at this level at any time this side of the title winning years. On 27 October 1951, Portsmouth beat Newcastle 3-1 in one of the three best Pompey matches that I have ever seen, the others being the Jubilee match of 1948 and the Newcastle Cup game of March 1952. The Newcastle game in October was a magnificent contest, with Reid getting two goals and Phillips one in an absorbing match. Milburn got a consolation goal for United, having been generally mastered by Froggatt that day. On 3 November 1951, Portsmouth won 3-0 away at Bolton, who were eventually to finish fifth. To put it mildly, the teams that Bolton fielded in the 1950s were tough, modelled, it seemed on their famous centre forward, soon to be the Lion of Vienna, Nat Lofthouse. One of their supporters I met in the Services boasted to me that Bolton took no prisoners. Well, maybe so, but there were normally casualties. So, we were very pleased to win there, with Phillips scoring twice and Reid once. Stoke were beaten 4-1 at Fratton Park the following week, and then on 12 November 1951, another away win followed, this time by 3-1 at Manchester United. A week later, a home victory was recorded when Tottenham were beaten 2-0 in a wonderful game, with Reid scoring twice, and Philips giving a brilliant display. After a November like this, talk of Portsmouth being Champions again seemed justified, but the seven games played in December yielded only one win, by 2-0 at Charlton. There was yet another home defeat, this time Liverpool won 3-1, an outcome made certain by Bob Jackson selecting the untried Brian Edwards at right back to mark the immensely gifted Billy Liddell, who ran rings round the novice, who never played at this level again. A 2-2 home draw with Burnley pleased nobody, not least because many spectators got saturated in a downpour. We were stunned to learn that Pompey had lost 4-1 away to Arsenal on Christmas Day. Froggatt returned after injury for the Boxing Day match. This ended in a 1-1 draw, but the reason that the game was remembered - though not by the Directors – was because of an appalling foul by one of the visiting players, Freddie Cox, obviously designed to seriously injure Froggatt, Pompey's talismanic figure at this time. Crowd trouble was very rare in those days, but after the match there was a demonstration by Portsmouth supporters about the incident. Froggatt missed the next two games, but, with Thompson in his place, Pompey drew 1-1 at Chelsea, and then won 1-0 at Manchester City to go top of the table.

Nobody had yet written Portsmouth off as a force in English football, and not surprisingly so, given the emergence of two players who seemed, at first sight, to be destined to be outstanding. They were Jackie Henderson and Phil Gunter. Though he was eventually to play in several positions in his long career at Portsmouth, at this stage Gunter was a tall, elegant right back, and I well recall Newcastle supporters telling us that he was certain to play for England. The most that Gunter ever managed was one England B cap, and all that he was ever widely remembered for in the longer term was for insisting that his Christian principles would not permit him to play in games held on Christmas Day or Good Friday. Like so many people who make public displays of their supposed virtuousness, Gunter's personal behaviour proved in practice to be much the same as the rest of us, and when this news got out this pleased in particular those Portsmouth supporters who not only wanted to go to Hell in their own way but also with excess displayed on the journey. The rest of us found it hard to forgive Gunter for wasting his talent and our time and damaging Pompey in the process. Nonetheless, Gunter looked a class act during his 17 appearances during the 1951-52 season, and everybody said the same thing about him, which was, of course, that he was one for the future, but, in later career, he was to attract a well deserved reputation for being a lazy player.

Jackie Henderson was a new, young player who attracted the attention of the newspapers from the moment he made the first team as the much needed replacement for Clarke. This was not surprising, since he possessed exceptional speed, and an excellent shot using either foot. This meant that he could be a threatening presence on both wings as well as playing down the centre, always at great pace. However, in an era in which, especially in the case of Scots, ball control seemed to come as second nature, that displayed by Henderson left a lot to be desired, notably in relation to trapping the ball. Henderson was given to trying to use his thigh to control the ball. Henderson eventually proved to be unloved by many Pompey fans and there were two main reasons for this. One was that such fans were used to the title winning team, which had in its ranks several outstanding players. For years afterwards, the level of expectation that Pompey players were supposed to live up to was exacting. In the case of Henderson, excessive early praise led to excessive disappointment, and, of course, few people like admitting that they have made a mistake of judgement. Those who had not jumped on the Henderson bandwagon in the first place, and who had merely regarded him as a promising player, were given to pointing out to Henderson's critics that, despite the prejudice against Anglo Scots evident in the ranks of the selectors, Henderson swiftly became a Scottish international. Indeed, he went on to win five caps for Scotland during his time with Portsmouth. The second reason for Henderson being eventually viewed with distrust by many Pompey fans was because of what seemed to me to be no more than a rumour. Clarke's ball control was excellent, and, indeed, he made it look effortless, and he was said to have offered to help Henderson to sharpen up his game only to have had his offer rejected, with Henderson supposedly saying to the veteran that as he had replaced him in the team that meant that he had little to learn from him. I doubted the veracity of this tale, and I recall that in the away game at Tottenham the following season, when Henderson was asked to play out on the left, and when Gordon Dale gave him some tips, Henderson responded, and, indeed, did so effectively, scoring twice. Nonetheless, however dangerous he

56

always looked, especially when Pompey counter attacked away from home, and even at the end of his career when I saw him play for Arsenal and Fulham, Henderson always had the air of unfulfilled promise about him.

If the behaviour of many Portsmouth supporters in relation to Henderson came to be self defeating in the sense that few thrive on discouragement, then, in the 1951-52 season, in relation to Len Phillips his treatment at the hands of a vocal section of the Fratton Park crowd was so negative that, at one stage, he felt forced to request a transfer. Phillips had been one of the youngest of the regular members of the title winning team, but now in his prime he placed more emphasis on holding the ball until he could distribute it to advantage rather than releasing it and risk losing possession. Critics of Phillips among the Portsmouth supporters plainly had no conception of what this immensely gifted player was doing or even trying to do. Though it might well be flattering to such critics to attribute to them even basic reasoning ability, what some of them may have come to feel was that, now he was a more senior player, Phillips was playing for himself and not the team. In other words, that he was becoming another version of Len Shackleton. The flamboyant Shackleton once scored six times for Newcastle in a 13-0 win over Newport County in 1946, and was to declare that Newport were lucky to get nil. Newport won the return game. At the end of the 1946-47 season, with Newcastle having failed to gain promotion from the Second Division, the Newcastle Manager, George Martin, transferred Shackleton to Sunderland, arguing that no club would win anything with Shackleton in their team. He was right, and Newcastle were promoted the following season. Phillips did play for the team, and he had already won two title medals, and Portsmouth ensured that he would continue to play for them by responding to the transfer requests by putting the relevant fee at a deterrent level. Phillips eventually relented and came off the transfer list. He never changed his style of play, but many of his former critics came to change their tune, without, of course, acknowledging this.

Oddly, some of those who had been less than admiring of Phillips were full of praise for another ball player, Gordon Dale, who had been recruited in the summer of 1951, becoming one of the very few players that Portsmouth had ever paid serious money for. Dale was one of the many skilful players at that time who were dubbed the Stanley Matthews of the left wing, and who never lived up to expectations. Dale only too often seemed to be injured, and not surprisingly so, given his slender build and the tactics adopted by many full backs when faced with a winger with his gifts. Years later, Aston Villa's Stan Lynn warned Liverpool's then youthful Tommy Smith, whom he was not even directly marking, that if he went past him again he would break Smith's leg. Smith, who was a hard case, laughed it off, but those with a more normal pain threshold could not afford to do the same. Gentler spirits like Dale could not expect much in the way of protection. Since it soon got out that recruiting Dale had been very much Bob Jackson's idea, there were those who wondered if the Manager was losing his way. Injury caused Dale to register only eight appearances in the 1951-52 season, and he was to be a frequent absentee over the next two seasons too. It was an exaggeration to say, as many did, that Dale spent most of his career at Fratton Park exhibiting his considerable skills in reserve games in the Football Combination, but, certainly at first, a cheap recruit, Marcel Gaillard, a fast and durable Belgian winger, had to be relied on, with mixed results.

After defeating Manchester City on New Year's Day, Portsmouth did not win away again in the First Division that season, merely drawing twice and losing six times. At home, five games were won, and there was one draw, and two defeats. In retrospect, the 2-0 home defeat by Sunderland on 26 January 1952 marked the beginning of the end of Pompey's title ambitions. Len Shackleton's goal for Sunderland was memorable. He broke clear from not that far from the half way line, and, with the entire Portsmouth crowd yelling 'offside,' and none louder that the Fratton End faithful who could not possibly tell from their vantage point, Shackleton drew Butler and lobbed the ball over the tall goalkeeper. He then turned away and strolled back to the centre circle, not bothering to check that the ball had gone under the bar and into the net, as, indeed, it had done. Fulham were beaten 4-0 in early February, with Henderson scoring with a spectacular back heel from a corner. Henderson could not seem to score ordinary goals. Bolton were crushed 3-0 for the second time that season. On 5 April 1952, a Pompey team minus Scoular, Froggatt, and Dickinson, who were on international duty, but marshalled by Flewin, beat the eventual Champions, Manchester United 1-0, with Reid scoring with a header from a corner. On Good Friday, Derby were beaten 3-1, with Froggatt scoring a remarkable goal, after running three quarters of the length of the field and dribbling round several Derby opponents. Though Portsmouth had by this time failed in their bid to win the F. A. Cup, they still seemed to have an outside chance of winning the title with four games to go. In the event, it would not have made the difference, even if all these games had been won. As it was, all four games were lost. Tottenham won the Easter Saturday away game rather more comfortably than the 3-1 margin suggested. The Easter Monday game at Derby was lost by the only goal. Next, Pompey lost at home to Preston 2-1 after leading by a Phillips header from a free kick. Much was to be written in praise of the football that Preston played in the 1950s, and with Finney in their ranks this was understandable, but Preston relied heavily on an offside trap to keep the goals against column down. On this occasion, Pompey were caught time and time again, and the last home game ended in frustration. For reasons lost on us, Jackson seemed to blame Reid and Harris for this defeat, and replaced them for the last match by Johnnie Gordon, another young man of supposed promise, and Terry Ryder, who had no promise at all. Burnley won that match 2-1. In the end, Pompey had to be satisfied with finishing fourth, no less than ten points behind Manchester United.

That Portsmouth would win the F.A. Cup had been an aspiration at the outset, but, as the tournament progressed, it soon became an expectation. In 1949, Pompey had seemed fortunate to reach the Semi-Final, but in 1952 their progress to the Sixth Round was magisterial. In the Third Round on 12 January 1952 at Fratton Park, before 41,093 spectators, Lincoln

City were crushed 4-0, with Gaillard 2, Clarke and Albert Mundy scoring. Then, in the Fourth Round at Meadow Lane on 2 February 1952, before 46,500 spectators, Pompey defeated Notts County 3-1, with all the goals coming in the first half from Albert Mundy, Gaillard, and Reid. Then, in the Fifth Round at Fratton Park on 23 February 1952, before 44,392 spectators, Pompey beat Doncaster 4-0 in a bitter match. Peter Doherty may well have been as great a player in his heyday as the old timers told me, but as Doncaster's Player-Manager his strategy was to encourage his team to work over the volatile Scoular to get him sent off. As far as I could make out, Scoular actually enjoyed the attention and more than gave as good as he got, but it was Miller, the Doncaster player, who got sent off for kicking Scoular in the vitals. Scoular was merely booked and carried on regardless. The football played was almost an optional extra, but Pompey made sure of progressing by winning 4-0, with Harris, Phillips, and Gaillard scoring with Doncaster helping out with an own goal. 'So, to Fratton Park, where Portsmouth meet the storming challenge of Newcastle, the holders,' wrote Geoffrey Green in *The Times* on the morning of the crucial Sixth Round match, 8 March 1952. 'Here should be the match of the Round,' Green observed without risk of contradiction: 'So much hangs upon it - Portsmouth with their chance for the Double of Cup and League: Newcastle full of determination and hoping to make history in the twentieth century by winning successive Finals. It is Newcastle's brilliance in attack against Portsmouth's half back line and all round balance. Both are outstanding sides in their own right and fashion, with great players. Both will be at full strength. Let the afternoon take care of itself, hoping that it will echo that October day not so long ago when these two sides fashioned a magnificent game in the League. Portsmouth won that day by 3-1. But Newcastle ... may this time survive.' This was a shrewd forecast on Green's part, giving him the option of the draw as well as a possible Newcastle victory. It seemed to me along with many others to be our year for the F. A. Cup, and, given our recent unconvincing form in the League, to some extent it had to be.

The official attendance for the Newcastle Cup game was 44,699, and the Portsmouth team lined up as follows: Butler; Gunter; Ferrier; Scoular; Froggatt; Dickinson; Harris; Reid; Henderson; Phillips; Gaillard. Pompey made the early running, and anybody who was present will still recall the brilliance of our opening goal. Geoffrey Green wrote about it in the following manner in *The Times* for 10 March 1952: 'Hardly had the struggle got under way on the heavy surface when the blow fell. From Gunter to Henderson the ball flowed swiftly out to Harris, and there was Gaillard moving in at lightning pace to head home a fiercely angled centre from the right.' Green commented that 'such a thrust would have knocked the heart out of most sides in a match so tensely balanced, but not Newcastle.' Indeed, to our alarm, Newcastle took the game to Pompey. Green detected what he saw as 'an unusual feature of the Newcastle plan' which was to use Walker and Mitchell as withdrawn wingers closely linking with the defence. Green wrote that 'Milburn more and more became the focal point of their attacks between the quick moving [George] Robledo and Foulkes.' Things seemed to me to be more straightforward than that. The legendary Jackie Milburn was 'the focal point' of the Newcastle attack anyway. In the League match the previous October, Froggatt had been the master, conceding to him only a late consolation goal. In this game, Milburn was king, and he scored three times. Milburn's dynamism was really why our 'great half back line of Scoular, Froggatt, and Dickinson,' and, hence, why Pompey were in danger of being 'cut to ribbons' at times. Green said that from the back Joe Harvey and Frank Brennan drove Newcastle forward, but I would have described Brennan as the rock at the back for United, and Harvey and Ted Robledo as driving them on. None of this should have mattered, because Pompey should have effectively settled the match before Newcastle opened their account. As Green recorded: 'With corner following corner, the equalizing goal had to come, though before it finally did in the last five minutes of the half, Portsmouth should have [gone] further ahead when Phillips sent through by Henderson, shot [straight] at Simpson ... Then, suddenly, Newcastle were level.'

61

It was Milburn, who seized on a half chance, and at the interval it was 1-1.

If the neutral Green found the second half to be 'breathtakingly exciting,' what did he imagine it was like for the partisan spectators? Pompey had yet another opportunity to command the game. Peter Harris put Gaillard through only for Simpson to dive successfully dive at the left winger's feet. Then with half an hour to go, Foulkes, intercepting when Froggatt had proved too adventurous, found Milburn with a reverse pass. Green wrote: 'Again, Milburn, with exquisite control and pace on the turn, broke free, and with a perfect chip shot from some twelve yards beat he advancing Butler, the ball glancing home off the angle of crossbar and post.' Now it was Newcastle's turn to wilt under a sustained assault. Pompey piled it on, and equalized with twenty minutes to go. Simpson could not hold a shot by Phillips [and] 'a square pass by Phillips across an open goalmouth let in Reid to crash home a low shot and it was 2-2.' So, the teams were level again, and, as Green said, the atmosphere at Fratton Park was 'on fire' as 'driven on by Dickinson and Scoular there came wave after wave of attacks, and it seemed to be Portsmouth, coming again, who would win. They might have done too had not Cowell headed a searing shot from Reid off [the] goal line.' That was Pompey's last chance. Green captured the critical moment expertly: 'With ten minutes left Milburn was in glorious stride again, shadowed by Froggatt and Gunter. Moving left, he suddenly checked and from the edge of the penalty area let fly an oblique left foot shot into the far corner of the net that left Portsmouth and everybody else open mouthed. Though [George] Robledo, taking a pass from Milburn, hit the back of the net a fourth time in the dying moments to make assurance doubly sure, it was that shot of Milburn's that had written *finis* imperiously upon a great game.'

'One would have wished that all the sceptics of this world could have been at Fratton Park on Saturday,' Green wrote afterwards. It had been 'a glorious game,' and Pompey had been 'generous and majestic in defeat,' and it is easy to agree to agree too that 'here was a grey afternoon touched by magic.' Even now, I have only seen one subsequent F. A. Cup tie that was the equal of Pompey versus Newcastle in 1952. This took place almost exactly twenty years later on 6 March 1972 before a smaller crowd of 43,937 spectators at Elland Road when Leeds United defeated Spurs 2-1 in the Sixth Round. Leeds, of course, went on to win the Cup in 1972, as Newcastle did twenty years before. I thought then and I think now that had Pompey beaten Newcastle in that justly famous game we would have gone on to win the Cup in 1952. The Newcastle supporters that we talked to also believed this, and tried to console us with the prospect of Portsmouth going on to win the title on the basis that on the day we had been the better team. In his memoirs, Milburn himself said that his performance in this Cup game was the best of his career, and, having seen all of the great stars of the English game I have never seen anybody play better. I would risk the assessment that Alan Shearer of the famous Newcastle centre forwards may well have been week in and week out the more consistent player, and one Newcastle obsessive once told me that he thought that Milburn was a special occasion player. Whatever the verdict, what was obvious was that on that March 1952 afternoon that Milburn was magnificent. So, the game ended and the relationship between the sets of the supporters was amiable in a manner that is hard to believe would be possible now. That said, though, far from the 'sceptics' being routed by the Newcastle Cup game, surely those in the Pompey camp were proved right. Several so-called stalwarts among the supporters that I knew I never saw again at Fratton Park. They acted as if they knew that Pompey were finished as a major force in English football, and, aside from a flourish in the 1954-55 season, they were proved right. The Newcastle Cup game of 1952 was a superb spectacle. That said, though, 8 March 1952 was the last day on which a Portsmouth team took the field with the aura of greatness around it. This was gone by the end of the game. It never returned.

DISAPPOINTMENT: THE 1952-53 SEASON

If *Match of the Day* had been in existence on the opening day of the 1952-53 season, then the lead item would almost certainly have been Portsmouth versus Blackpool, who both ranked as major clubs at the time. Blackpool won the game 2-0 and with some comfort, and they went on to win the F. A. Cup the following May in what became known as the Stanley Matthews Final, despite Mortensen scoring a hat trick for the winners. Portsmouth's Cup ambitions did not last beyond the Third Round stage. A 1-1 home draw with Burnley on 10 January 1953 was followed by a 3-1 defeat at Turf Moor the following Tuesday. I learnt about Pompey's Cup exit from a bus driver I knew, who was armed with information obtained from the stop press of *The Evening News*. When my face dropped, he said to me, 'You didn't expect us to win up there did you?' Since I was not looking for an argument, I just shrugged, but, privately, it seemed to me that once you started to treat such games as impossible to win then you would never get anywhere. Such were the League results following the opening day defeat that Pompey had badly needed a Cup run to bring to life what turned out to be a disappointing season from the beginning all the way down to its sour end. Of the 42 League games played, Portsmouth won 14, drew 10, and lost 18, which meant that they obtained 38 points and finished fifteenth. Pompey scored 74 goals, of which Harris scored 23 times in 41 games, which was impressive, but the goals against tally was 83, which was disgraceful.

Portsmouth won just one of their first eight fixtures, with that victory being a 2-0 home win at the expense of Manchester United on 6 September 1952. United were rebuilding their team at the time, and it looked like it too. The evening match against Arsenal on 17 September 1952 proved to be a remarkable game. Arsenal were to be the eventual Champions, and they were leading 2-0 and seemed in control when, late on, Froggatt was moved up to centre forward, and ran Ray Daniel and the rest of the Arsenal defence ragged. Froggatt scored with a spectacular header, and then the flustered Daniel pulled him down to concede a penalty, from which Phillips scored with a wild shot that went in off the bar to make the score 2-2. Then, on 20 September 1952, Portsmouth won 5-0 at Bolton, Harris scoring twice. 'Pompey Feast Off Trotters' ran the jubilant headline in *The Football Mail*, but at home the following Saturday all Portsmouth could manage was a 1-1 draw with Aston Villa, with Phillips missing a penalty. A draw at Sunderland, thanks to an own goal, was followed by a 2-1 win over Manchester City, Harris getting both goals, and a 4-2 away win at Stoke, with Harris scoring twice again. Then on 25 October, Preston, following a 5-0 home defeat against Manchester United, crushed Portsmouth 5-2 at Fratton Park, with Finney running riot. It was humiliating. We could scarcely raise a cheer when Reid got a late goal with a clever header. On the boat home, I sought out Zigger Holmes to ask him when, if ever, Pompey had conceded five goals at home before. Apparently, Derby had scored five at Fratton Park on our first season in the top flight, and then not long before Christmas 1936, Arsenal had also won 5-1 against us in a home game. That was the beginning of the end for the then regular goalkeeper, Jock Gilfillan, and Zigger thought that Ernie Butler's career was now effectively over, and, indeed, a 3-2 defeat at Burnley the next week saw the last of him. Norman Uprichard, a Northern Ireland international, was signed from Swindon, and many people came to believe that he was to become Portsmouth's best ever goalkeeper. I was not alone in thinking that some of Uprichard's popularity with the Pompey fans owed something to his alcohol consumption, which seemed to match even their own. As a goalkeeper, he was certainly an excellent shot stopper, but his form was too erratic for me, and we got a taste of this characteristic when, on his debut in the 2-1 home victory over Tottenham on 8 November 1952, Uprichard contrived to put through his own goal. A spectacular away win at Sheffield Wednesday followed a week later by 4-3, with Froggatt getting the better of the local hero Derek Dooley, at least according to *The Football Mail*. Was this the turning point? Would Pompey now set off on a run to re-establish themselves in the top half of the Division?

Portsmouth actually embarked on a dreadful sequence of six straight defeats, five of them by the odd goal, followed by a 3-0 defeat at Derby on Boxing Day, and a 2-2 home draw against them the following day. Given that Derby looked a good bet for relegation even at this stage, Pompey were plainly in difficulties.

There had been rumours of a dressing room bust up between Scoular and Froggatt. Though doubtless Scoular expressed the criticism more forcefully, what this dispute was supposed to be about was Froggatt having lost the speed to play the attacking centre half, which allegedly meant that he could not get back in time to do his defensive work. Since Froggatt's adventurousness had been less and less in evidence, it seemed to many of us that Scoular was looking around for a grievance, having become increasingly fed up with Manager Eddie Lever's schoolmastery style of regime, which was accompanied by a style of play that was sometimes attractive but more often ineffectual. Lever seemed to be fed up with Scoular, who was dropped for a couple of games, and put in a transfer request. In the home game with Derby, at one stage when a ball went high in the air, Scoular did a handstand and bicycle kicked the ball clear. This was play acting, of course, though Scoular knuckled down to more disciplined performances in Pompey's successful battle to avoid relegation. This escape owed nothing to Portsmouth's away form, which comprised defeat after defeat, aside from coming back to secure a 3-3 draw at Tottenham, and a single goal win at Cardiff, Froggatt scoring. After the Fratton Park crowd had slow hand clapped the team during a tedious 1-1 draw with relegation favourites Stoke, followed by a 4-0 beating at Preston, the Directors seemed to be alarmed and found the money to actually sign another player, Charlie Vaughan, a veteran centre forward from Charlton, who scored in his first game, a 2-1 home win over Burnley. Fortunately, starting with and including a 2-0 win over Chelsea, Pompey had earlier gone on a nine game unbeaten run at home which included seven wins and two draws. Some of the wins were spectacular. Sunderland were crushed 5-2 with Harris scoring a hat trick, and Sheffield Wednesday were also beaten 5-2. When Pompey were 5-0 up at half time in that game, a Wednesday exile told me he feared that Portsmouth would score ten, but, of course, they eased off. Another exile, his father in fact, told me that the sun being in the Wednesday players' eyes explained the first half rout, though given that the sun had not set in the meantime it remained unclear why the Pompey players were not blinded too. A week later, Newcastle were beaten 5-1, and two of the Pompey goals were especially memorable. As if to ensure that Newcastle, his preferred destination, noticed his talents, Scoular made certain that he scored by treading on the left hand of goalkeeper Simpson to stop him from preventing the ball from going over the goal line and into the net. Henderson scored a quite stunning goal. Cutting in from the left, he hit a ferocious right foot shot into the far top corner of the net. It was a breathtaking goal, and, to our amazement, Jackie Milburn joined in the applause.

In the final home game on 2 May 1953, though, Pompey spoilt it all with a wretched display. Efforts had been made to rearrange the game for another day, but it ended up being played on Cup Final day, with a crowd of only 18,765, the smallest attendance since 1939. Those of us who had the loyalty to turn up were rewarded by having to watch Middlesbrough run riot. Relegation candidates until their 5-0 victory over Manchester United the week before, Middlesbrough seemed set on celebrating, or, at least, our former player, Delephena did, and he took Pompey apart, in particular humiliating left back Stephen, conventionally one of the favourites of the Fratton faithful, though this particular display was deemed to be literally unforgivable. Middlesbrough won 4-1 on merit. We were surprised that Pompey scored at all. I had thought that a miss from a yard out by Gaillard in front of an open goal in the Cardiff home game on 22 November 1952 (Pompey deservedly lost 2-0) was the worst miss that I have ever seen from a professional player, but Vaughan's miss in this match was even worse. He was only inches from the goal line itself and tried to flick the ball home and completely missed it. Dale eventually scored with a half hit shot. Portsmouth's performance was both lazy and disgraceful, and afterwards many of the fans were very angry, and, of course, the more thoughtful in our ranks were very worried about where exactly Pompey were going. They seemed to have good cause for their concerns, given that though Middlesbrough had escaped relegation this season it was obvious that they were likely to go down the following year. Yet, they had trounced Pompey at Fratton Park. So, where did that leave us? We feared going nowhere, and at some speed.

ANOTHER RELEGATION BATTLE: THE 1953-54 SEASON

If the summer of 1953 is remembered at all by those who were alive at the time it was because of the Coronation, or because England defeated Australia at cricket to win back the Ashes with Denis Compton, as if God had decreed it, scoring the winning runs at the Oval. I was aware of these events, but my clearest recollection is that it was the first summer in which I did not look forward to the start of the new football season. The previous season had been a poor one, but, instead of strengthening the team, Portsmouth transferred Scoular to Newcastle, without a replacement. One could see that Pompey had to replace their title winning players sooner rather than later, but Scoular was still at his peak, as he was to show by playing for Newcastle for the rest of the decade. So, Scoular was far from finished, though Eddie Lever wanted to be finished with him, and to play pure football. After Scoular's departure, yet more former stalwarts among the Pompey supporters I knew were never seen at Fratton Park again. Lever did not seem to mind Pompey playing the role of the good loser, and Scoular was a winner, and, if it came to it, by what means were available. After he had led Newcastle to victory in the 1955 F. A. Cup Final, the B.B.C. television commentator commended Scoular for running across and showing the trophy to the defeated Manchester City fans in the belief that this was a sporting gesture. Of course, what Scoular was doing was rubbing it in that City had lost.

Of the 42 First Division games that Portsmouth played in the 1953-54 season, 14 were won (13 of these victories being home wins), 11 were drawn, and 17 were lost. Thus, Pompey obtained 39 points and finished fourteenth, which was one more point and one place higher than in the previous season. Pompey scored 81 goals, but conceded no less than 89. Peter Harris scored 21 goals in 40 First Division appearances, Gordon scored 18 times also in 40 games, and Charlie Vaughan scored a dozen in 21 games. Injuries meant that Pompey had to call on no less than 32 different players for their League games, including Keith Ames and Rodney Henwood, whom few had heard of before or after. Goalkeeper Uprichard was injured yet again and played just twice, and no less than three others replaced him in goal at various times: Ted Platt, Mervyn Gill, and Charlie Dore. Platt had been an Arsenal reserve, much as Uprichard had been at one time, but there the similarity ended. Platt had the reputation of being a practical joker, and tales of his japes amused some people over the years, but all I cared about was that Platt was not much of a goalkeeper. The Directors just wanted a cheap option. They got one in every sense.

When the fixture list came out, I wrote off the three of the first four games on the basis that they were away. Portsmouth duly lost at Liverpool (3-1), Chelsea (4-3), and to newly promoted Huddersfield (5-1). I expected Pompey to win the home game against Sheffield United, the other promoted team, but the outcome was a 4-3 away win. Jimmy Hagan was still there to run the show for United in a manner that Scoular would never have allowed, and what was even more worrying was the evidence at the centre of Portsmouth's defence that Jack Froggatt was not the force he had been. Jack was kept in the team, but Reid was moved back to centre half, eventually to good effect. The harsh reality was that Pompey were bottom of the league after four games, and that sixteen goals had been conceded. Portsmouth then recorded a couple of home wins over Chelsea (3-2) and Aston Villa (2-1) respectively, followed by a rare point at Blackpool (1-1), before another away defeat at Wolves, the eventual Champions (4-3). Before the return game with Blackpool at Fratton Park, the Pompey faithful had made it clear to the Portsmouth Directors that they would not tolerate the proposed transfer of Froggatt to Arsenal, and the Directors backed down. The general opinion on the ferry back home was that the Directors would wait their time, and then Froggatt would be sold off later in the season. This was what happened. Sentiment played its part in the demonstration, but my attitude was that if anybody had to be sold out of Scoular and Froggatt it ought to be Jack because he was the wrong side of thirty, and Scoular was younger than him by a couple of years or so. Against that, I did not see the point of selling either of them without replacements of the same standard, and who might they be? Froggatt could also play a multitude of positions, and, for

69

example, in the 4-4 draw with Blackpool he played on the left wing, as he did to good effect in a 4-1 win over Sunderland the following Saturday. Portsmouth's results were all over the place. Pompey scored four times in the second half at Hillsborough to secure a 4-4 draw with Sheffield Wednesday, but then lost 2-0 at home to Middlesbrough, who had conceded eight goals at Charlton the previous week, and who were later to be relegated. The next away game at Bolton was lost 6-1, with Harris getting a consolation goal from a penalty. Then came Pompey's third home defeat in just nine home games at the hands of Preston by 3-1. Finney ran rings round Ferrier, who had a reputation for dealing with that particular genius better than most, but not this time, and Ferrier never played again. Pompey were bottom of the table, and frankly deserved to be.

The turning point came at Newcastle on 21 November 1953, when Pompey got a 1-1 draw which marked the beginning of a ten match run that comprised four wins, five draws and only one defeat, that inflicted by Sheffield United at Bramall Lane just before Christmas by 3-1. Len Phillips had been languishing in the reserves, but he was drafted into the half back line for the Newcastle game, really to try to fill the gap left by Scoular. Reid was moved back to the central defence, where he was to spend most of the rest of his career. In at left back came Jack Mansell, who had played brilliantly for Cardiff against Peter Harris a few weeks before. With Ferrier by this time a shadow of his former self, several of us thought that Mansell would be the ideal replacement. To our amazement, the Directors took positive action and recruited him. The switching of Froggatt to centre forward was less of a success, though he did score in Pompey's 1-1 home draw with Manchester United, an achievement given the masterful display of Allenby Chilton, commonly remembered merely as a stopper centre half, but whenever I saw him he was much more versatile than that. Next on the list was away to West Bromwich Albion on 5 December 1953. Froggatt was dropped, though it seemed unlikely to make much difference, given that Pompey had lost on their last four visits to The Hawthorns. More than this, Pompey had not even scored. It looked hopeless. West Brom were either going to be Champions

70

or runner up to Wolves. When somebody, on the basis of the scores in the stop press of the local paper, told me that Pompey were 1-0 up at half time, I thought that it was a misprint. I found the 3-2 final score in our favour every bit as hard to believe. It was a famous victory, even if we all laughed when Gordon, the scorer of two goals, tried a bit of false modesty when he said about taking away this particular unbeaten record that 'somebody had to do it.' The following week, Pompey played Liverpool at Fratton Park, and won 5-1. Harris scored a hat trick in a brilliant display of opportunism. The Sheffield United defeat followed, and then came a couple of 1-1 draws with Tottenham in the Christmas games. The Boxing Day game at Fratton Park was memorable for the outplayed Spurs contriving to hold on to a 1-0 lead until the last minute. Alf Ramsey at right back for Tottenham had a deserved reputation as a gifted and thoughtful player, but this close to the end of his career he found Henderson's raw pace too much for him and he tried to kick Henderson out of the game. Being Scottish, Henderson was not intimidated. Pompey's centre forward Vaughan seemed to the crowd to miss chance after chance. Then in the very last minute Henderson hammered in yet another cross and Vaughan dashing forward placed a rocket header past the previously unbeatable Ditchburn and into the corner of the net. When I got the ferry back to the Isle of Wight, one of my father's friends, a painter and decorator, who had been too ill to stay to the end, and who had never seen Pompey lose in his life, asked me if we had equalized. I was able to tell him that his record was still intact. The next game and the first fixture of 1954 was home to Huddersfield, and revenge was taken for the beating at Leeds Road in August. Pompey won 5-2, no mean feat against a side destined to finish third in the table. The game finished in a remarkable manner too. Huddersfield's Metcalfe missed a penalty at the Milton End which would have made it 4-3, and Pompey went straight to the Fratton End for Vaughan to score and, thus, complete a hat trick. Oddly, Vaughan never played for Pompey in a home league game again. Then came the F.A. Cup, and, showing uncharacteristic optimism, I convinced myself, though nobody else, that Portsmouth stood an excellent chance

71

of a good Cup run, and, who knows, even of winning the trophy itself. History was on my side, or so I thought. In 1929, Pompey got to the Final. Five years later, we had done the same. Five years after that, Pompey had won the Cup. The Second World War prevented this sequence from being immediately repeated, but in 1949 Pompey had reached the semi final. On the Fry Five Year Plan, in 1954 Portsmouth were due for an extended Cup run. My father informed me that fighting relegation came first, and that I was daydreaming. At half time of the Third Round home tie with Charlton on 9 January 1954, it did look as if the great man was right. Pompey were 3-1 down. A second half rally witnessed Pompey secure a 3-3 draw. So, then it was up to the Valley on the following Wednesday, and Pompey won 3-2, Harris scoring twice, and a youth scheme product, Mike Barnard scored the other goal. If you believed the newspapers, the return of Flewin to central defence explained the victory. If you believed the Pompey supporters who made the trip, Flewin was just his former ruthless self, only older. In the Fourth Round, Pompey drew Scunthorpe away. Special trains descended on the Lincolnshire town on 30 January 1954. People came back with tales of untold riches to be found in Scunthorpe, though it was iron and steel that was being produced there, not gold. Platt was injured in the game, some thought deliberately, and Reid went in goal. Pompey held out for a 1-1 draw, Harris, of course, scoring. The replay was another draw, this time 2-2. Victory would have been certain according to the Pompey faithful if a Scunthorpe shot had not hit a ridge of ice and thus defeated Mervyn Gill, our third or fourth choice goalkeeper. I have to admit that I was beginning to lose count by this stage. The second replay was at Highbury. The Scunthorpe players were bullish in the newspapers. Pompey would not turn up and so on. Eddie Lever relied on experience, with not just Flewin being played but Froggatt too. Gordon Dale also emerged from the shadows, and was said to have given a display of artistry that defied the muddy conditions. Froggatt scored twice, and Henderson and Harris once to ensure that Pompey won 4-0. So, on to Bolton for the Fifth Round on 20 February 1954, and a 0-0 draw was obtained. Confidence was high for the replay at Fratton Park. The Cup Final defeat by Bolton in 1929 was cheerfully forgotten. So was the absence of Flewin, who had played his last game. Bolton had never won at Fratton Park. Well, they did this time, by 2-1. I have to say that I could not believe it. Froggatt missed an open goal, and beat his fists on the turf in frustration. It made no difference. We were out.

In the meantime, and contrary to the fears of many, the Cup run such as it was had not adversely affected Pompey's battle against relegation, which had the same character of ineptitude away from home, together with increasing reliability at Fratton Park. Thus, at home on 23 January 1954, Wolves, the prospective Champions, were beaten 2-0. Such was Harris's form that Wolves had moved Billy Wright, the then England captain, across to mark him, but it made no difference. On 13 February 1954, Manchester City were beaten 4-1, with Froggatt scoring twice. Then Burnley were beaten 3-2, after having led by 2-0 at half time, and Bolton were also beaten 3-2 after leading 1-0 at the interval. Victories over Sheffield Wednesday (2-1) and Newcastle (3-1) and an Easter Monday home draw with Arsenal (1-1) followed. Then, with Pompey safe, despite persistently losing away games, came the last match of the season at home to West Bromwich, who were to be runners up in the League and destined to win the F. A. Cup the following Saturday. Pompey won 3-0, in part thanks to a brilliant save at 0-0 executed by yet another goalkeeper, Charlie Dore, whose appearance always reminded me of the then famous American film comedian Danny Kaye, and, some unkind souls thought, only too often played like him. Harris scored twice, but what stuck in the mind was a stunning display by Gordon Dale, who reduced the West Bromwich right back Rickaby into a nervous wreck to such an extent that he lost his place in the following week's Cup Final, and, thus, as it turned out, a winner's medal. Dale made the third goal, which was one of the best that I have ever seen. He floated the ball as if on a piece of string towards Reid, who had moved up from central defence, and who volleyed the ball from thirty yards past Sanders and a foot under the bar to score to the exultation of the Fratton End. We went home full of the joys of Spring. That Pompey had finished a modest fourteenth did not matter. Next season would be different. All we needed to do was to keep up our impressive form at home, currently 12 games without defeat, and, surely, we were bound to improve away. That we had won just 6 of the 50 away games played since the beginning of 1952 was cheerfully forgotten. Most of us on the ferry home thought that Pompey would finish something like sixth the next season, but it was to be better than that.

NOT HUNGRY ENOUGH: THE 1954-55 SEASON

When my father and I tuned in to Sports Report on B.B.C. radio at 5 o'clock on 21 August 1954, we were both delighted and surprised to hear that Portsmouth had beaten Manchester United 3-1 at Old Trafford. Dale and Henderson had scored for Pompey, and, less intentionally, so had a United player with an own goal. The game had been played in driving rain, and Pompey had been without Dickinson, still a current international. The team had been Norman Uprichard, Alex Wilson, Jack Mansell, Len Phillips, Duggie Reid, Reg Pickett, Peter Harris, Johnnie Gordon, Jackie Henderson, Mike Barnard, and Gordon Dale. Dickinson eventually replaced Pickett, and Wilson was to lose his place to Tommy McGhee, a right back with pace and skill, who had been discovered playing football in the Royal Navy, and supposedly signed by Pompey in dramatic manner on Portsmouth and Southsea railway station. Otherwise, the team that won at Old Trafford was essentially that which was to make Portsmouth's last serious bid to become English Champions once more.

Fresh from the opening day away win, Pompey played home games against Huddersfield (4-2) and Wolves (0-0), before losing three away games in a row at Huddersfield (2-1), Aston Villa (1-0), and Bolton (3-!). It did look at this stage as if Portsmouth had thrown away the benefits of the Old Trafford victory as the team sank into mid table. There then followed one of the only two sequences of good results of the entire season. This one set Pompey up for what turned out to be a challenge for the title. We went eight games without defeat. This run started inauspiciously enough with a 2-2 home draw against Sunderland on 11 September 1954, but then Pompey beat Bolton 1-0 thanks to a Harris goal the next Wednesday. Next up was the annual trip to Tottenham, with the result being a 1-1 draw. Reid scored from a free kick, hitting the ball past Ditchburn's right hand into the bottom corner. Ditchburn virtually had to dig the ball out of the net. Less to his credit, Reid missed a second half penalty. He tried to place the ball instead of relying on his usual pile driver. Anyway, we returned home pretty pleased at the way things were going, and this sense of progress was added to by a 2-1 home win over Sheffield Wednesday, followed by what had become a rare point at Preston, Barnard scoring. The next home game proved to be memorable. Pompey beat Sheffield United 6-2. Harris scored no less than four times. I can still mentally picture him limping in to head his fourth goal. Pompey had played spectacularly well in this game, but they were ordinary in the following away game at Arsenal, being fortunate to win 1-0, with Harris getting the crucial goal with a downward header in front of the North Bank. We were delighted to win at Highbury, and this victory was followed by yet another home win against Leicester City by 2-1. Froggatt played for Leicester, and he got the hero's welcome he deserved, though on the day he played poorly. Harris scored again - twice.

That home victory marked the end of what had been a good run, even if, after going down by a single goal at Burnley, Portsmouth followed this up on 6 November 1954 with a 5-0 thumping of Everton at Fratton Park, a result rendered all the more remarkable by the fact that Harris was not among the scorers. The great man was on target the following Saturday at Maine Road. Manchester City had developed the Revie Plan, a tactical arrangement which entailed Don Revie playing in a withdrawn centre forward role. This departure from the playing formation favoured in those days was, of course, intended to throw City's opponents off balance. This did not work in Pompey's case. Gunter, deputizing for Reid at centre half, did not man mark Revie, and left others to pick him up. So, then it was back to Fratton Park, where Portsmouth had gone no less than 20 games without losing in a league game. On 20 November 1954, Cardiff ended this run with a 3-1 victory that owed something to Pompey being reduced to ten men when Dickinson broke his ankle, an injury that kept him out of action for over three months. The following Saturday witnessed a 4-1 defeat at Chelsea. Few took Chelsea seriously as title contenders, including the home supporters that we spoke to. Their attitude seemed to be that Chelsea had never won anything and never would. All the same, Chelsea defeated Pompey comfortably in our opinion, and it was a long journey home. After that defeat, some of us wondered if Portsmouth's inconsistency meant that we were less serious title contenders than we hoped, and the unpredictability of the team was emphasized the following week when West Bromwich were thumped 6-1 in a marvellous exhibition of attacking football. Harris only scored twice. This stunning victory on 4 December 1954 was followed by a run of seven league games in which Pompey only won once. Away from home, Portsmouth lost at Newcastle 2-1, and drew 2-2 at Blackpool, Wolves and Sunderland respectively. Pompey drew the return game with Manchester United 0-0. On 27 December 1954, Portsmouth defeated Blackpool 3-0. That was also the score at half time, and we all expected a hatful, but the game petered out, with the veteran Harry Johnston at the heart of the Blackpool defence expertly closing things down. Jimmy Armfield, who subsequently became a distinguished England full back, made his debut for Blackpool that day, and years later I had the opportunity to ask him what he remembered about the match. He recalled the impossibility of marking Dale with his magical ball control. Other defenders seemed to manage through the use of calculated violence, but Armfield played it straight and got the run around. On 5 February 1955, Pompey suffered a traumatic 3-0 home defeat at the hands of Tottenham. I remember the London newspapers heavily praising Spurs and, in particular, a player called Johnnie Brooks, whom they seemed to think was the coming man. Brooks never arrived. The consensus among the Pompey faithful was that Spurs were no better than they had been in the White Hart Lane game, but that Portsmouth had played very poorly. In the midst of this bout of league games, Pompey went out of the F. A. Cup at the Third Round stage, despite being one of the favourites because of our league position. Bristol Rovers had got to the Sixth Round of the Cup in

1951, even taking Newcastle, the eventual winners, to a replay, with their supporters being given to singing a song called *Goodnight Irene* at length and to no obvious purpose. On 8 January 1955, with this dire ballad in the background, Pompey lost 2-1 at Eastville on 8 January 1955, with somebody called Roost getting a late winner. By common consent, Uprichard was to blame for this goal. Since I did not think that Pompey had the resources to mount both a title challenge and also to make a serious bid to win the Cup, I was not as dismayed as many Pompey fans were by this setback. However, it had occurred to me that, given the way that they were behaving, Pompey might never win the Cup again, and I was finding the campaign to be Champions to be increasingly unconvincing.

Just when some of us were about to write this campaign off, Portsmouth followed the home defeat to Spurs with a run of six wins in eight games. On 12 February 1955, Pompey won 3-1 at Sheffield Wednesday, thus completing a double. There then followed, in the welcome absence of Finney, a rare home win over Preston by 2-0. On 5 March 1955, Newcastle, including Scoular, were also beaten at Fratton Park, in this instance by 3-1. A week later, meeting up again with another hero in Froggatt went very differently. Pompey lost 4-0 to Leicester City at Filbert Street, and Froggatt ran the show, thus exacting revenge for being thrown out. A Leicester fan who saw this game praised the talents of the supposedly finished Froggatt to the skies in a later conversation with me in the Services, and the best that I could come up with as a reply was that Jack had been vastly better in his prime. The following Saturday witnessed a home defeat by Burnley 2-0, with the crucial goal being the result of a blunder by Reid that let in Pilkington to score. We thought the title bid was all over, but then Pompey defeated Everton away (3-2), Manchester City at home (1-0), and then, on Good Friday, Charlton (2-0) at Fratton Park. Portsmouth were making a heavy weather of their title challenge, but with only seven games to go we were still serious contenders together with Chelsea and Wolves. On the way back from the Charlton game, our little group concluded that Pompey needed ten or eleven points from these seven games to take the title. Portsmouth only managed six points in this quest, getting off to a poor start by losing 3-1 away to West Bromwich, and then drawing 2-2 at Charlton. So, the odds were already stacked against us when we faced Chelsea at Fratton Park on 16 April 1955. Pompey had to win the match to have any chance of taking the title, and the outcome was a 0-0 draw. The London newspapers thought that Chelsea had the better of the game, and, for once, I agreed with them. On the following Saturday, a Harris goal put Pompey 1-0 up at Cardiff, but, typically, the home side were allowed to equalize. Then, Portsmouth had a mid week game against Aston Villa, the original match having been abandoned because of fog the previous February with Aston Villa leading 2-1. This time, Pompey were winning 2-1 when, with characteristic carelessness, Uprichard misjudged a shot which he anticipated going over but which hit the crossbar and a Villa player called Thompson ran in to slip the ball home. On 30 April 1955, Portsmouth completed the double over Arsenal by beating them 2-1, which meant that on the Monday all Pompey had to do in order to finish as runners up was to draw in their final fixture at Bramall Lane. Sheffield United won 5-2, and thus took their revenge for the humiliation that they had suffered in the autumn. If Harris had not scored late on, Pompey would have finished fourth.

Of the 42 games that Portsmouth played, 18 were won, 12 were drawn and 12 were lost, meaning that Pompey obtained 48 points and finished third. At home, as in the previous season, Portsmouth won 13 times, drew 5, and lost 3. Away, Pompey won just 5 times, drawing 7 games and losing 9. Overall, Pompey scored 74 goals, with Harris getting 23 of them in 41 appearances, a remarkable ratio for a conventional winger; but, on the other hand, 62 goals were conceded. Pompey finished four points short of the title in crude figures, but the unimpressive goal average meant that the gap was really five points. I still think that Pompey would have won the title if Dickinson had been able to play more than 25 of the 42 games, and had Phillips managed more than the 31 appearances that he made before an injury when on England duty ended not just his season but effectively his career. Reg Pickett provided capable cover for the pair of them, but Pompey's cause was scarcely helped by the fact that Phillips and Dickinson only played in the same team 14 times. I am not saying that the Portsmouth team of 1954-55 was remotely as good as the title winning teams of 1948-49 and 1949-50 when, after all, most of the better players were much younger, and there were a lot more of them. The point was that Pompey did not need to be that wonderful to win the title in the 1954-55 season. Everybody knew that Manchester United's Busby Babes were going to rule English football in the near future, but this was a season too soon for them. The hard truth about the Pompey team of 1954-55, like that of 1951-52 was that they were not hungry enough for success. Like that team too, they often played more entertaining football than the only great team that Portsmouth ever produced - but football is not about entertainment: it is about winning.

Though, of course, we would all have preferred it if the Portsmouth players had raised their game to become Champions again, nobody could write off a season in which Pompey had finished third. Away from home, Pompey could not be trusted, but, say, winning at Arsenal still meant that we counted for something. We gloated about that victory, of course, but when we got back to Waterloo as my father read down the list of the results, he stopped at the Third Division North, and drew attention to the plight of Derby, who had been serious rivals to us in our Golden Age. If Derby could collapse like that, why not us? I was determined to enjoy my last year or so of freedom before going off to do my National Service, and so I did not rise to the bait and discuss the matter. The fate of Derby never left the back of my mind, though, and as the following season progressed it became clear that Pompey were heading the same way down. All the same, all that had seemed a long way off during the previous autumn at Highbury. When it was obvious that Pompey were going to win, several of the Arsenal people called out that we would be relegated. I laughed out loud. I was soon to find that my world was going to change, and, of course, for the worse.

TOWARDS THE EDGE: THE 1955-56 SEASON

The summer of 1955 was to be the last one for a very long time during which I looked forward to the next football season with even mild optimism. There were plenty of warning signs about the long term future, or, at least, a minority of us thought so, and nobody expected Portsmouth to actually win anything. Nevertheless, Pompey still ranked as a major club and most supporters I knew thought in terms of Portsmouth finishing something like sixth, seventh or eighth in the 1955-56 season. Of their 42 League fixtures, Portsmouth won 16, drew 9, and lost 17, which meant that they obtained 41 points and finished twelfth. Pompey scored 74 goals (with Harris getting 23 goals in 41 appearances) but 85 were conceded. If the 1955-56 season for Portsmouth could be summed up in one word it would be inconsistency.

Portsmouth got off to a mixed start, losing 1-0 at Huddersfield on 20 August 1955, beating Wolves 2-1 four days later in a spectacular and exciting evening match at Fratton Park characterized by all out attack on the part of both teams; and then a 3-3 home draw with Blackpool that was almost as entertaining. It must have been in this match that when Jack Mansell laid Stanley Matthews low with a harsh tackle, Dickinson was reported to have said to Mansell that we did not play that way at Portsmouth. Unless the likes of Flewin and Scoular were being erased from the history books in the manner of Stalin, it would have been nearer the mark for Dickinson to have said that Pompey did not play that way under Eddie Lever. Anyway, a midweek away defeat at Wolves (3-1) in what *The Evening News* described as a classic encounter did not offer encouragement to those of us who made what was by now the familiar journey to Stamford Bridge on 3 September 1955. Chelsea, the reigning Champions, dominated the first twenty minutes. It looked like being a repeat of last year's beating, though the Pompey defence marshalled by Reid managed to hold out. I have no idea whether or not what happened next surprised the rest of the 48,273 crowd, but it certainly surprised me. Pompey cut loose and proceeded to crush Chelsea, with the left wing pairing of Derek Rees and Pat Neil leading the way. A local boy, Neil was thought at the time to be immensely promising player, able to operate on both wings. Like many others before him, Pompey had discovered Rees a year or so earlier playing in Services football.

Rees seemed too small to me to succeed as a centre forward, but he had sufficient skill to play elsewhere as Alf Ramsey recognized in later signing him for Ipswich when Pompey let him go. Ramsey was also to sign Reg Pickett when Pompey later discarded him. For some reason, on this particular afternoon, Chelsea allowed Pickett to run the game. Pompey were 3-0 up at half time, and ran out 5-1 winners, with the Chelsea goal very much a late consolation effort. The Portsmouth scorers were Harris (2), Rees (2) and Henderson. After the match, on hearing our South coast voices, several of the Chelsea fans came up to us to congratulate us on Pompey's display. No doubt, if it had been the 1970s or 1980s, the Shed End types would have tried to knife us, probably for pleasure. It was a different world then. That said, though, Pompey's win at Chelsea that sunny September 1955 afternoon proved to be the best display that Portsmouth gave in any away game that I saw for over half a century, even if it was also one of those games where you had the feeling that everything that Pompey tried came off. So, we all looked forward to the following Saturday and the Bolton home game, hoping for a repeat performance. We were to be disappointed. Bolton ran the match, leading 3-0 until Pompey rallied near the end to get an unlikely 3-3 draw. Harris scored twice, one of his goals being a brilliant cross shot off the far post. So, off we went to Arsenal on 17 September 1955 not knowing what would happen. Pompey's first half display was appalling. Tommy Lawton headed down a corner and Doug Lishman lashed it in the net to put Arsenal 1-0 up, and we feared, the way that things were going, that this would be the first of many. After the interval, it was a different game. Henderson had been the worst player on the field, but he suddenly tore Arsenal apart. Shots from him rained down on the spectators at the Clock End. Harris (2) and Rees actually managed to score to give Pompey a 3-1 victory. We did not know this at the time, but this was to be the last time that Pompey ever won an away game at Highbury. More immediately, on 23 September 1955, Pompey defeated Everton 1-0 at Fratton Park, and then Sunderland 2-1 in another home game a week later, before losing at Newcastle by the odd goal. There then followed two dreadful defeats. On 15 October 1955, Birmingham won 5-0 at Fratton Park. This Birmingham team was destined to reach the 1956 Cup Final, and it may well have been the best team that City ever fielded, finishing sixth in the top flight. The 'Brummie Bashers' were certainly one of the toughest teams I have ever seen even by the violent standards of those days, and they swept Pompey aside. The experiment of playing Rutter at centre half proved to be a disaster. In the manner of a traffic policeman, he might as well have waved the 'Bashers' through. As it was, they just ignored him. The following Saturday, Pompey were beaten 6-1 at Charlton. That Uprichard was injured yet again was some excuse for this drubbing. A week later, as if to underline their inconsistency, Pompey outplayed Tottenham to win 4-1, and then on Guy Fawkes Day 1955 Portsmouth defeated Sheffield United 3-1 to record what proved to be their last win at Bramall Lane for the rest of the century. There then followed a four game run in which Pompey scored no goals and secured one point, a 0-0 home draw with Luton in a game that tested the soul.

Then the season turned around again, with a run in which Portsmouth went six games without defeat. On 10 December 1955, in an exciting game which the visitors largely ran and then effectively threw away, Pompey defeated Manchester United 3-2. United were winning until the last five minutes, but their defence increasingly failed to contain Henderson, and in trying to clear a shot from him Mark Jones the United centre half drove the ball into his own net for the winning goal. That game sticks in the memory because it proved to be the last time that I saw the Busby Babes because seven of them - including Jones - were to die in the Munich Air Crash not much more than a year later. This victory over the prospective Champions was followed a week later by another home win, this time by 5-2 over Huddersfield, who were destined to be relegated. Henderson got two goals this time. There then followed four games in a fortnight. Pompey had several bogey teams whom they rarely seemed to defeat, and top of the list during the immediate post war period came Blackpool. So, when Pompey recorded a 3-2 away win at Bloomfield Road on Christmas Eve 1955, we were delighted at our first victory there since 1933. We were less surprised that

Harris scored twice. Since Pompey had not won at Villa Park since 1932, nobody expected Aston Villa to be defeated on Boxing Day 1955. Yet, Pompey won 3-1, Harris only scoring once. In the return game the next day, Pompey were 2-0 up at half time thanks to (almost inevitably) Harris and also Gordon. Those of us who thought the game to be over were wrong. Villa rallied and earned a 2-2 draw. On New Year's Eve 1955, Chelsea were the visitors and those expecting a repeat of the away result were again to be disappointed. Chelsea were deservedly 3-0 ahead in no time at all, and some of us wondered if they would exact literal revenge for the drubbing they had endured the previous September. We were wrong again. In a pulsating match, it was Pompey's turn to rally this time, and the outcome was a 4-4 draw, with both Harris and Henderson scoring twice. Though Portsmouth had been as high as third during the Christmas period, nobody with much sense believed that we would finish there. So, interest turned towards the possibility of an F. A. Cup run, especially when we learned that Len Phillips would be making his comeback on 7 January 1956 in the Third Round home tie with Grimsby Town from the Third Division North. Pompey won easily enough by 3-1, but, after showing some of his old skills in the first part of the game, Phillips was eventually reduced by a recurrence of his knee injury to being a virtual passenger, and his career was plainly over. Hopes of a Cup run were also at an end when West Bromwich away came out of the hat for the Fourth Round. There were to be special trains and so forth, but my father had the offer of some overtime on the Saturday concerned in late January 1956, and, like me, he had no wish to go. That two such stalwarts were unwilling to make the effort aroused sour comments from several people who were to go missing permanently in the years to come, but we had come to distrust Pompey on such occasions, certainly away from home. A 4-1 defeat at Manchester City followed by a 4-0 beating at Bolton did not point to anything other than a Cup exit at The Hawthorns, and, sure enough, those who did make the trip came back dismayed after a 2-0 defeat, with much moaning about the legitimacy of the penalty conceded. In the midst of all this, on 21 January.1956, as if to emphasize Portsmouth's inconsistency,

Arsenal were crushed 5-2. The newspapers told us that this was to be the comeback day for the Arsenal legend, Alex Forbes, but it was Peter Harris who dominated the show, scoring twice. A fortnight later, Pompey won 2-0 at Everton, and, reportedly in some style, which was just as well because this was to be Pompey's last league win at Goodison Park that century. A 4-2 away defeat at Sunderland was followed by a 2-0 defeat in midweek at the hands of Newcastle, who, in front of the lowest crowd since the War, recorded their first win in a league game at Fratton Park since 1931. This match, which took place in bitterly cold conditions on 22 February 1956, has a place in the record books because it was the first ever Football League game to be entirely played under floodlights. Ironically, it was the first Portsmouth home league game that I had missed for five years, and I could scarcely believe that Pompey had lost. On the Saturday, a last minute goal meant a 3-2 defeat at Birmingham, but a hat trick by Rees resulted in a 3-1 home win over Burnley. Rees also scored in a 1-1 draw at Tottenham, with Spurs seeming distracted by an imminent Cup semi final. The season then drifted to a close. Of their last five home games, Pompey registered just one victory, a 4-0 win over Charlton on Easter Saturday, one day after a fortunate 1-1 home draw with Cardiff in which the play was dictated by Trevor Ford. As if the underline Pompey's irritating inconsistency, Portsmouth won the return game at Cardiff 3-2. The remaining away games were all lost, and so it came to the last home match of the season, against Manchester City on 28 April 1956. Instead of trying to win the match against a team who were due to play in the F. A. Cup Final the following Saturday, Manager Lever decided that letting Duggie Reid have another outing as a forward would be a fitting way to mark the end of his playing career. Since Reid had not played in such a role for over two years, and he had not played in the first team at all since December, this was sentimental behaviour on Lever's part. Reid should have saluted the crowd from the sidelines and we could have saluted him back. A few years earlier, the great cricketer, Wally Hammond had been persuaded to make a comeback against his better judgement, and he was to admit that, when fielding, he was reduced to praying long before the end that the ball would come nowhere near him. Reid played in much the same manner that April day. Moved to the back eventually, he seemed all at sea, and I prayed for the final whistle to end his misery and my own at watching him struggle. City did not just have one eye on the following week's Cup Final they had both eyes, but they still won 4-2. Don Revie was to be the architect of City's victory in the 1956 Final, but in the game at Fratton Park the week before Revie was the worst City player on the field, though he earned our gratitude when capping a dreadful display by missing an open goal late on. So, for Pompey supporters, the 1955-56 season ended on a sour note. The great days were already fading into the past, and there was every cause to fear the future.

PART II: SUPPORTING AN ORDINARY JOE CLUB PORTSMOUTH 1956-2008

CHAPTER 4: LIVING THE NIGHTMARE: PORTSMOUTH 1956-1961

INTO THE ABYSS

'I was living the dream.' So Peter Ridsdale, the then Chairman of Leeds United, famously said as he led his club into bankruptcy in the early twenty first century. Roughly fifty years before, if somebody had asked me how I felt about supporting Portsmouth in the years 1956 to 1961, it would have hit the nail on the head if I had said that 'I was living the nightmare.' For the 1955-56 season proved to be the last in which Pompey ranked as a major club. On the boat going back to the Isle of Wight after the Manchester City defeat on the last day of that season I got an early and unwelcome taste of the bitterness among the Pompey faithful that this collapse in status engendered. Quite who started this heated debate on that April evening remained unclear, but I made the mistake of taking part. On one side were those - whom we can call the Pessimists - who maintained that Portsmouth were going nowhere fast; and they were ridiculed by the other fans - whom we can refer to, out of kindness, as the Optimists. Zigger Holmes and my father were the only Pompey supporters present who took my side as I unwisely abandoned my previous policy of being the amiable bystander in such discussions, though one deferred to in matters that were tests of memory. The Pessimist argument was that the season just finished was yet another in which we had done nothing in the F.A. Cup, and that it was the third season out of the last four in which Pompey had won fewer games than we had lost. We had conceded more goals in the 1955-56 season than we had in the two title winning seasons combined. The style of play that the Lever regime preferred made us only too vulnerable to the more physical teams, and, in particular, we had become a soft touch away from home. With Phillips forced to retire through injury, and Reid, too, because of age, there were just Dickinson and Harris left from the title winning team, and no sign of any replacements of comparable quality emerging from what passed for Pompey's youth policy, or from the transfer market in recent times - with the honourable exception of the gifted Jack Mansell - given that the Board of Directors plainly had no serious money. Barely credibly, what money they did have was being spent on rebuilding the Fratton End. The existing structure was ramshackle, but it served its purpose, and radically improving the team and not the ground should have been the priority. So, the Pessimist case was that unless there was serious recruitment of new players allied to changes in playing strategy, especially placing more emphasis on defence, Pompey were heading for trouble, meaning relegation to the Second Division, perhaps even worse. Look what had happened to Derby.

The Pessimist case might have been better presented by Zigger Holmes or by my father and not by somebody still at the Grammar School and yet to do his National Service and thus, by the harsher tests that prevailed in those days compared with now, by somebody who qualified as a man. Against that, the Optimists simply did not want to listen to anybody. They were in the majority, and they believed that Portsmouth had a divine right to a place in the elite of English football, and that all was well. What was obscured by the heat of the argument was that what the supporters thought mattered little anyway because the only power that they possessed was to walk away, which, to my disgust, eventually the Optimists did, to a man. The power lay with the Board of Directors in whose good judgement, at least at this stage, the Optimists placed their trust, whereas to people like me these Directors bore the main responsibility for having led Pompey to the brink of the precipice. From this exchange of views, I learnt the truth of the maxim about blame the messenger, and also, what should have been obvious to me, that most football supporters only want to hear good news about their club, and, never mind the hard evidence, to be offered hope.

Further than this, the logic of my position was simply to give up being a Portsmouth supporter in 1956. It was just as well that I did not do so because spending a couple of years in the ranks in the Armed Forces in the 1950s, as conscripts were forced to do, when you were not the 'one of the lads' type was scarcely fun anyway. Supporting Pompey gave me an identity, and my knowledge of, and continuing interest in, football gave me something in common with the overwhelming majority of my unwanted comrades. As it happened, calculation of this kind did not enter into it, primarily because in 1956 it seemed to me that, having experienced wonderful times with Pompey, even if those times were fast fading into the past, then I ought to stand by Portsmouth in the dark days to come. To put the matter mildly, this proved to immensely harder to do than I expected. To paraphrase the notorious admiring remark attributed to Sidney and Beatrice Webb about Stalin's tyranny in Communist Russia, I had seen the future for Portsmouth Football Club, and I knew that it would not work.

THE NIGHTMARE YEARS

[A] The 1956-57 Season

Portsmouth's record in the 1956-57 season was disgraceful. My family and several of my friends wrote to tell me that I was lucky that my R. A. F. duties cut down on the number of Pompey's fixtures that I could see. Eventually, after training, I was posted to the Aden Garrison, and I could see no fixtures at all. Since Aden as a long term posting scared the hell out of even some of the toughest Servicemen that I have known, I might have been better off being able to indulge my self pity watching Pompey lose most of the time. As it was, Pompey won just one of their first ten fixtures, defeating Sheffield Wednesday on 25 August 1956, mainly, in my opinion, because an Isle of Wight man called Roy Shiner, playing for Wednesday, missed a sucession of easy chances. The preferred explanation for Shiner's failings from the rest of the Island contingent was that Roy remained a Pompey supporter at heart. This may have been just as well, given that Pompey only recorded two further wins (defeating Aston Villa 5-1 and Charlton 1-0) in the first half of the season. As I was surrounded by Everton supporters in my R. A. F. billet at the time, I did not relish going to see Pompey play at Goodison Park on 10 November 1956. Everton dominated the game and led by 2-0 until late on when, against the run of play, Gordon and Rafferty (with an excellent header) scored for Pompey, and Henderson had a shot cleared off the line in the last minute. My Everton comrades assured me that with luck like that Pompey would avoid relegation, and, whether ot not by good fortune in the sense that there were two even worse teams around to save them, Pompey did, indeed, survive.

There was little relief from the enveloping gloom, however, and I well remember that on successive Saturdays in early 1957, when stationed at Hereford, buying a sports paper at the local bus station, and learning in the first instance that Pompey had been defeated at home in the F. A. Cup by Notts Forest from the Second Division by 3-1, and then the next week that Portsmouth's struggle to avoid relegation had not been helped by a 7-1 defeat at Preston. Tom Finney assured readers of one newspaper that Pompey had played some good football, but that they had played it too slowly. Neither a fellow Pompey fan nor myself reading this comment had the slightest idea what Finney was talking about, and we wondered if he did. Of our 42 games in the then First Division, Portsmouth won just 10, drew 13, and lost 19, scoring 62 goals, and conceding no less than 92. So, Portsmouth obtained 33 points, and finished ninetenneth out of 22 clubs. No fewer than seven home defeats were suffered, including a 5-2 defeat by Leeds, for whom, some good judges later told me, John Charles was said to have been magnificent. I can express no worthwhile opinion about Charles, given that I only saw him play twice. The first time was in a friendly match in which Pompey beat Leeds 4-0 in 1956, which Charles, understandably, took lightly, and the other time was nine years later when, well past his best, he played at Fratton Park for Cardiff and missed an open goal. Charles once told a friend of mine that the two best teams that he ever saw were the Portsmouth title winning side and Revie's Leeds. I would have described them myself as two of the best teams that I ever saw, but I was grateful for the great man's comments. Anyway, as far as the 1956-57 season was concerned, besides the seven home defeats, Pompey endured no less than twelve away defeats. Pompey suffered a 6-0 beating at Wolves, a 5-0 defeat at Blackpool, and a 5-1 loss at Manchester City. That Pompey were not relegated was partly explained by the fact that Portsmouth did the double over both Charlton and Cardiff, the two clubs who did go down to the Second Division. The wins at the Valley and at Ninian Park were the only away victories that Pompey recorded in the League. Portsmouth defeated Cardiff by 1-0 on Good Friday by 1-0 at home, and by 2-0 on the Easter Monday. Peter Harris scored all three goals. I looked forward to the next season with dread.

[B] The 1957-58 Season.

The 1957-58 season proved to be the only one since the Second World War in which I was unable to see Portsmouth play. This was because I was serving in the Middle East with the R. A. F. The football results eventually reached me via the Forces radio network and British newspapers would reach Aden a week late. My parents also sent me copies of the Portsmouth *Football Mail* on an irregular basis. My mother included several copies in a Christmas parcel which arrived many weeks later. By that time, the cake that was also enclosed seemed to me to be actually moving because of the wild life that it had attracted. I declined to eat it, but my Scottish comrades showed no such reticence, devoured the cake, and, to my amazement, showed no ill effects. Of the 42 games in the First Division that Portsmouth played, 12 were won, 8 were drawn, and 22 were lost, with 73 goals being scored, and 88 being conceded. Pompey obtained 32 points, and finished twentieth out of 22. If Portsmouth had lost the last home game of the season against Sunderland by 9-0 instead of 2-0, Pompey would have been relegated in their place.

That result on 1 May 1958 represented Portsmouth's fifth home defeat of the season. That Pompey won just two away games came as no surprise, though few would have predicted an early season 5-3 win at Tottenham just a week after a 5-1 home victory over Spurs, or, for that matter, that Pompey would win by 3-0 against the reigning Champions, Manchester United at Old

Trafford, though the task had been made easier by United being weakened by international calls, which were no longer much of a problem for Portsmouth. The home victory over Spurs witnessed two goals from Ray Crawford, a local born player, who had done his National Service in Malaya, and who was, as a result, dubbed The Jungle Boy by *The Daily Express*. Another young man of promise was Derek Dougan from Northern Ireland, whose performance in a 1-1 draw with Wolves in direct opposition to Billy Wright, the then England captain, so impressed the old timers so much that they were still describing one trick that Dougan pulled at Wright's expense when I got back home not far short of a year later. Otherwise, aside from a 5-1 drubbing in the Fourth Round of the F. A. Cup away at Wolves, only the 7-4 defeat away at Chelsea matched the humiliations of the previous season. Striving to listen for the result on the barrack block's temperamental radio, I hoped that I had misheard the Stamford Bridge score that Christmas Day, but no such luck, and I learnt later that a then unknown called Jimmy Greaves had scored four times for Chelsea. The next day, the radio informed me, correctly once more, that Pompey defeated Chelsea 3-0. Far from signalling a revival, Pompey lost at home to Preston two days later. Early in the season, Pompey had lost 4-0 at Preston, and there were 4-1 defeats too at the hands of Birmingham away and by the newly promoted Notts Forest at home, but, nevertheless, the Directors seemed to think that Pompey were safe by early March because Jackie Henderson was suddenly sold to Wolves. No doubt, Henderson's many unreasoning detractors were pleased by this act of crass stupidity, which was added to by Henderson's inevitably cheap, and also older, replacement, Alex Govan, proving so inept that he had to be sold on after just eleven appearances. Pompey could not seem to do anything right. Somehow, though, with six games to go it seemed a reasonable assumption that Portsmouth needed just one point to be sure of staying up. As the reader will by now guess, five of the six games were lost, and one point was all Pompey secured. It came when Peter Harris scored a late equaliser to earn a 3-3 draw against a Manchester United team devestated by the Munich air crash. So, Sunderland were relegated for the first time in their League history. Portsmouth had never been relegated as a League club either, but that this proud record was going to end merely a year later was made certain when Portsmouth replaced the pleasantly ineffectual Eddie Lever as Manager by a prize idiot.

[C] The 1958-59 Season

There are many candidates for the title of the worst season in Portsmouth's history this side of the Second World War, but, having lived through all of them, my vote goes to the 1958-59 season. This was under way before I returned from Aden in an R.A.F plane that seemed to be held together by string and chewing gum, and which was packed to the roof with cargo. 'Ammunition,' a Sergeant on the flight informed me, 'If we hit the deck, we've had it.' Quite why ammunition was being transported to the U.K. in such bulk was not explained, but, in the end, it made no difference. We landed safely at Lyneham, and, once demobbed, I made my way back to the Isle of Wight. I had more to think about than football, above all getting a job, but eventually I came across the Pompey loyalists, and the mood had changed dramatically over the past nineteen months that I had been abroad. In the Isle of Wight of my youth, for most of us most of the time the mood was one of sunny side up, but the hard core Portsmouth supporters that remained were by now an embittered bunch, and, to a man, they told me that they hated Eddie Lever's replacement as Manager, Freddie Cox, whom they believed, correctly as it turned out, would preside over our relegation to the Second Division, and that we would be very lucky if the slide stopped there. As might be expected, I found it easier to have earlier predicted this outcome than to live with it when it happened. I still went to as many Pompey games as I could, despite my father having become seriously ill, and with Saturday being the best time to visit him in the cancer ward. I most certainly did not enjoy going to the games, finding it harder and harder to tolerate the bitterness that came to dominate the atmosphere at Fratton Park. This overflowed during the home game with Notts Forest on 3 January 1959, which Pompey lost 1-0, being fortunate that the eventual F.A. Cup winners missed several chances. The crowd turned on Reg Cutler, one of Cox's signings, with a venom that bore no relation to the player's performance. I have always thought and still do that treating one of your own players like this was counter productive. Cutler could not help being a mediocre player. The responsibility lay with Cox for hiring him, and with the Directors for hiring Cox.

The Cox era began with Portsmouth losing their opening home game with West Ham by 2-1, watched by a crowd of 40,470, followed by two away defeats at the hands of Aston Villa and Notts Forest, in the latter case by 5-0. Then, in the return game against Aston Villa on 3 September 1958, Pompey won 5-2, with Peter Harris scoring all five goals. Zigger Holmes told me later that Harris's feat was largely explained by left winger Ron Newman having the game of his life. It seemed that Harris's achievement was not unique, because somebody called Alf Strange had also scored five times for Pompey in a game in the 1920s. As ever, Zigger was correct in saying this, and also in his prediction that both Pompey and Villa would be relegated. Portsmouth then drew at home with Chelsea 2-2, won at West Brom 2-1, which proved to be Pompey's only away win of the season, and then drew at Blackpool 1-1. The methods that two Cox imports, Basil Hayward and Tommy Casey used to subdue Stanley Matthews in the game at Bloomfield Road led the great man to vow that he would not ever play against Portsmouth again. Hayward was a lumbering oaf, though, sadly, it turned out, by no means the only natural Third Division player by this time featuring in the Portsmouth ranks. That said though, the win away at West Brom led to talk in the newspapers about there being a New Pompey, largely on the basis, it seemed, that two further Cox recruits, Ron Saunders and Harry Harris had scored Portsmouth's goals. The return game at Fratton Park on 17 September 1958 represented my welcome back into the Portsmouth fold, and the supposed New Pompey proceeded to be 5-1 down to West Brom at half time, eventually losing 6-2. I thought that Ronnie Allen had a superb game for the visiting team, who deserved to win more heavily. Allen owed one of his goals entirely to the assistance of the ridiculous Hayward, whose intended back pass turned out to be an ideal cross for Allen. In the second half, with the game already easily won, West Brom only bothered to pay any serious defensive attention to Peter Harris, as if the other attackers were nobodies, which, of course, they were. On the ferry back to the Isle of Wight afterwards, a former girlfriend tried to talk to me about the game, but, pleased though I was to have any form of female company after spending 599 days with the R.A.F. in a desert, I found it hard to say anything at all, least of all something of value, and I noticed that around me most people were reduced to silence.

Of the 42 games in the First Division that Portsmouth played in the wretched 1958-59 season, Pompey won 6, drew 9, and lost 27, scoring 64 goals and conceding the disgraceful total of 112 goals. Pompey obtained 21 points, and finished last out of 22 clubs. Thus, Pompey were relegated, and very much deserved to be. Aside from the heavy defeats at the hands of Notts Forest and West Brom already noted, Portsmouth suffered a 7-0 beating at Wolverhampton the day after losing 5-3 to them at Fratton Park, a 6-0 defeat at West Ham, a 6-1 thrashing at Manchester United, a 5-1 home defeat by Newcastle, and a final day 5-2 beating at Arsenal. Pompey somehow defeated Swansea and then Accrington Stanley in the F. A. Cup, before losing at Burnley in the Fifth Round, but this did not distract from the carnage of the League season. Seventeen of Pompey's miserable total of 21 points came from the first 18 games. The last time that Portsmouth won a league game not just at Fratton Park but anywhere was when Pompey defeated Burnley 4-2 on 22 November 1958, after which Portsmouth took just one point (a 1-1 draw with Birmingham) from the last 12 home games. Of the last 12 away matches, Pompey drew three (at Chelsea, Tottenham, and Leeds) and lost the remainder. Portsmouth lost every one of their last nine fixtures home and away, to thus finish off a season in which Pompey set a record at this level by failing to win in 24 successive games, one which stood until Oxford United did even worse in the 1987-88 season, when Portsmouth were relegated once more.

[D] The 1959-60 Season

Nobody that I knew among the Portsmouth supporters expected Pompey to bounce straight back after being relegated to the Second Division, and almost everybody feared immediate relegation to the Third Division. The feeling that everything was going against Pompey was added to when a serious illness forced Peter Harris to retire in the early weeks of the 1959-60 season, During that season, Portsmouth won 10, drew 12, and lost 20 of their 42 Second Division games, scoring 59 goals and conceding 77. Pompey thus obtained 32 points and finished twentieth. Pompey started off with a 0-0 draw at Middlesbrough, and then secured their first win of any kind in a league game for nine months with a 2-0 away victory at Lincoln. Portsmouth then lost their opening home game against Swansea by 3-1. Swansea deserved to win, though their task was made easier by some poor goalkeeping on the part on the part of Dick Beattie, whose recruitment from Celtic in the summer had been deemed a coup by Cox. He seemed to find the Glasgow club's willingness to part with Beattie to be a mystery, but one of my Celtic friends later said to me that Beattie had been transferred out because he let in too many suspiciously soft goals. His line was that Beattie was gifted, but a crook, which assessment was to be borne out. Lincoln then won the next home fixture, leading many of us to wonder when Pompey would next record a victory at Fratton Park. The answer proved to be the 1-0 win over Plymouth on 17 October 1959, just short of eleven months since the Burnley victory, which, incidentally, had been undeserved. Pompey won just six times at home all season, including a bizarre 6-3 victory over Middlesbrough, including Clough, on the Saturday before Christmas. To the amazement of his detractors, Cutler played very well on a difficult surface, and, indeed, ran the match. Everything Pompey tried came off. It was a freak result. Another oddity was that Pompey also somehow beat Bill Shankly's Liverpool 2-1 at Fratton Park on 12 March 1960, having already drawn 1-1 at Anfield. Another uncharacteristic result was a 4-1 away victory at Cardiff, a club that was to win promotion. A Third Round exit from the F.A. Cup following a 3-0 away defeat at the hands of Sheffield United fitted in rather better with the general pattern of results. After a 5-4 home defeat at the hands of Bristol Rovers in early February, Cox made great play about conducting an inquiry into how Pompey could possibly lose after scoring four times. The lack of any form of serious defensive organization would seem to be the obvious answer, though there were those who believed after another home defeat, this time by Derby, at the end of the same month that Beattie had thrown that particular game. Certainly, he had translated a goal kick into what was a pass to a Derby player, who had promptly scored. The general opinion was that with types like Beattie and wretched outfield players like Sammy Chapman and Ron Howells, Pompey did not need to be bribed to lose, given that they almost always lost anyway. This piece of cynicism missed the point that successful betting has to be about certainties, not just probabilities, and Beattie, Chapman, and Howells were all later to be sent to prison for football corruption, though only in Beattie's case was this related to Pompey. What could not be disputed was that the current Portsmouth team was so poor that the Club was only spared another relegation because, scarcely believably, Bristol City and Hull City had even worse outfits, and it has to be said that the home games that I saw against these two appalling teams were probably the worst games of professional football that I had seen down to that time. Pompey rounded off the fixture list by being thrashed 6-1 at Charlton.

[E] The 1960-61 Season

The 1960-61 season was awaited with dread, and rightly so. Portsmouth won 11, drew 11, and lost 20 of their 42 Second Division fixtures, scoring 64 goals and conceding no less than 91. Pompey thus obtained 33 points, and finished in twenty first place, meaning that they were relegated. Only Lincoln City finished below Portsmouth. The opening game of the season was against Lincoln at Fratton Park, and, though Pompey won 3-0, most people I talked to shared my opinion that both teams were relegation fodder. In the second game, which was away at Luton, Pompey fought hard, and Beattie played very well. In the last minute, Turner for Luton pulled the ball down with his hand and volleyed the ball into the net as a joke. The referee gave a goal, thus granting Luton a 1-0 win. Beattie was reported in the newspapers as having shed tears of frustration.

Three days later, on 27 August 1960 to be precise, Pompey played Southampton for the first time since 1927. I had neither visited the Dell before that day, nor seen Southampton play at all. The Saints had been in the Third Division since 1953, but they had become Champions of that Division in 1960, and the youth policy that their gifted Manager, Ted Bates had pursued seemed to be paying off at last. I had no experience of local derbies, but what I did know was that those returning the previous season from the first meeting with local rivals Brighton since 1924 and from a defeat had not enjoyed the experience. It had been made clear to me then by my fellow loyalists that preferring the company of my girlfriend to supporting the lads was close to blasphemy. A year later, and minus the girlfriend (and not surprisingly so since she would have easily won a Marilyn Monroe contest even up against Marilyn herself), I had no good reason for missing the Southampton away game, and, moreover, my father, at that time deemed to have recovered from lung cancer, though the specialist had no idea why, wanted to go. As it happened, he was too ill to travel, but I still made the mistake of travelling. The game was a nightmare from start to finish. Two of Bates's young prodigies, Terry Paine and John Sydenham, tore Pompey apart. Pompey were 4-0 down at half time. If the Saints, in the manner of professionals, had not decided that they had done enough, Portsmouth might well have conceded ten goals before the game, mercifully, came to an end. As it was, Pompey lost 5-1. The return journey back to Portsmouth was a miserable experience. The train was packed to the roof with Pompey supporters, all of whom were strangers to me. In the classic Hitchcock movie, *Strangers on a Train*, two people meet, and one of the characters played by Robert Walker, who just happened to be mad in real life, believes that he has convinced his fellow traveller played by Farley Granger that all their problems would be solved if the two people who were making their lives a misery were murdered. So, why not swap murder victims? As both murders would be motiveless, they would get away with it. Walker went ahead with his scheme, but

97

Granger did not. The difference with the strangers on the train coming back from Pompey's humiliation at the Dell that August day was that everybody wanted to murder the same person - Freddie Cox – and, thus, save Pompey from relegation. The general opinion on the ferry back to the Isle of Wight was that the Board of Directors would soon see sense, and that, dead or alive, Cox's services would soon be dispensed with. My line was that the Directors would eventually have to dismiss Cox - but that they would do this too late. As so often, my attitude pleased nobody.

As it happened, Cox survived until February, probably because, combined with inertia on the part of the Directors, Pompey somehow won their first five home league games, and made some progress in the first ever League Cup tournament. Manchester City and Chelsea were both beaten in League Cup games at Fratton Park, and Cox told *The Football Mail* that these victories meant that good times were on the horizon, and that he was well on the way to building a promotion team. More sensibly, the general opinion among the Pompey faithful was that the defeated clubs concerned had little or no interest in taking part in the League Cup, and the results meant nothing. The 1-0 win against Chelsea was to be the last time Pompey defeated a team from that club in any game in the twentieth century. The run of home League victories mentioned earlier followed on from that over Lincoln and involved Luton (3-2), Stoke (1-0), Sunderland (2-1), and Norwich (3-0). As had become familiar, Pompey more than compensated for such results by only winning one away game all season, on 17 December 1960, almost inevitably at Lincoln (3-2). In terms of away humiliations, that at the Dell had competition in further 5-1 defeats at Plymouth and at Scunthorpe, the latter marginally representing an improvement on the previous year's 6-2 thrashing. At Charlton on 1 October 1960, Pompey lost 7-4, with a home player called Johnnie Summers scoring five times. Four weeks later, Pompey lost 6-2 at Derby. There were 17,595 spectators present, and in years to come, given the number of people who wanted to tell me about what it was like to watch this drubbing as a Derby supporter, I came to wonder if I had met all of them. Pompey managed a fortuitous 1-1 home draw with the Saints on New Year's Eve. A week later, Peterborough from the Fourth Division dumped Pompey out of the F.A. Cup at Fratton Park 2-1, and there then followed eight successive defeats in Second Division games. Only 7,272 bothered to watch Clough get a hat trick when Middlesbrough won 3-0 at Fratton Park on 28 January 1961, and 9,178 endured a further 2-0 home defeat at the hands of Plymouth a week later. Cox was sacked, and his temporary successor as Manager was Bill Thompson, one of the heroes of the famous last day victory over Aston Villa to clinch the title in 1950. Eleven years too late, Pompey at last secured the services of Alan Brown, and Johnnie Gordon was brought back from exile in Birmingham. Pompey promptly defeated Leeds 3-1, and, indeed, only lost one of their last eight home games, and that to promotion certainties, Sheffield United, who outclassed them. George Smith, who had been a coach at United then became the Portsmouth Manager, and, though, only one of the remaining five games was lost, Pompey were relegated to the Third Division, back where they started over forty years before.

THE CHOPPING BLOCK YEARS

During the seasons 1956-57 to 1960-61 inclusive, Portsmouth played 210 League games, won only 49, drew 53, and lost no less than 108. Pompey scored 322 goals and conceded no less than 460 in getting relegated twice in five seasons all of which were spent fighting relegation. This record was abysmal. I did not think so at the time, but, in retrospect, it would have been better if, instead of winning all three of their Easter 1957 games, Pompey had lost the lot. As it was, Portsmouth somehow beat Wolves, and Peter Harris played Superman in the two games against Cardiff, and Pompey stayed in the top flight. If Portsmouth had been relegated at the end of the 1956-57 season, Pompey would have gone down with a poor team, but one that might well have held its own in the Second Division, as the two clubs who were relegated actually did. As it was, when Portsmouth were relegated two years later, Pompey had an utterly demoralized, drained, and weakened team fit only for further relegation.

99

The Board of Directors had to take the main blame for Portsmouth descending so swiftly from being Champions of England to one of the chopping blocks of English football. When Pompey lost 3-1 to Brighton early in the awful 1959-60 season, one of the Directors said how he wished that Pompey could sign players like Curry, who had scored a hat trick for Brighton. So, why didn't they sign this cheap Newcastle reject? The answer was that, having squandered the resources built up in the good years, the Board of Directors ran Pompey on Third Division money, and it was not surprising that the club ended up at that level. Those of us who had long criticised Portsmouth for being just a selling club got it right. In the autumn of 1958, with Pompey in obvious relegation difficulties, the Directors transferred Johnnie Gordon to Birmingham for a knock down fee. Gordon had his critics, but he was the best midfield player that Portsmouth had produced this side of the Golden Age, and if that was evidence of poverty of talent, then buy somebody better rather than selling the player cheaply and without replacement. Then again, when, at the end of the 1957-58 season, the Board of Directors finally dismissed Eddie Lever, they replaced him with the man who turned out to be the worst Manager in Portsmouth's history, Freddie Cox. A despised figure among Pompey supporters anyway because of his infamous foul on Froggatt back in 1951, Cox was an absurd appointment. When a member of the Board was asked by one bewildered supporter why Cox had been selected as Lever's successor, all the man could come up with was that Cox had once taken Bournemouth to the Sixth Round of the F.A. Cup. Lever had wanted to play pure football, which was impractical. Cox wanted to play Third Division football. Out went the young players of any class - Ray Crawford and Derek Dougan - and for small fees. When dismissed, Eddie Lever begged the Directors not to sell Crawford at any price, but they preferred to listen to Cox. Alf Ramsey, the then Manager of Ipswich, signed Crawford, who proceeded to score no less than 204 League goals for that club, and to be a member of the Ipswich team that won the Second Division title in the 1960-61 season and then became the English Champions the following season. Crawford also went on to play for England. Cox plainly

100

found working with lower division hacks like Basil Hayward, a discard from Port Vale, to be a more comfortable experience. The Pompey supporters hated types like Hayward, and showed this in the Newcastle home game on 11 March 1959, when Jimmy Scoular cleverly fouled him, and then feigned innocence. The entire Pompey crowd hooted with laughter. Though now in a Newcastle shirt, Scoular was still a hero, whereas the very presence of Hayward in Pompey's team was an unwanted reminder of the Club's desperate decline. Everything went wrong. With Cox in charge, the young players developed under the club's belatedly established youth policy - the Sparshatt Plan - were brought into the sourest of atmospheres. It was not surprising that none flourished. Cox's absurd game plan seemed to be to take Pompey down to the Third Division and then take them back again. He performed half his task. When, against Manchester City on 7 March 1959, Pompey threw away a 2-0 lead to lose 4-3, Cox protested that the Portsmouth players thought that they were a football team. Nobody else did. Few would pretend that Cox's inheritance as a Manager was other than an unenviable one, but his own performance in that role was so disgraceful that he could hardly have done more damage to Portsmouth Football Club if he had been paid deliberately to inflict it by, say, Southampton.

When, five dismal losing seasons before, Portsmouth had played Manchester City in the last match of the 1955-56 season, the attendance had been 24, 684. When, already doomed to relegation, Pompey played Derby in the last match of the 1960-61 season, 9,966 were present. Among those who witnessed a token 3-2 win were all three Pessimists who predicted the ruination of Portsmouth Football Club. It would make a fine ending to this sad story if the Optimists had been there too to confess their sins, but none of us had seen any of them at a Pompey game for at least a couple of years. In some ways, Portsmouth's fall from grace was summarized by an incident in the second half of the home game with Manchester United on 30 March 1959, which Pompey eventually lost 3-1. As if the player of old, Peter Harris destroyed the left side of the United defence, and cut the ball back to give Ron Saunders, Cox's idea of a

101

replacement for Crawford, an open goal. With all the time in the world, Saunders steered the ball wide. Harris just stood there with a mixture of despair and astonishment written all over his face. Those of us who stayed loyal to Pompey during this dreadful period in the Club's history knew how Harris felt. My father once caught the mood of the loyalists exactly in one of our conversations when he was on the cancer ward. I took him the most recent copy of *The Football Mail*, containing, of course, news of the latest humiliation for Portsmouth. As he surveyed the wreckage, he spoke for all of us when he said: 'We've certainly paid a price for our little bit of glory haven't we?'

CHAPTER 5: THE LITTLE POMPEY EXPERIENCE: 1961-2002

AN ALTERNATIVE REALITY

After five years of utter misery, spending the 1961-62 season in the Third Division proved to be a relatively pleasant experience, since it became clear early on that Portsmouth were going to be immediately promoted, almost certainly as Champions.

Pompey did not lose a home game until April, and there were early away wins at Q.P.R. (1-0) and Crystal Palace (2-1), in the latter case after falling behind. A 3-0 defeat in the First Round of the F.A. Cup at Palace in early November proved to be an unwanted reminder of Pompey's limitations even at this level. If remembered at all these days, Budgie Byrne is thought of as a West Ham player, but then he was a Palace man. Byrne ran the match. In those days, the fans were not segregated, and, fortunately, after my Service experience, I was skilled at handling the banter at my expense, helped by the reality that the earlier League victory was what really mattered. One of my friends, a Selhurst Park regular, said to me afterwards that he did not take the Cup result very seriously. As he put it, Palace had never won anything that mattered, and he (correctly) predicted that they never would, whereas Pompey had won major trophies in their time. Pompey had at least been something. This was a generous thing to say, but what was already evident to the thinking Pompey fan at least was what Anthony Minghella once called the tyranny of Portsmouth's back to back title winning team of the immediate post war period, whose achievements dwarfed what had gone before, and showed every sign of doing the same to whatever followed. How long could we carry on living like parasites on the achievements of the team that Flewin had led to greatness? Was it going to have to be for ever? It certainly looked like it.

The majority of the Pompey supporters seemed to think that the impetus provided by promotion from the Third Division would take us straight through the Second Division, and back into the top flight, where, of course, they believed, Pompey 'belonged.' I thought and feared that what would come next would be the living death of spending season after season in the Second Division relegation zone, followed, most probably, by even greater humiliation, on the basis that you can only stagnate for so long. Sadly for me, and for everybody else in the ranks of the Portsmouth supporters, this was more or less what happened. On the face of it, there was no need for this to have been the case. The abolition of the maximum wage in 1961 did not have an immediate and dramatic effect on the shape of English football, and this seemed to be more than a matter of the retain and transfer system surviving intact all the way down to 1978. Of course, in the end and in general terms the big battalions were bound to benefit most from the removal of the wage limit because of the revenue emanating from their higher attendances, and, for example, Liverpool immediately made their escape from their long exile in the Second Division. Liverpool soon won the title twice more and their first F.A. Cup, and they went on to dominate English football from the early 1970s all the way down to 1990. It was the advent of the Premier League from 1992 onwards that finally reduced the Ordinary Joe clubs to the status of onlookers. Before that, Clough worked his miracles at Derby and Notts Forest, and, without much in the way of expenditure or support, Ipswich won three major honours in the first twenty seasons after the wage limit was removed. To illustrate the more immediate situation, the England team that won the World Cup in 1966 comprised Banks (Leicester), Cohen (Fulham), Jack Charlton (Leeds United), Moore (West Ham), Wilson (Everton), Ball (Blackpool), Stiles (Manchester United), Bobby Charlton (Manchester United), Peters (West Ham), Hurst (West Ham), and Hunt (Liverpool). Of the four undisputed world class players in that team - Banks, Moore, Wilson, and Bobby Charlton - only Charlton and Wilson played for clubs that at the time most would have expected to be an important force in English football in the long run. As for the World Cup winning team as a whole only

Stiles and Hunt needed to be added to their names, though Ball soon afterwards moved to Everton, who had what passed for real money in those days.

So, at least at first, the overall picture was more complex than expected, though several then famous but smaller clubs were soon sentenced to a life of perpetual mediocrity. Since, at the time that the maximum wage was initially removed Portsmouth had a bigger prospective support base than all but about a dozen clubs, at first sight there was always hope for Pompey, but with a Board of Directors that was impecunious even by the modest standards of the time it was always going to be hope deferred. To judge from their behaviour and conversation on the journey to and from, for instance, the Peterborough match in early December 1961, as well as at the game itself and on other similar occasions, the great majority of Portsmouth fans chose to ignore this reality. They were in the process of constructing a form of dream world in which winning minor games like that at the London Road ground by 1-0 that day were great events, and that success in the world of English football was defined as getting the better of Southampton, who did not matter and never would. Over the years many people who came into contact with the Portsmouth supporters put it to me that most of them were mad, and that season after season of continued failure would ensure that they would get madder, and I would end up the same unless I gave up my addiction. If they could have been bothered to reply to this form of criticism instead of treating it dismissively, I suppose that such supporters could have responded by saying that the level and intensity of their loyalty to Pompey merited admiration rather than derision, given that without this support Portsmouth Football Club might well go under, and that while there's life there's hope. The difficulty was that, say, belting out the Pompey Chimes and - despite what passed for their performances - 'getting behind the lads' did not alter the harsh reality that those running Portsmouth lacked the means to enable the Club to be the serious force in English football that they had been in anything like the near future.

Since I ended up as a University Professor as well as continuing to be a Pompey fan, eventually I had to live with many people thinking me mad twice over, which I found amusing, given my belief that taking yourself, or, most certainly, other people's estimates of you, in any respect seriously serves no useful purpose. More immediately, what that Peterborough trip brought home to me was that I was already a creature from the past, relating, as I did, to the older generation, who had lived through the glory years, and much of it in my company. There was nothing mad about them. As I saw things, the people running Portsmouth had allowed Pompey to become no more than a history book club. For me and those old timers who still went, Portsmouth being relegated to the Third Division was a disgrace, but one that we chose to live with. It was during the trip back and forth to Peterborough that I realised that those of us from the great days were slowly but surely becoming a minority among what could be called the regulars, the people who turned up come what may. The newcomers that I eventually got to know were usually drawn from Pompey supporting families, but what might be called the ambience had changed. The ambience, though, needed a name. Little Pompey syndrome fitted the bill. It added up to an alternative reality in which, say, winning by a Ron Saunders goal at Shrewsbury on 3 March 1962 was of world shattering importance. If those prepared to live in this dream world were numerous enough - which they were - then Pompey would always have a support base. If you could redefine success in this way, then, say, losing home and away in the same season to Grimsby was solely a test of loyalty, and one to be passed before setting out for, say, what turned out to be a goal less draw at Watford, and another test to be passed.

Those of us who were uncomfortable with Pompey being consigned to the dustbin of history tried to cast around for a way out of being defined in this way. Some looked to the example of Ipswich, who were able to make the impressive progress they did by appointing Managers like Alf Ramsey and, later, Bobby Robson, much as Pompey had done in the past in the case of McCartney and Tinn, and, of course, management skills of this order were essential anyway. Pompey, however, had lost the

106

knack of finding and then appointing such talented people. Above all, of course, it was the Club's poverty that was most undermining. As one of the old timers from the Isle of Wight, who knew a couple of the Directors socially, said to me after yet another bitter defeat, these people were well meaning, and, indeed, ardent Pompey supporters themselves. The problem was that they had no money - and what can you do without money? Those who argued against me and this old timer would have had a point, at least at this stage of the evolution of English football, if they had said that money did not guarantee success, and that this was not surprising given that as always there were only a small number of major honours to be won. What they preferred to argue - and, of course, needed to believe, because otherwise there was no hope - was that money did not buy success *per se*. In those days, the favourite example given was that of Sunderland in the 1950s. What did the so called Bank of England team achieve? Didn't they get relegated in the end? Sunderland were in fact laid low by corruption, with players ensuring at times that the Club was in relegation trouble in order to attract illicit payments so that this fate was avoided, and, in the end, they miscalculated, and down Sunderland went. Pompey had then gone down too, of course, without resorting to this behaviour. The advent of the Premier League eventually killed off the Ipswich form of success, though, of course, long before that it had become obvious that, for example, the smaller Lancashire clubs could no longer compete with the biggest clubs without the backing of a rich benefactor. Blackburn demonstrated this in the 1990s, once armed with Jack Walker's money combined on his part with a willingness to leave playing matters to the professionals. Walker's reward was to live to see Blackburn win the Premiership, and the Club's first major honour since 1928. Blackburn's fierce and once impressive rivals such as Burnley, Blackpool, Bolton, and Preston proceeded to win absolutely nothing. As far as the second half of the twentieth century was concerned, Portsmouth contrived to end up in the same unenviable situation, despite not having serious rivals to compete with, as the smaller Lancashire clubs did in the shape of the Liverpool and Manchester clubs, and with the advantage of a

107

much bigger prospective support base than the ordinary Lancashire clubs. The only way out was the rich benefactor route, and even then one needed such people to be honest and unwilling to intervene in team matters, an unlikely combination of virtues. As time went on, it has to be said that a small minority of Pompey fans got so bored that they resorted to violence to liven up the games, with the outfit concerned being called the 657 Crew.

When Len Shackleton published his memoirs, he left a blank page to represent what the average Director of a football club knew about football, and I must admit that when I came to write this book I was tempted to do the same for Portsmouth's history between 1956 and 2002. The Third Division title was won in 1962 and 1983. Pompey got to the semi-final stage of the F. A. Cup in 1992, and took Liverpool, the eventual winners, to a replay, but lost. That was about it, really, when one considers nearly half a century of Pompey's history. In principle, one could compose what would these days be called a useful lower half of the Premiership team from some of the players who appeared in a Portsmouth shirt during that half century, even, possibly, a squad. In practice, there were never enough of them around at the same time to constitute a team that would impress anybody but the devoted Portsmouth fan, meaning somebody who had come to accept, and, it seemed, in some cases, even to enjoy living the nightmare of the Little Pompey existence. So, duty calls, and, given that nobody who was not seeking a cure for insomnia would want the full details, we will summarise the Little Pompey years. We have already set the scene with our review of the dire 1956-61 era, and there seems to me to three natural divisions in the rest of this story: namely, 1961-1973, 1973-1988, and then 1988-2002.

POMPEY 1961-1973: GOING NOWHERE SLOWLY

What the Portsmouth Manager, George Smith called 'my team of old men' won the Third Division Championship in the 1961-62 season. Pompey were unbeaten in their first 12 matches, and later had a run of just one defeat in 19 games, before fading near the end when losing half of their last 8 games.

108

All told, though, Dickinson, Gordon, Alex Wilson and all but one of their colleagues did their job admirably. Smithy, as everybody called the Manager as if they knew him, made much of having introduced discipline into the ranks of the Pompey players, requiring them to run around during training with sandbags on their backs and so on. The goalkeeper Dick Beattie seemed to have escaped Smithy's notice, which was unfortunate because Beattie was a crook, being involved with a betting syndicate. Beattie had seemed to me to do his best to throw a home game against Newport in September, and he did succeed in ensuring that Peterborough won 3-0 at Fratton Park in the driving rain on Easter Saturday 1962. The Fratton End barracked him for his behaviour, and we learnt later that Smithy and Beattie had a fight after the match, no doubt after accusations had been made. Beattie was dropped, and later transferred. Since Peterborough proved to be his next club, they proved to be less perceptive about Beattie than either Smithy or the Fratton Enders. Beattie rewarded Peterborough for employing him by making sure that they lost a home game against Q.P.R., throwing the ball out to an opposition forward, who scored the winner. Beattie eventually went to gaol for nine months for his corrupt behaviour in these games involving Peterborough. Most Portsmouth supporters seemed to conclude that as Pompey had won the Third Division title despite Beattie playing for the other side some of the time, and so from now on it would be onward and upward. After the first five games of the 1962-63 season, Portsmouth were top of the Second Division, and *The Observer* wrote as if Pompey were going to return to the top flight straightaway. The results did not match these expectations, but, as the harsh winter eased a little by the beginning of March, Pompey seemed to be engaged in what could be called a pseudo promotion push. This involved no serious prospect of actual promotion, but, overall, since there were more wins than defeats, an artificial atmosphere of hope was generated. For the 1962-63 season, anyway, this all ended with a 4-2 defeat at Southampton on a pitch so heavily sanded that some of us half expected to see Rommel and the Afrika Corps among the team changes. Dickinson could certainly have used such reinforcements as he proceeded to play the Saints largely on his own. Notably inept was Armstrong, a goalkeeper whom Smithy had signed from Barrow, being unaware for some reason that Armstrong had a deserved reputation for being unable to deal with crosses from the left. It turned out that crosses from the right were a problem too, and Pompey were lucky to avoid a much heavier defeat. The defeat at The Dell proved to be the first of nine successive losses, which turned Portsmouth from supposed promotion contenders into relegation candidates. Pompey just about scraped together enough further points to survive, which was just as well because in the final game Portsmouth were thrashed 7-0 by Chelsea, who, fortunately for the visiting fans such as myself, chose to effectively declare with half an hour to go. So, Pompey spent the 1963-64 season still in the Second Division, and, thanks to a six game run of five wins and a draw in the autumn, there was another pseudo promotion push. Saunders scored 33 goals, and a fast winger called John McClelland impressed at times, but a collapse at the end meant a mid table finish. Smithy fell out with Saunders, who was transferred, and also with the irritating Gunter, who was deported to Aldershot, and, without effective replacements, Pompey were lucky to escape relegation in the 1964-65 season. Indeed, on the final day, which was also Dickinson's fortieth birthday and the occasion of the last of his 764 league appearances, Pompey needed at least to draw at Northampton to stay up. Gordon hardly helped matters by putting through his own goal, but Alex Wilson got a late equaliser. So, Pompey survived, though to say that this was to fight another day would misrepresent the climate of torpor and hopelessness that had come to envelop the club.

That the Board of Directors did not have even moderate financial resources at their disposal was emphasised when, following complaints from visiting teams about their quality, the floodlights had to be replaced, and this was only paid for by the Supporters Club raising the money. This was, of course, a ridiculous state of affairs, and the Directors had some cause to thank Smithy for diverting attention from their own uselessness by regularly provoking controversy. This behaviour convinced many Portsmouth supporters that Smithy had gone mad. When

32,407 turned out for a home game with Southampton on 13 October 1962 (which Pompey were fortunate to draw 1-1), Smithy maintained that Saints supporters had constituted half of the crowd. To judge from the reaction to the goals, more than three quarters of the spectators were Pompey fans. Smithy went on to say that there should be attendances of this order at every home game, which, of course, there would have been, only a dozen years after the Golden Age, if Portsmouth had anything resembling a team worthy of the name. It seemed to me that hard core regulars could argue that it was your duty to turn up as often as possible, but, of course, they put their money where their mouth is, whereas football insiders never do so, being known to say in praise of a game, for instance, that 'I would have paid money to watch that game' - the rest of us have to pay anyway. Smithy was spelling out the reality, though, when he said that 'I'm managing here on Third Division money.' In the summer of 1963, all Smithy felt able to do when trying to strengthen the team was to go back to Crystal Palace, his former club, and make signings from that club's free transfer list, with a small fee being paid for Brian Lewis, a midfield player of some gifts and much indolence. Lewis became popular with the crowd, and plainly remembered this in later life when, dying of cancer, he requested to be buried in a Portsmouth shirt. One of the free transfers, Roy Lunnis, was later to be charged with having run off with an old lady's handbag in London when he should have been training with Pompey. It seemed to me that Lunnis needed all the training he could get, given that the old lady ran after him and caught him. Another Palace recruit, with the wonderfully Dickensian name of Alfie Noakes, whom some unkind souls thought to be, despite the increasing competition, the worst player ever to wear a Pompey shirt, only lasted for a handful of games. The Football Mail hailed the advent of Lewis and even Lunnis, when present, as The New Pompey, but Smithy was tired of the current set up, and during the wretched 1964-65 season he devised a new playing structure for the club, which tried to bring into balance revenue and expenditure, naturally enough by cutting down on spending. Smithy persuaded the Directors that the club needed no more than sixteen players, with some

111

additional amateurs to fill in in the event of an injury crisis. The reserves and the youth team could be dispensed with.

Smithy told the Pompey supporters that the youth team would not be missed because all you got around Portsmouth was fish in the sea. Smithy did not explain why, despite its similar coastal location, Southampton had contrived to develop a more than useful youth scheme. The fish remark convinced even more Pompey supporters than before that Smithy was off his rocker, but I did not subscribe to this popular thesis. My line was that Smithy's perpetual Army Sergeant act was numbingly boring. Smithy was an aggressively ignorant man who believed that he had a monopoly of (the reader will have guessed it) common sense. All this meant was that Smithy and his kind had a particular outlook, because, of course, if the term common sense meant anything in specific terms almost everybody would think much the same. Sadly, discussion of the Smith Plan tended to concentrate on the issue of the viability of a sixteen man squad, and the Club and Smithy put it about that Portsmouth were leading a football revolution. Where Pompey led, the argument went, most other clubs would be sure to follow because of pressure to balance the books, since Smithy thought that football was in the midst of a financial crisis, when, as it turned out, it was on the brink of a short lived boom in the wake of England winning the World Cup. We were soon told, accurately or not, that, earlier in the century, Celtic had experimented with a one team structure, but this example, if true, did not support the case because, plainly, Celtic had later chosen to abandon the plan, and, anyway, that club could prospectively draw on much of Scotland to sustain its recruitment. To put the matter gently, Portsmouth were not that important, and few were surprised that only Brighton and Carlisle among contemporary clubs ever thought it worthwhile to adopt Pompey's one team formula, and then, of course, as Portsmouth were eventually forced to do, abandoned the idea. The obvious flaw in the Smith Plan was that under its aegis Pompey could neither breed nor buy serious players. Such funds as would be made available for transfer market activity would be those released by any surplus that emerged from the difference between expenditure and revenue

112

from gates. Thus, the supporters were solely sustaining the system, as had been the case with renewing the floodlights. Quite what function the Board of Directors had come to serve was unclear, and if, as it was put to me, they were there to entertain visiting Directors, surely hiring a catering company could have fulfilled that role.

Whatever the Pompey supporters thought, the Smith Plan went ahead, and Portsmouth drifted on. The threat of relegation hovered over the 1965-66 season, not least after an 8-2 thrashing at Wolves. With Wolves 6-0 ahead at half time, and with a snow storm having rendered the game into a farce, the Pompey supporters clamoured for it to be abandoned, but without success. With ten games to go, instead of the familiar late season collapse, Pompey proceeded to win 6 and lose only 2. On the final day of the season, there was a pitch invasion after Portsmouth had beaten Bury 4-0 at Fratton Park, with Gordon the captain being chaired from the field by a wildly cheering crowd. This behaviour led those of us who were sober, or pretending to be, to wonder what this crowd would do if Portsmouth actually won a game or a trophy of real importance, but, of course, there was no prospect of that. By the time that the 1966-67 season started, I was on the move from London to the North of England to take up an academic appointment at the University of Leeds, where, with my usual sense of adventure, I was to spend the rest of my working life. The general opinion among my friends and acquaintances, and especially the former Northerners, was that anybody voluntarily leaving the Swinging London of the 1960s was off his trolley. As it happened, the girls of Leeds were only too pleased to wear their mini skirts and mini dresses in defiance of a climate that might well have tested the resolve of the Red Army. I soon ensured that I owned a coat for the first time in my life, and one which, in some contrast with the thigh high coats of my female companions, made me look like a character from *Dr Zhivago*. Leeds proved to be a cheap place to live, which was just as well given what passed for university pay, and when I got married (and very happily too) I was able to buy an excellent house for a sum which would have probably purchased no more than a garden shed in a comparable area of London. One

113

advantage of living in London, though, was that I could nip down to Portsmouth easily enough, whereas now for most of the time I lived the life of an exile, being sentenced to mainly watch Pompey play in the North and Midlands. The 1966-67 season proved to be very boring anyway, being memorable solely for being the only season in Portsmouth's history in which Pompey got more away points than they did at home. Aside from Everton all those years before in my R.A.F. days, my first Portsmouth game in the North at this level anyway was at Rotherham in September 1966. To travel was one thing, to arrive was another as was demonstrated by the then Rotherham railway station, which had a wartime look about it, as if a scene from *The Great Escape* was about to be played out. I instinctively looked for the escapers from Stalag Luft 3. Would Richard Attenborough be stopped by the Gestapo checking the tickets? In fact, at the gate, there were just the usual apathetic British Railways ticket collectors. The Millmoor ground was close to the station, with what looked like a scrap yard in between. The game was appalling, but, at least, Pompey won 1-0, Cliff Portwood scoring. Portsmouth coasted along in the Second Division, and held out for an hour in a Fourth Round F. A. Cup tie at Tottenham, before losing 3-1 to the eventual Cup winners. Spurs friends who contacted me afterwards made fun of the enthusiasm of that the Pompey faithful displayed in supporting such a poor team. *The Times* wrote us off as 'homespun Portsmouth.'

Then, out of the blue, the 1967-68 season witnessed Pompey making a pseudo promotion push in the Second Division, which, down to Christmas, offered the possibility, though no more than that, of a flying visit to the top division. Portsmouth also made it to the Fifth Round of the F. A. Cup before losing to the eventual winners of the trophy, West Bromwich. I am told that the scorer of the winning goal in the Final, Jeff Astle has had a bridge in or near West Bromwich named after him, but I have to confess that I have never noticed this. Following most journeys away from The Hawthorns, I am usually concentrating on recovering from the result. Aside from the Third Division title winning season, the 1967-68 season was the only one that I remember with any affection in the dire period between 1956 and

1978, though I found it hard to take the promotion talk very seriously. Portsmouth started off with a 9 game unbeaten run, and after that the results were much the same as usual. That Pompey were not the familiar pushover was mostly explained by Bobby Kellard, previously an anonymous winger, and George Smith (no relation), signed from Barrow, having been brought together to form a combative central midfield combination, winning the ball more often than not and also more often than not distributing it to their colleagues. In attack, the former England player, Ray Pointer, together with Ray Hiron, recruited from Fareham Town, and the skilful Albert McCann, and Nicky Jennings, a winger from Plymouth, also combined to comprise a useful front line. In defence, Roy Pack, an Arsenal discard, and George Ley were good full backs, and in goal local product John Milkins was reliable. The problem was in central defence where Ron Tindall and Harry Harris were not good enough. When increased attendances made money available for strengthening the team as it faded after Christmas, Smithy had the opportunity to reshape the defence. Instead, he signed Mike Trebilcock, a striker from Everton, who had scored twice in the 1966 F. A. Cup Final and done little since. I saw Trebilcock play for Everton at Leeds the week before Smithy signed him. Early on, Trebilcock raced down the left wing, showed the ball to Paul Reaney, beat him, and crossed the ball just too high for Joe Royle to get in a header. Reaney had a deserved reputation for being one of the few full backs not to be made a fool of by George Best, though, of course, the methods used to stop that particular genius were of the anything goes variety. So, predictably, the next time that Trebilcock tried to get the better of Reaney he was stopped in his tracks, and he made little contribution after that, being substituted. Even from the safety of the stands, I had some sympathy with Trebilcock for having little taste for dealing with the sophisticated violence dealt out by Revie's defence, but it was evident that the man would be even less effective against the crude violence that was dished out regularly in contemporary Second Division football. When Trebilcock scored the winner for Pompey in an F. A. Cup replay with Fulham, I was on the receiving end of much criticism, but I stuck to my guns, saying that Trebilcock was, if anything, a special occasions player. We needed defenders, but if Smithy had to recruit an attacker, how about a regular goalscorer? Trebilcock proceeded to score just once in 13 Second Division games. So, the season just faded away. I still remember at Hull, where a fine display of goalkeeping from Milkins ensured that Pompey got an undeserved point, that, when McCann got the equaliser, the Pompey faithful gave their rendering of what was then a familiar chant:

'Mr Smith, Mr Smith,

Is it true that Pompey say,

They're going to win Division Two.'

They attempted to repeat this, and may well have brought this off, though it was difficult to tell because of the gales of laughter from the Hull fans that the first rendering induced. On the train back from Boothferry Park afterwards to the ridiculously named Hull Paragon Station, even this thick skinned Pompey loyalist, who had taken beating after beating and still came back for more, reflected on what depths Portsmouth had sunk to that even Hull supporters could deride the idea that Pompey could win a minor honour like the Second Division title, and, of course, they had got it right.

Despite the receipts from the Cup run (which included home gates of 44,050 and 42,642) and higher league atttendances anyway, Smithy announced that Pompey would have to be financially cute to get through the summer, and, as if to make sure, absurdly transferred Kellard to Bristol City. The namesake Smith was also later to be transferred out, thus destroying the midfield, and rendering the 1968-69 season worthless. The 1969-70 season was effectively over in the first week, during which Pompey lost three times, including a 5-1 home defeat at the hands of Sheffield United, the manner of which was utterly humiliating. I was one of the few that made it up to Birmingham for the next game, to be rewarded with a 1-1 draw. Once it was clear that Pompey were not, for once, going to play the role of sacrificial lamb, the home crowd turned on their Manager, who was none other than Stan Cullis. He just sat there head bowed, as if in shame. Smithy later made it clear that he was outraged by the crowd's behaviour, maintaining that he would have retaliated, as, indeed, he did when the time came. Smithy argued that Cullis merited respect for what he had achieved at Wolves in the old days. Cullis's memoirs were rightly called *All For The Wolves*, however, and Smithy did not explain why Birmingham fans should be grateful for his past achievements at a rival club. Then again, what made Smithy's argument even more peculiar was that he was always telling Portsmouth fans to forget about past glories, though these were, after all, their own glories, and learn to love being a chopping block outfit. During Pompey's last home game of the 1969-70 season, which Norwich won 4-1, there was a demonstration against Smithy by those who had paid to sit in the South Stand. Smithy responded with a demonstration of his own, with swearing and crude gestures. When he calmed down later, Smithy revealed that he had warned the Pompey players against taking the match too lightly, given that Aston Villa and Preston were sentenced to relegation, thus making Pompey safe. The Portsmouth players took no notice. Smithy stepped down as Manager at the end of the season. The local sports paper was later to catch up with him in retirement, and he was still on about his one team plan being the future for football, which was facing financial disaster, you mark my words, and so on. Nobody but a fool would rule that out - eventually - but football always has been about the short term and results, and Smithy seemed to forget that his plan had been designed to help impecunious Directors to keep things going, and not some sort of moral crusade. The local paper wrote of Smithy walking off along the cliffs accompanied by his dog. Given Smithy's managerial talents, one had to fear for the future of the dog.

Nobody with much sense expected Smithy's successor as Manager, Ron Tindall, to be a success in the job, because there was too much of the nice guy about him, and also because the Club remained poverty stricken. Tindall was eventually to restore the reserve and youth team structure, and more immediately he was allowed to sign Norman Piper, a good midfield player, and a couple of defenders from Burnley, one of whom - Fred Smith -

117

proved to be a good signing. What little excitement that the wretched 1970-71 season provided came in the 1-1 home draw in the F. A. Cup Fourth Round against Arsenal, the eventual winners. To the delight of the 39,659 crowd, Pompey equalised in the last minute, with Trebilcock, inevitably, scoring. The replay was lost 3-2. The league programme was devoted to avoiding relegation to the Third Division. Tindall thought that 35 points would do this, and a bonus system was devised that would kick in once this meagre total was achieved. As the team inched its way to towards 35 points, few should have been surprised that the pressure proved too much for the players. Luckily, falling one point short was not a disaster, and, indeed, Pompey achieved safety at Birmingham, where just before the end of an execrable game an unexpected equaliser from Hiron gave Portsmouth the necessary point. The only light hearted moment in the grim 1971-72 season came in the F. A. Cup Third Round away game at Boston. Since joining the Football League, Pompey had not lost a cup tie to a non-league club, a record that owed something to having rarely played many of them. The solitary goal was credited to Jennings, though it seemed to me that a deflection from the bald head of Boston's Jim Smith, a future Portsmouth Manager, had proved decisive. That only 5,885 turned up for the last home game was an indication that even the Pompey faithful could not take much more of the Second Division relegation zone. The attendances in the first half of the 1972-73 season proved to be as poor as the performances, and, after Pompey contrived to lose at home to Sunderland after being ahead with two minutes to go, the attendance for the next home game against Middlesbrough was an alarming 4,688. The reward for those who turned up was a 0-0 draw. In the Directors' Box, though, was a supposed benefactor, John Deacon, who was soon to join the Board, and who put up the money to resign Kellard. Pompey slowly climbed away from relegation trouble. Kellard led the way in the midfield, and he gave an excellent display in a remarkable 5-0 win at Preston. The team was still a poor one, though, as was borne out when Pompey contrived to win just twice in the last thirteen games of yet another season to forget.

POMPEY 1973-1988: THE DEACON ERA

In the role of its Chairman for the fifteen years down to 1988, the property developer, John Deacon was eventually to become one of the most hated men in the history of Portsmouth Football Club. This followed from his behaviour in excessively raising the expectations of the fans and then failing to deliver. Like everybody else, I hoped that Deacon was the saviour that Pompey needed, though I did wonder from the outset quite why, if he was as wealthy as he was reputed to be, Southampton had previously turned him down when he had tried to join the Board of Directors there. Southampton had shown themselves, if only in recent years, to be a well run club, and I guessed that their Board's reasoning in rejecting his overtures was that Deacon had enough money to destabilise their club, but not enough to translate it into a more important one. In other words, he was more trouble than he was worth. Beggars cannot be choosers, of course, and at the time that Deacon approached the Directors the situation at Portsmouth Football Club was so desperate that they had little choice about welcoming him aboard. 'Fasten your seatbelts, it's going to be a bumpy ride,' Bette Davis famously said in *All About Eve*, and it would have been prescient if Deacon had said much the same. At first, Deacon spent heavily by the standards that Pompey were used to, and, to a much lesser extent, those of that era. To replace Tindall as Manager, Deacon brought in John Mortimore, who had earlier been no. 2 at Southampton. The signings that were made were done the wrong way round. A team should be built from the back, but only one of the first three signings made was a defender - Phil Roberts from Bristol Rovers - who soon showed that, whatever his abilities he possessed as a full back, defensive qualities were not among them. That Ted Bates, the shrewd Southampton Manager, allowed Pompey to sign Ron Davies, a Welsh international striker, from the Saints suggested that he believed that a serious knee injury meant that Davies was finished. Davies disputed this verdict, but Bates was proved right. The signing of Peter Marinello, a winger from Arsenal for £100,000 was thought to be evidence of Deacon's ambition and resources. Marinello had been hailed as the new George Best, and, indeed,

119

he was of slender build and he had dark hair. There the resemblance ended. Marinello had skills, but Arsenal had written him off after he had missed a golden scoring opportunity in a European Cup game against Ajax, and Pompey were the only club that came in for him. So, it should not have been a surprise that the results were unimpressive. The first win came at Carlisle in mid September, but Pompey's away form was as poor as usual, and so was the defensive work. In December, action was taken, and Paul Went and Malcolm Manley were expensively recruited from Fulham and Leicester respectively to solve the central defensive problem. When I learnt that Deacon had been involved in the relevant scouting missions, my heart sank. He needed to trust the professionals. Went seemed to me to be the eternal young man of promise, and Don Revie had been interested in him as a player at one time, but Went rarely delivered. As for Manley, such were his gifts that, at first sight, there was cause to wonder why one of the bigger clubs had not tried to sign him, but Leicester fans told me that this was because of his injury record. At first, the strengthening of the defence seemed to work, and a 2-1 win at West Bromwich in mid December proved to be a pleasant surprise. A well deserved 4-0 beating at Bolton at the end of the month added a touch of reality. The rest of the season was only enlivened by what passed for a Portsmouth F. A. Cup run. Pompey reached the Fifth Round. In the midst of the coal miners' strike that effectively brought down the Heath Conservative Government, Portsmouth travelled to Notts Forest, backed by a large contingent of supporters. Pompey lost 1-0, with one of the stalwarts from the Smith-Tindall era, Eoin Hand, needlessly giving away a penalty. That Hand was in the team at all was explained by Manley being absent because of an injury that effectively finished his career. After that, the 1973-74 season drifted to a close, with Deacon's random style of expenditure having improved Portsmouth's standing by just two places in the Second Division. As if to emphasise that the Deacon regime did not know what it was doing, Milkins the goalkeeper was replaced by an older man in David Best, who had been thrown out by Bobby Robson at Ipswich as being no longer good enough.

Portsmouth made their usual start to the 1974-75 season, but Deacon wanted something better for his money and dismissed Mortimore, replacing him by Ian St John as early as September. St John had been a great player with Liverpool, and, though his limitations off the field were to be paraded regularly on television later, he had done so well as Manager at Motherwell that there was some talk of him being Revie's successor at Leeds. Taking what turned out to be poor advice from Bill Shankly, St John chose to come to Portsmouth. Deacon told him that there would be plenty of money available in the transfer market, and took St John for a drive to see the site of the new football stadium that he intended to build on what had been the Portsmouth Airport. In retrospect, and in principle, one could see the sense of this idea, but the more immediate priority was surely the team, floundering in the Second Division. There was also the matter of Deacon's finances. As part of its attempts to appease the then rampant trade union movement, the Heath Conservative Government had imposed a tax on development land. Deacon did not think that a Conservative Government would do such a thing, but that of Heath had been behaving in a socialist manner since the infamous U Turn of 1972, and Deacon should have seen this particular body blow coming. So, soon Deacon was denying that he had ever promised St John money to spend on transfers, and the new ground idea was forgotten. Pompey were in a mess. St John organised the team to chip out the results necessary to avoid relegation. Manchester United were somehow persuaded to sign Davies and let Pompey have George Graham as a replacement. Though well past his best, of course, Graham was to do a good job as a target man for a couple of years. The only game of the 1974-75 season worth remembering was a 2-0 win at Sheffield Wednesday, with the normally subdued Marinello outstanding. At the end of the season, there was a clear out, mainly for financial reasons, but getting rid of Hiron one season too early was a mistake. That the 1975-76 season was going to end in relegation was obvious from the outset, to judge from the dire performance Portsmouth gave in an opening day defeat at York, a club that was to be relegated with them. Pompey only won nine games all season, not winning a home game until victory over Carlisle on 10 January 1976. That the league attendances averaged five figures was remarkable, and no less than 31,722 turned out at Fratton Park to watch the Fourth Round F. A. Cup replay with Charlton on 27 January 1976. The team rewarded them by losing 3-0. Pompey's relegation coincided with Southampton winning the F. A. Cup. The Saints captain who lifted the Cup was Peter Rodrigues, who had been the victim of Marinello's skills in the Hillsborough game the previous year. There was to be no such revival for Portsmouth, and early in the 1976-77 season, Deacon's cash flow problems led to the local newspaper launching an SOS Pompey appeal to keep the Club in existence. The fans rallied round and the necessary money was raised. With Marinello having returned to Scotland, the only asset that remained was Went and he departed for Cardiff. One piece of good business that St John was able to do in the transfer market was to persuade Crystal Palace to exchange David Kemp for Graham, and 'King Kemp' - as the Fratton Enders called him - proceeded to score 36 times in 73 league and cup games, no mean feat in such a poor team. St John also showed skill in bringing on young players and he deserved the credit for converting Steve Foster from an ordinary central striker into a central defender who eventually was to play for England. Chris Kamara, Peter Denyer, and Keith Viney were among the better youth players who showed promise at this time. The results were poor, though, and, with relegation threatening, St John was dismissed with three games to go. He was replaced by Jimmy Dickinson, at the time the Company Secretary. As St John pointed out, Jimmy had never disguised his distaste for modern football or made much effort to watch it, implying that in making Jimmy the Manager Deacon had made a fool of himself. I never doubted that Dickinson would fail in the job, much like his mentor Eddie Lever had done, on the nice guy principle. Worse than this, it was no secret that Jimmy was a natural athlete who could have made his mark in several sports, not least tennis, and now he was taking on responsibilty for a Portsmouth squad that had many mediocrities in its ranks. He would not be able to understand why they could not do what came to him easily. You did not have to be particularly perceptive to foresee that it would all end with Jimmy having a heart attack. The trouble was that Pompey could not afford to hire anybody else, and the fans made the best of things, unfurling a banner at the Milton End declared that 'Jim'll fix it,' and Pompey just avoided dropping into the Fourth Division. Barely credibly, the players asked for financial rewards for this feat. Of course, relegation to the Fourth Division had been merely postponed, and this took place at the end of the 1977-78 season, which was appalling. That Dickinson transferred Kamara to Swindon led to controversy, but otherwise apathy reigned. Some feared that the humiliations of the Third Division programme would be added to by an F. A. Cup defeat at the hands of non league Bideford, but Pompey won the game just as they had done when facing Minehead the year before. Frank Burrows was imported from Swindon as the Coach, and with Dickinson he attempted to reshape the team which, in terms of quality, for the most part resembled the Hampshire League sides we had seen play against Pompey's third team at Fratton Park in the immediate post war period near the end of the season after the first team game had finished. There was still a market for the capable Kemp, of course, and in his place Colin Garwood was recruited from Colchester. It made no difference. Long before the end, it took an effort to go to the games, and when it came to the last match of the season at Rotherham on 29 April 1978 there were few Pompey fans present to see the debut of Alan Knight, a sixteen year old goalkeeper. When Denyer got the only and thus winning goal, no more than twenty people celebrated.

As I walked away from Millmoor, Edward G. Robinson's dismissive 'You're all washed up' line addressed to the hapless Fred MacMurray near the end of the classic movie *Double Indemnity* was in my mind. There was no point in trying to pretend that celebrating the thirtieth anniversaries of the title winning years in the Fourth Division was anything but a humiliation, but, knowing my fellow Pompey supporters as I did, I knew that many of them would dress it up in some way. When I was asked what the future held for Portsmouth, my line was that the Fourth Division gave us the opportunity to regroup over, say, a couple of years, and then we would make our way slowly

123

and unsurely up the ladder to reach the top flight within ten years, before then coming to rest in the Second Division relegation zone because of lack of money. This turned out to be one of my better predictions, but at the time it attracted derision. This response looked to be justified at first when if it had not been for a late equaliser at Hartlepool from Steve Davey to give Pompey a barely merited 1-1 draw, Portsmouth would have been bottom of the entire Football League by the second weekend of the 1978-79 season. Soon, though, the defence in particular was sorted out, with Peter Mellor, imported from Fulham, proving to be a capable goalkeeper at this level, and it seemed to me that if the central defender Foster had not been injured late on in the season, Pompey might well have been promoted at the first time of asking. Others thought differently, and in the ridiculous setting of The Shay (which had trees at one end of the ground) on 3 March 1979, when Halifax deservedly won 2-0, many in the sizeable contingent of Portsmouth supporters among the 'crowd' of 1,741 turned on Jimmy Dickinson. The Pompey old timers were furious at this treatment of the great man, and this was the nearest that I ever came to walking away from the whole wretched business. Dickinson was not cut out to be a Manager and he never wanted the job anyway, and at Barnsley the end of the same month (following a 1-1 draw and easily the best Fourth Division match I ever saw) Jimmy had a massive heart attack. Frank Burrows took over as Manager, and in the summer, with Foster transferred to Brighton for a record fee, the money was used to sign defenders Steve Azlewood, John McLaughlin and Archie Styles, and midfield men Joe Laidlaw and Terry Brisley. Not all of Burrows's other dealings in the transfer market proved worthwhile, but Pompey got off to a flying start with ten wins in the first dozen games, followed by a 3-1 win at Huddersfield, the eventual Champions, on 13 October 1979. Portsmouth won the return game with Huddersfield by 4-1 as well, but Pompey tried to play football at this level, and Mick Buxton, the Huddersfield Manager adopted a more pragmatic style and it worked. Injuries, notably to Azlewood, disrupted Pompey's promotion bid, but so did laziness, and, with Portsmouth trailing at half time at Port Vale appropriately enough on April Fool's Day 1980, Burrows told the players that there was no more that he could do. It was up to them. Pompey eventually won that game 3-2, but I wrote Burrows off after that evening game, even though it marked the beginning of a six match unbeaten run that ended in promotion. After Pompey won 2-1 at Halifax, some Bradford City fans I chatted to, who had for their own reasons gone to see the game, told me (a) that they feared that Portsmouth were going to pip them for promotion, and that (b) they were amazed that the Pompey fans had turned up in such numbers at such a distance and that these fans were plainly completely mad. I suggested that it might be sensible not to convey opinion (b) to the fans concerned. Anyway, Bradford City somehow managed to lose their last game at Peterborough, and Pompey won their final fixture at Northampton 2-0, helped by the reality that at least two thirds of the crowd were Portsmouth supporters. That Pompey had only managed to gain promotion from the Fourth Division in fourth place by virtue of goal difference seemed to me to be cause for apology and not exultation, but, sure enough, jubilant celebrations were held in Portsmouth's Guildhall Square. Deacon delivered what seemed to be a Martin Luther King impersonation, with the promise that he would deliver on his 'dream' of bringing top flight football to Fratton Park. In this manner, the Fourth Division experience came to an end, with many Pompey supporters later forgetting that it had involved two seasons and not just one, and trying to pretend that we crushed the opposition week in and week out. Beating Scunthorpe 6-1 in August 1979 was often cited, but what about the failure to beat the same team in any other of the games at this level, not least the poor and losing display in the away game the following January? What was so wonderful about, say, losing 1-0 at Lincoln? Yes, it was an experience to go to Spotland, and see Pompey win on both occasions, and Rochdale remain one of the few clubs never to have beaten Portsmouth, and so I regard them - and Spotland, come to that - with some affection, but the notion that the Fourth Division was all 'good fun' which took hold later did not accord with the reality.

The bookmakers made Portsmouth the favourites for immediate promotion from the Third Division, and Pompey

125

started off with four wins, even a couple of them away, but it soon became clear that it was going to be a long haul, and a 3-0 defeat at Rotherham at the end of January 1981 really finished things off. Functional Rotherham went on to win the Third Division title, and footballing Portsmouth eventually finished sixth. More important in many ways was the Fourth Round League Cup away tie with Liverpool on 28 October 1980. The Liverpool Manager, Bob Paisley, old enough to know better, scoffed at the idea that Pompey would bring 16,000 supporters with them to Anfield. If only to be difficult, that number came, of course, providing about half of the attendance. The overriding problem with Portsmouth never was its prospective support base, but the Club's lack of financial backing which was reflected in the low quality of the players. The size of the task facing the Club in striving to count for something once more in English football, or, indeed, at all was obviously a considerable one. On the night, though much was made of the brave fight that Pompey put up, the fact was that Liverpool won 4-1, and reality kicked in. If the 1980-81 season fizzled out, that of 1981-82 never got going in the first place. To the extent that anybody remembered it at all later, it was the season when Pompey seemed to draw all the time - nineteen times in fact - and in the end finished thirteenth after spending much of the season struggling to avoid becoming one of the relegation candidates. The 1981-82 season witnessed Alan Knight finally replacing Mellor as Pompey's regular goalkeeper. Knight gave several fine displays in a string of dire away games, the best of those displays being at Doncaster. Though Burrows had made some shrewd signings since the Fourth Division days (notably the midfielder Bobby Doyle, the utility man Mick Tait, and the striker Billy Rafferty) the results were unimpressive, and Bobby Campbell replaced him as Portsmouth's Manager. Campbell always wanted Pompey to play with style. A reconstruction of the squad followed in the summer of 1982, with the main signings including central defender Ernie Howe from Q. P. R.; striker Alan Biley from Everton; and the young and very promising future England midfield player Neil Webb from Reading. Portsmouth began their 1982-83 Third Division programme with a spectacular 4-1 opening day victory

126

over Sheffield United at Fratton Park in the sunshine. It was marvellous stuff, and I told anybody who would listen that Pompey were going to be promoted as Champions. Portsmouth matched the historical formula of winning at least half of their first twelve games. That said, though, some results (notably, a couple of early home defeats, a fortuitous away draw at Huddersfield, and a 4-0 beating at Southend) led me to think that Pompey were going to make a meal of winning the title, and missing several penalties on the way did not help the cause. A 5-1 defeat at the hands of Bristol Rovers at Eastville in admittedly dreadful conditions was worrying too, and so was a 2-2 draw at Bradford City, where two opportunist goals from Biley gave Pompey an undeserved point. The combative Tait got the winner at icy Chesterfield, and eventually following a 1-0 home win over Oxford on 22 January 1983 Portsmouth strung together seven straight wins. This run was followed by four games without Pompey scoring a goal. Something had to be done, and the midfield player Kevin Dillon was recruited from Birmingham, and the striker Nicky Morgan from West Ham. There were eleven games left, and, though only the home game with Bradford City (0-1) was lost, the title was not secured until the last game when Pompey won 1-0 at Plymouth. Such was the rampant atmosphere that one Plymouth supporter told me later that he did wonder what would have been left of Home Park if the Pompey supporters had been denied their prize. Biley got the winning goal, and, indeed, scored 23 times in 46 games, working well with Rafferty in a team that played some attractive football at times, but which was too inconsistent to suggest that a further promotion would follow at once.

In what passed for a learned discussion in the gents lavatory at half time at Doncaster on 30 April 1983, and with four more games to go, the Portsmouth fans present agreed that, aside from Knight, the defence simply was not good enough for the Second Division. Richard Money, formerly of Liverpool, would have been a more than useful recruit had not injury cut his career short. Instead of other defenders, Mark Hateley, a young and promising central striker, was recruited from Coventry. This looked very much like a Chairman's signing to me. The following

127

June, Hateley was to become Pompey's first England player since Dickinson was last capped in 1956, and soon he was to be transferred to A. C. Milan. So, Pompey had Hateley for the 1983-84 season only, and he scored 22 times in 38 appearances. With Biley chipping in 16 goals too, Portsmouth's problem was not scoring goals. Indeed, Pompey scored 73 times, but, as the Doncaster lavatory analysts had predicted, the trouble was at the other end with no less than 64 goals conceded, absurdly half of them at home. Campbell lost his job, of course, and the youth team coach Alan Ball was to be his replacement. Nobody doubted that Ball had been a great player. Indeed, when Alf Ramsey said that Martin Peters was the model for the player of the future it seeemed to me that he should have nominated Ball instead. I have never seen a better first time passer of a football than Ball, and with either foot too. I saw him play many times, and it was a privilege. That said though, I did not welcome him as a Manager. I would have preferred somebody with more experience. I doubted that a man with a poor disciplinary record would be able to run a disciplined squad. Further than this, having read his ghosted and ghastly autobiography, unforgivably called *It's All About A Ball*, it was evident there that Ball was convinced that he had a special knack of dealing with football's 'bad boys.' I was in no mood for experiments, and I also feared that there was some substance in remarks made to me by a contemporary of Ball's when he was at Everton. His line was that Ball would never be able to keep sufficient distance from the players. Even worse, Ball was one of those people who required others to be utterly 'for' him or they were defined as being 'against' him, which seemed to me to be a poor basis for management. The prediction that no team run by Ball would ever win a trophy proved to be a correct one. Anyway, Deacon ignored advice from people like me, and Ball was let loose on the transfer market with the money from the Hateley transfer. Good as his word, Ball mainly recruited the misfits of football, the 'mongrels' as he and Mick Channon termed them, the talents that others could not channel. To the rest of us, the film *The Dirty Dozen* was simply a Hollywood fantasy in which Lee Marvin moulded a bunch of dangerous headbangers into a fighting unit with which

128

to undertake an impossible mission successfully. To Ball, *The Dirty Dozen* might as well have been reality.

Whatever others in football thought of him, he soon became the much loved Bally among the majority of Portsmouth supporters, and the drinking culture that he promoted within the Club did not bother them, of course. The love affair was mutual, with Bally going on record as expressing admiration for Pompey supporters as real men, the sort that go to war. Without feeling warlike myself, whatever my private reservations, I always publicly supported Bally against those outside the Pompey fraternity who criticised him, and I was pleased at least at first by his recruitment policy. At Second Division level certainly, Noel Blake from Birmingham and Billy Gilbert from Crystal Palace formed a physically formidable central defensive partnership, with the latter being a very skilful player. Into the midfield, Bally brought Mick Kennedy from Middlesbrough, whose well justified reputation for violence obscured his two footed skills. Up front, Bally misguidedly signed Scott McGarvey from Manchester United to replace Hateley. You had only to look at McGarvey to see that he would fail, and one hoped that rumours that Bally had the opportunity to sign Mark Hughes instead were untrue. Portsmouth already had several able players in Knight, Webb, Dillon, Doyle, Biley and Tait, and, as the season progressed, added two wingers to the list: namely, Vince Hilaire and Kevin O'Callaghan. Ironically, given my scepticism about Ball, I have to concede that the 1984-85 season proved to be one of those that I enjoyed most between the mid 1950s and the early 1990s. The scene was set for me at least by a couple of early season away wins, both by the only goal, at Leeds and Birmingham. These were bitterly contested games, and Pompey could be said to be playing post - Ramsey modern football for the first time. Portsmouth started off with a ten game unbeaten run, including seven victories. The next two games were lost, and things were never quite the same again, though few would forget Blake's dramatic winner in the last minute of the home game with Huddersfield in December, or, a week later, Biley's two goals to secure victory over Oxford in time added on because a Pompey nutter dressed as Santa Claus had invaded the pitch. New Year's

129

Day 1985 was not such fun for Pompey when, in a home game played in a gale, a four goal lead was thrown away. This 4-4 draw meant the end of promotion hopes, according to the despairing Ball, but it was the later home defeats by Birmingham and Manchester City in April that really undermined the bid to secure the third and final promotion place. Pompey got more points at home than away, but the number of defeats in each case was the same. The team did not give up, and a Tait header won a brutal match at Blackburn, and then Carlisle were beaten. Everything depended on the last day of the season, 11 May 1985, and, as in 1927, it was between Manchester City and Pompey for the final promotion place. Ten thousand Pompey fans turned up for the game at Huddersfield, which Portsmouth won in some style by 2-0. O'Callaghan got an extraordinary goal, dribbling from the halfway line past man after man. Webb set up a classy goal for Hilaire. It made no difference. City crushed Charlton 5-1, and they were promoted.

Much of the optimism generated by the 1984-85 season among the ranks of the Portsmouth supporters - including myself - was only justified if the obvious weaknesses in the team were remedied. Otherwise, the 1985-86 season would have much the same outcome as its predecessor, and, indeed, Pompey finished fourth once more. Portsmouth had done little in the way of recruitment in the summer of 1985 because, as Ball explained, the selling clubs were talking telephone numbers. That's why it was called a transfer market. Chairman Deacon did actually say that once the Hateley money was used up, there would be no more to come, but, of course, nobody wanted to listen. Inevitably, actions spoke larger than his often ignored words. With Webb having, not surprisingly, insisted on advancing his career by going to Clough's Notts Forest, nobody was brought in for him, and without Webb the team lacked sophistication in its play, becoming merely combative and much less stylish. Pompey needed a striker, and the obvious target was Mick Quinn of Oldham, 'a bit of a pudding,' as one Newcastle fan later said to me, but the best available at this level. Pompey made do with Mick Channon, once a major player but now very much in the veteran stage. By the end of October, Pompey were top of the table and had won eleven games, drawn two, and lost only at Oldham, but a wretched November marked the turning of the tide. Ball could not seem to prioritise, and Pompey got involved in a form of marathon League Cup combat with Spurs from which Portmouth emerged victorious, only to collapse in the next round to Oxford. Despite Pompey's August victory over Norwich, I always fancied the East Anglian club to finish top because in Woods, Watson and Bruce they had defensive talent that Pompey lacked. So, it had to be second or nothing, and nothing it proved to be. Quinn was at last signed in March, and got half a dozen goals, but it was all too late. Few had taken Wimbledon seriously as promotion rivals, and when the home game with them came around in late March one Pompey fan favoured the media with the opinion that the visiting team consisted of ten basketball players and a dwarf. One of tall men, John Fashanu broke Dillon's cheekbone, and, according to him, the Pompey players tried to get even in the tunnel afterwards. Fashanu thought this was marvellous, and expressed the hope that he would play for Portsmouth one day. This 1-1 draw did not mark the end of the promotion drive. That came with a 3-2 home defeat inflicted by Leeds on 5 April 1986. Pompey had been 2-0 up at half time, and Channon later confirmed that Ball had told the players that the game was far from won, but they took no notice. Three weeks later, a 0-0 draw at Sheffield United in an appalling match merely confirmed that Pompey were sentenced to another season of Second Division football. Forgivably, Ball wept with frustration.

The 1986-87 season was to see Pompey finally promoted to the top flight in an atmosphere of anti climax. Three years before, I recalled a Pompey fan laughing about the fact that Pompey had Hateley and Arsenal had to make do with the fading Paul Mariner. Now, Pompey no longer had Hateley, and the veteran Mariner had been recruited as his latest replacement. Portsmouth were top of the table at the end of October, and their home form was good all season, with 17 wins, 2 draws, and just 2 defeats. Pompey's ambition at Fratton Park was to somehow get the lead and then kill the game off, and it usually worked. Away from home, however, Pompey often looked unconvincing, and lost more games than they won, and their reputation for indiscipline did them few favours away from Fratton Park. At Sheffield United in December, Pompey had three players sent off to United's one, losing only 1-0 thanks to a Mariner own goal. Mariner only scored five goals at the right end all season, and Portsmouth were heavily dependent on Quinn who scored 22 League goals, despite spending some time in prison for a driving offence. The Pompey fans sent him more cakes than even the rotund Quinn could devour. The hard truth was that Portsmouth nearly threw away promotion once again and staggered over the line by default, when Oldham lost at Shrewsbury. The players celebrated in excessive style, lost the final match of the season at home, and finished six points down on the Champions. Few Pompey supporters trusted Chairman Deacon to come up with the money in the summer of 1987 to reconstruct a squad which had too many players who had plainly reached their ceiling. Deacon's detractors were right, but what they did not allow for was for him to suddenly embark on putting what money he had into a basketball team. Deacon's attitude was that he could do what he liked with his own money, calmly forgetting that without the SOS Pompey iniative he would not have a football club anyway. As far as that club was concerned, Deacon told Ball that he could sign seven players, but four of them had to be free transfers. One of those who cost money, Barry Horne, proved to be an impressive recruit to the midfield, but the team needed at least half a dozen new players of that calibre. Instead, Pompey recruited players like Ian Baird, a classic non striking striker, well described as the poor man's Joe Jordan; and another natural Second Division player in Terry Connor as his partner. Of the free transfers, Clive Whitehead did a good job, and the same could be said of defender Kevin Ball, a promotee from within. To balance the books, Deacon tried but failed to sell Quinn, and successfully insisted on getting rid of Tait and one of the wingers. Hilaire would not have been missed, but Ball chose to get rid of the more gifted O'Callaghan, whom he did not get on with. Then, before a ball was kicked, it was announced that a knee injury was going to rule out Noel Blake for half the season. Absurdly, Ball was forced to replace him in central defence with Mariner for the opening game at Oxford, which was duly lost 4-2. I thought that Pompey were relegated there and then, and results like losing 6-0 at Arsenal a fortnight later seemed to confirm this. I had intended to go to this game, but the state of the garden after a long holiday demanded my attention. My children ran out regularly to keep me up with the score, which was kind of them. Pompey only won four home games all season, and three away. One of the away wins was by 2-0 at Southampton on 2 January 1988, with Kennedy running the show. Deacon reacted by insisting that Kennedy was transferred to Bradford City, either because he desperately needed the money or to get at the 'Deacon Out' protestors who were shouting at him all the time by this stage. Pompey somehow got to the Sixth Round of the Cup, and Ball seemed convinced that we would stay up until Portsmouth's appalling performance at Sheffield Wednesday in March. Pompey should have lost by ten goals instead of by 1-0 that day: and they would have done but for a spectacular display of shot stopping by Knight, who somehow managed to better a superb performance from him on the same ground four years earlier. A fortnight later, Pompey won 1-0 at Tottenham in one of the strangest games I have ever experienced. In close to silence, and to the evident amazement of the Spurs supporters, Ball and the Pompey players expended almost as much energy shouting abuse at each other as they devoted to playing. For the final match at Old Trafford, which Pompey were lucky to lose to Manchester United by only 4-1, our supporters were packed into the visitors' end like sardines and I thought that we were fortunate that the game was not marked by tragedy.

POMPEY 1988-2002: WAITING FOR GODOT

Samuel Beckett's *Waiting For Godot* must be the most overpraised play in the history of the theatre. Its central theme was that life is boring. Well, most of the time it is bound to be boring - but, of course, it is vastly better than the alternative. That said, though, I have to confess that the period 1988-2002 in Portsmouth's history did make me wonder many times if Beckett had got it right after all. John Deacon made way for Jim Gregory as the Chairman in the summer of 1988. Deacon had been found

133

to have senile dementia, which led the more generous spirited among the Pompey faithful to believe that the onset of this dreaded disease accounted for his increasingly strange behaviour in recent years. Jim Gregory had done an impressive job when he ran Q.P.R., and, at first, some of us hoped that he would do the same at Fratton Park. However, Gregory proved to be a sick man and Blue Star Garages, his main business, soon proved to be in poor shape too. Gregory should have got rid of Ball as Manager at once, but instead let him loose in the transfer market where he signed more 'mongrels' in the form of Warren Aspinall and Gavin Maguire. Ball was sacked in early 1989. The new Manager, John Gregory had little idea what he was doing, and Pompey were fortunate not to be relegated to the Third Division, finishing twentieth at the end of the 1988-89 season. Pompey finished twelfth in the 1989-90 season, and seventeenth in that of 1990-91. Frank Burrows had returned as Manager in place of John Gregory in early 1990, but the squad he inherited contained several very distasteful and indolent players whom he could not tolerate working with, and in the summer of 1991 he made way for the experienced Jim 'Bald Eagle' Smith.

Jim Smith had hardly set foot in Portsmouth before the fans told him that Pompey were doomed to relegation. Since Portsmouth's youth team had recently got to the semi-final of the F. A. Youth Cup, Smith's reply took the form of what about the young players Pompey have got? Sure enough, Darren Anderton, Andy Awford, Kit Symons, and Daryll Powell were all included in the team on the opening day of the 1991-92 season at Blackburn. The locals were full of talk about the money that Jack Walker was putting into Rovers, but as far as the game on 17 August 1991 was concerned Pompey had the better of things, with Anderton scoring with a looping shot that Mimms should have saved. Paranoid as ever, we thought that the referee kept the game going until Blackburn equalised. That said, though, the season proved to be pleasant enough, with Pompey only letting in 12 goals at home and 51 goals overall in 46 fixtures. At home, Pompey won 15, drew 6, and lost just 2 of their games, and the overall total of 59 points was only 5 short of that which earned Blackburn a place in the play offs, and, in their case, promotion.

Pompey might have made it in their place, instead of finishing ninth, but for an exciting run in the F. A. Cup. Most of us were relieved that Pompey survived a Third Round trip to Exeter with a 2-1 win, followed by a 2-0 home win over Leyton Orient, and we thought it was all over when Middlesbrough forced a 1-1 draw in the Fifth Round at Fratton Park. Ayresome Park had been like a graveyard for Pompey most of the time this side of 1949, but the evening of 26 February 1992 witnessed the turning of the tide. To our amazement, Pompey won 4-2, with some extraordinary goals, including one from Anderton direct from a corner. So, it was on to the Sixth Round and a home tie with Notts Forest. The media made much of Brian Clough never having managed an F. A. Cup winning team. 'Never mind about Cloughie, neither have I,' responded 'Bald Eagle,' and an early goal from McLoughlin gave Pompey victory by 1-0. So, it was on to Highbury on 5 April 1992, and a semi final against Liverpool. 'Pompey, Pompey, who are they?' the Liverpool fans chanted in response to the repeated renderings of the Pompey Chimes. Well, they soon found out, with Portsmouth taking the lead near the end when a through ball from Neill found Anderton, and he slipped the ball into the bottom corner. Awford needlessly conceded a free kick which gave Liverpool their equaliser. Liverpool showed little sign of scoring in the replay at Villa Park, being held comfortably by the Portsmouth defence. When, near the end, Beresford surprised the Liverpool defence with a pull back from what looked like a lost cause, McLaughlin, seemingly taken by surprise himself, tamely hit the ball against the underside of the bar with Grobbelar beaten. Liverpool won 3-1 on penalties, to the relief of the media, who did not want two Second Division teams (the other being Sunderland) in the Final. The Pompey team at Villa Park was Alan Knight, Warren Neill, Kit Symons, Andy Awford, Ray Daniel, Chris Burns, Alan McLoughlin (Warren Aspinall), Martin Kuhl, John Beresford, Colin Clarke (Guy Whittingham), and Darren Anderton. Though Pompey had fielded better players in some positions at various times in those years (notably Webb and Hateley) that particular team as an entity seemed to me to be the best team to represent Portsmouth between 1956 and 2002. After the Highbury game, Anderton was asked by the media: 'When are you going to move to a big club?' and, as if it was 1956, came up with the wonderful reply: 'But I am at a big club.'

It turned out that Jim Gregory no longer had the resources ro run an Endsleigh First Division club, as the second level of English football was now misleadingly called following the formation of the Premier League. Beresford was transferred to Newcastle, and Kuhl to Derby, and, at a fee that savoured of desperation, Anderton was transferred to Spurs. In part exchange, Spurs let Pompey have Paul Walsh, a gifted player who achieved little during the first half of the 1992-93 season, an observation that was true of his team mates too. Down to the halfway stage, Pompey were consistent at home and poor away, though Whittingham was scoring freely, getting hat tricks at both Bristol City and Luton. In an absurd game at Oxford on 3 November 1992, Pompey were 5-3 ahead with a minute remaining, but managed to only draw 5-5, in part due to local product Stuart Doling giving away a stupid penalty. 'Bald Eagle' was said to have tried to strangle Doling in the dressing room afterwards. Pompey marked the halfway stage of the season by winning 4-2 at Derby, usually another unhappy hunting ground, and reaching 37 points. The Walsh-Whittingham combination cut loose in the second half of the season, and Pompey threatened to win automatic promotion at one stage, even catching previously runaway leaders Newcastle for a day, but the early season results were what cost Pompey dear. Everybody remembers the 4-1 defeat at Sunderland on 1 May 1993, with Butters and Walsh getting sent off, but what about losing 4-1 at relegated Brentford on 1 September 1992, or that wretched 3-0 defeat at Grimsby on 31 October 1992? Anyway, it all came down to the last day of the season, and this time Pompey did beat Grimsby 2-1 to reach 88 points, but West Ham beat Cambridge 2-0 to take automatic promotion on goal difference. Pompey had lost both games against West Ham. The defence only let in an average of a goal a game overall, but attention tended to be centred on the achievements of the ever present Whittingham who scored 42 times, which meant that he had beaten the record of 'Farmer' Haines. After Pompey lost in the play offs against Leicester,

136

Whittingham insisted on leaving, and joined 'Big Ron' Atkinson at Aston Villa, and, thus, wasted his career.

After the near miss in 1993, Portsmouth experienced a succession of seasons that not merely tested the loyalty of the Pompey supporters: they tested the soul. Portsmouth's idea of a replacement for Whittingham was the veteran Leeds striker Lee Chapman, who soon cleared off once he realised that Portsmouth was not on the District Line. The 1993-94 season was anonymous, with Pompey finishing seventeenth in the Endsleigh First Division, though a great deal of fuss was made when, within a matter of days in January, Pompey drew away at Blackburn in the F. A. Cup, and then drew away again in an exciting League Cup game at Manchester United. The replays were both lost, of course, and, just to rub this in, Walsh, the scorer of both Pompey's goals at Old Trafford, was transferred to Manchester City for a routine fee. Gerry Creaney from Celtic was supposed to be his replacement. He proved to be talented, but idle. Creaney's consistency as a goalscorer was one reason why Pompey managed to finish as high as eighteenth in the League in the 1994-95 season, the only highlight of which was an away win in the League Cup at Everton by 3-2, with Creaney scoring twice. With Fratton Park in many respects semi derelict by this stage, the Gregory regime stirred itself, and came up with a scheme for a new ground, located in Farlington, and called Parkway. I submitted supporting evidence to the planning inquiry myself, and I had my usual influence, with the plan being turned down by the then Conservative Government in late 1994 because the retail element would lead to too much competition with other shops, and because the development would disturb the natural habitat of Brent Geese who flew there from Siberia. Predictably, these birds soon found another home, but too late to save this imaginative scheme. For some time, Jim Gregory had been too ill to take an active part in running the Club, and control was ceded to his son Martin Gregory. Some described this man as a mediocrity, but events in the 1995-96 season showed that this was a needlessly generous assessment. In the first week of the season, Pompey sold Symons and Creaney to Manchester City. Since Creaney had been scoring at the rate of about a goal every other game, Pompey were bound to struggle up front, and since Symons was instrumental (along with the redoubtable Alan Knight) in keeping the goals against column in check, what followed from this behaviour was obvious. Relegation or, at best, a near miss was on the cards. When I suggested this to the Pompey faithful after a 3-2 defeat at Derby with several games to go, the kindest of the responses was that I was on another planet. Pompey avoided relegation on the last day of the season only by goal difference, winning 1-0 at Huddersfield, Deon Burton scoring. Meanwhile, a Northern Consortium had made serious efforts to buy the Club, aiming to develop the Fratton Goods Yard and, with it, the now dilapidated Fratton Park, which had for some time had both the Fratton End and the Milton End open to the elements. Martin Gregory tried to play hard ball in the financial negotiations, and, when this failed, for no obvious reason he appointed Terry Venables as the Portsmouth Chairman. Venables had a reputation as a coach, and in that role he had taken England to the semi final stage of Euro 1996, but he did not have the sort of money to get Portsmouth out of the second level of English football or to keep them in the Premiership. So, his appointment was pointless, and, indeed, short lived. Oddly, the 1996-97 season was not too bad by Portsmouth's humble standards, with Pompey finishing seventh. This did not lead to the current Manager, Terry Fenwick being hated less than before, but everybody was surprised and pleased when Pompey reached the Sixth Round of the F. A. Cup. Leeds United had won at Arsenal in the Fourth Round and, understandably, seemed to think that beating Portsmouth at Elland Road would be no problem. Pompey won more comfortably than the 3-2 scoreline suggested, and much was made of Venables supposedly having given the players a coaching master class. The belief was that he would come up with a repeat performance that would enable Pompey to get the better of Chelsea at Fratton Park in the next Round. The key to the Elland Road victory, though, aside from complacency on the part of the Leeds players, was the use of Paul Hall as a withdrawn central striker. There was no point in using this approach against the current Chelsea team, since it would give central defender Frank Leboeuf too much freedom to spray the ball around. This was exactly what happened, and Pompey lost 4-1.

When Portsmouth Football Club decided to celebrate its Centenary in 1998, it was in stark contrast to the events of fifty years before. Instead of this time defeating the reigning English Champions, Pompey just about managed a 1-1 home draw with an anonymous Birmingham team. That this sad response to the call of history took that form was fitting enough for the Club that had translated itself into Little Pompey. The 1997-98 season witnessed the departures of Fenwick and Venables, and the eventual return of Alan Ball as Manager, and a relegation battle only settled on the final day. Over the years, Pompey had made the Second Division relegation zone under its various names into a way of life, and so most of us believed that somehow we would escape the drop. That said though, a run of seven games with just one point from late December 1997 onwards did suggest that this time we were wrong. Alan Ball's body language during a merited 3-1 defeat at Crewe on 14 February 1998 suggested that he thought that his decision to return to Portsmouth had been a mistake. The performance of the team was so bad at Crewe that, at first as a joke, the Pompey supporters stepped up their manic level of backing, and when, for no obvious reason, this soon seemed to work in terms of results, they kept this up all the way down to a last day 3-1 win at Bradford City that enabled Portsmouth to stay up and send Manchester City down. A Leeds fan who accompanied us to the game at Valley Parade thought the support given was insane in its intensity. Well, maybe so, but the much loved 'Johnnie Lager' Durnin got a couple of goals, and the midfielder Sammy Igoe played the game of his life. Quite a few among the Pompey faithful convinced themselves that the 1998-99 season would be different, which it was in the sense that Pompey only escaped relegation this time by goal difference. The only interesting game of a dire season was when Pompey won 1-0 at Notts Forest in the Third Round of the F. A. Cup, with Alan Knight in goal for the last time and with Pompey supporters providing the majority of the crowd. Since Martin Gregory was unwilling for whatever reasons to sell the Club to the Northern Consortium, he preferred Portsmouth to go into adminstration, and the new owner became a Serb American called Milan Mandaric. The Pompey supporters convinced themselves on the basis of no evidence at all that Mandaric was nothing less than a billionaire, having made his money his money in no time at all in Silicon Valley. Mandaric soon became much loved by the Portsmouth faithful, who would sing 'There's only one Milan' to the confusion of supporters of other teams who had heard, of course, of Inter Milan and A. C. Milan. My opinion was that Mandaric's first move should have been to dismiss Ball and get a better Manager. As so often, this left me in a minority. When I returned from holiday for yet another visit to Barnsley on 28 August 1999, I was assured that 'everything's different, Geoff.' It looked like much the same team to me, and, indeed, with the help of some poor refereeing, Pompey rewarded the loyalty of the faithful by losing 6-0. To the amazement of some Barnsley supporters I knew, the majority of the Pompey fans danced around the ground. Three weeks later, there was the excitement of a trip to Tranmere Rovers, scene of many a beating in the past, and Pompey were 4-0 up shortly after half time. Barnsley was forgotten, and so was the fact that Tranmere were allowed to score two late goals. Things went from bad to worse, and Ball was dismissed before Christmas, though not before, for some reason, selling the two best midfield players. Jeff Peron simply vanished and Alan McLoughlin was transferred to Wigan, which seemed to be much the same fate. Ball's eventual replacement as Manager was Tony Pulis, who ensured that Pompey finished as high as eighteenth place.

The Mandaric era had started off poorly and this continued in the 2000 -2001 and 2001-2002 seasons, with Pulis soon being discarded only to be initially replaced as Manager by one of the characters on the Portsmouth scene, a local product originally and now a much travelled player, Steve Claridge. When in a managerial role at Millwall in 2005, Claridge was dismissed even before the season started. Claridge was given longer to fail at Portsmouth. Claridge's memoirs are well worth reading, not least about his time as a player at Birmingham. To hide from the bookmakers to whom he owed money, Claridge was forced at one stage to sleep in his car. Needing more money, he tried to negotiate with the Birmingham administrator, Karren Brady, while she was walking her dog. To judge from his account, Claridge did not seem to grasp that Brady took him much less seriously than the dog. Claridge was a much better player than his dishevelled appearance suggested, but it was no surprise that he proved to be inept as a Manager. This was also true of his successor, Graham Rix, who had been a successful coach at Chelsea. Being number two, though, in his case proved to be not the same as being number one. Portsmouth were extremely lucky not to be relegated at the end of the 2000-2001 season. Winning just two games out of the last dozen did not help the cause, of course, though the enthusiasm of the Pompey fans was still in evidence, not least at Blackburn on 29 April 2001, when the thousand or so who made it up to Ewood Park on a Sunday dominated the place with their singing. A loan player, Lee Sharpe, formerly of Manchester United, told one of my friends that this display of loyalty was evidence of insanity. Whether this was so or not, Pompey lost 3-1. According to one of the players, Mike Panopoulos, a couple of draws with Birmingham and Fulham had convinced the team that they had been doing quite well. Panopoulos had originally been signed by Alan Ball on the basis of video evidence, and it was generally believed even by his admirers that Ball had signed the wrong Panopoulos. Anyway, the Blackburn defeat made it imperative that Pompey won the next home game with fellow strugglers, Crystal Palace, but Palace won 4-2. All now depended, yet again, on the last day of the season. I predicted that Pompey would beat Barnsley by the 3-0 score needed, and that Palace would fail to win by more than 1-0 at Stockport, a very depressing location I knew only too well from my travels. So, we would be safe. These results were exactly as predicted. I was hailed as a genius. Years of negativity and cheap cynicism on my part were forgiven. Few seemed to notice or care that it was Huddersfield who went down, thanks to losing 2-1 at home to Birmingham, a result that I had most certainly not anticipated.

The Pompey fans were assured by Graham Rix that everything would be different in the 2001-2002 season. They were certainly different for him, given that, for example, he was no longer in sole charge of player recruitment. It was Mandaric himself who signed the Croatian midfield player, Robert Prosinecki, formerly of Real Madrid, as a present to the fans. When he could be bothered, as at Barnsley in late September, Prosinecki still had more than enough class for the second level of English football - but where he could not stir himself, such as at West Brom the following February, he was useless; and it was unclear whether or not Rix was allowed to leave him out of the team. Further than this, Mandaric had appointed the former West Ham boss, Harry Redknapp, as Director of Football, and, fairly obviously, as Rix's eventual successor. It had been Harry, and not Rix, who had recruited the striker Peter Crouch from Q.P.R. Crouch scored around a goal every other game, and he really did his stuff in the away games. With or without Rix's approval, Harry was sent to Japan to run the rule over the national goalkeeper, Yoshi Kawaguchi. Harry confessed that in the game he saw Kawaguchi never touched the ball in the first half, and Harry had fallen asleep in the second half because of jet lag. Nonetheless, Kawaguchi was signed. The idea seemed to be to make money by filming the games in which he played and selling the material to Japan. Since TV rights had already been sold to ITV Digital, this scheme was a non starter, and soon nobody would admit authorship. Meanwhile, Kawaguchi made his debut against Sheffield Wednesday away, and conceded a goal inside a half a minute. A couple of goals from Crouch ensured victory in that game, but, sooner rather than later, Pompey were once more in relegation trouble. Following a humiliating 4-1 home defeat in the F. A. Cup at the hands of Leyton Orient, Kawaguchi was dropped, and Pompey were forced to rely on the veteran David Beasant to fill the gap. Pompey were not safe from relegation until they secured a 1-1 away draw at Crewe in mid March. In the last minute, for no obvious reason, goalkeeper Beasant went walkabout, and quite how one of the Crewe players missed what was literally an open goal in his absence nobody knew. Rix was sacked the following weekend. Harry Redknapp then took over.

CHAPTER 6: MINI REVIVAL: PORTSMOUTH 2002-2008

A FOOTBALL MAN TO THE RESCUE

The popular image of Harry Redknapp, and one cultivated by Harry himself in alliance with the media, was that of the Cockney 'character,' or, if one prefers, amiable rogue. Harry tended to be commonly perceived as being football's Arthur Daley, as in the classic television series *Minder*. Why I welcomed the appointment of Harry Redknapp as Manager of Portsmouth was not because of its comic possibilities, though the jokes were often very good. The well honed Arthur Daley act was amusing, but it did not matter. What did matter was that Harry was a football man. He knew English football from top to bottom. Everybody in and around the game knew who Harry was, and, having been anonymous for so long, at last Pompey had an identity worth having again.

When Harry was once asked by Portsmouth supporters why the West Ham team in which he played in the 1960s achieved so little, despite having Bobby Moore, Martin Peters, and Geoff Hurst from England's 1966 World Cup winning side in their ranks, Harry's explanation was that 'we spent too much time down [at] the Black Lion Pub.' Harry was a much better player than he was later commonly considered to have been, and I say this having seen Harry compete against the vicious Leeds defence of the Revie era. If, as some have suggested, Harry was a less skilful player than his son Jamie Redknapp, he had very real pace. I recall an evening match at Leeds in the late 1960s when Harry provided a superb cross for Hurst, who instantly hit a flat volley into the bottom corner of the net. It was a superlative goal, but, as the West Ham Manager, Ron Greenwood would have noted, it was a consolation goal. Leeds had swept West Ham aside 4-1. That sort of thing happened rather a lot, and after the turn of the decade Greenwood seemed to get fed up with the Black Lion drinking school, and Harry got moved on into the

143

Wilderness. In former times, discarded Hammers were transported to Torquay, and Budgie Byrne even ended up, fat as a pig, in South Africa. Harry was banished to Bournemouth. He was in his mid twenties.

Harry always tends to be associated with West Ham as a player, but he spent more of his senior playing career at Bournemouth, eventually ending up as Manager there in 1983. There was a famous F. A. Cup victory over Manchester United to celebrate in 1984, and Bournemouth were Third Division Champions in 1987. It seems likely that Harry was never the same man after a horrendous car crash in Italy when he was there for the 1990 World Cup. Harry was lucky to survive. That Bournemouth were relegated in 1992, and in financial disarray, tended to be forgotten by Harry's numerous media admirers. Harry moved on to West Ham, and he was Manager there by 1994, though quite how and why he replaced Billy Bonds in that role remains unexplained. Harry was said to dislike being portrayed as a wheeler dealer, but that he had this reputation at West Ham was not surprising, given that, according to my record books, in his seven years as Manager there, Harry was involved in transfer deals relating to 134 players. Most famously of all, the transfer of Rio Ferdinand to Leeds United in 2000 saw Harry up against Peter Ridsdale, the then Leeds Chairman, in the relevant negotiations. It was not really a contest. As is well known, Harry played his part in talking the fee up from £12M to £18M. To Harry's credit, of course, the youth policy he had pursued had led to the emergence of Ferdinand in the first place, as well as, for example, Joe Cole and Frank Lampard. Though, in the opinion of his critics, Harry's dealings in the transfer market savoured of activity for its own sake, it was the case that when Harry was in charge at West Ham, the Hammers finished fourteenth, tenth, fourteenth, eighth, fifth, ninth, ninth, and fifteenth. Harry later told the Pompey supporters that at West Ham his aim was the modest one of finishing above Spurs, and this was done three times. In the summer of 2001, rumour had it that Harry expected to secure a generous new contract for himself. The West Ham Board of Directors decided instead to sack Harry, who was said to have burst into tears. There was the

144

consolation, though, of substantial compensation, and Harry, who had first met Milan Mandaric when in America, was soon installed as Director of Football at Portsmouth.

'We must clear the deadwood,' Harry had said about what passed for the Portsmouth first team squad when he first came to Fratton Park, and, though he felt 'a bit like a fish out of water' in the role of Director of Football, this otherwise worthless role did give him the chance to assess the players over time, and to work out how, once he became the Manager, he was going to change the defeatist culture that had dominated the Club for decades. When the players did a lap of honour after losing the last home game of the wretched 2001-2002 season to Watford, they threw their shirts into the crowd. I was delighted by Harry's reaction, which was to say that, after the disgraceful performance that the team had given, the crowd should have thrown the shirts back. Harry made it clear that he thought the squad was rubbish, and soon there were rumours that he had fallen out with the captain Shaun Derry, who, despite compelling evidence to the contrary, believed himself to be a gifted player. Derry was soon transferred out. The first thing, though, that Harry did on becoming Manager in March 2002 was to agree to the transfer of Pompey's best player, Peter Crouch to Aston Villa. This was justified on the basis that the fee of £4.5M was 'silly money,' and, thus, well worth having, given that Harry thought that the transfer market at the Nationwide League level could only go down in the near future. What Harry had guessed was that the ITV Digital deal would collapse in the summer of 2002, and that Pompey's rivals at the second level of English football would be unable to compete in the transfer market. Harry brought in Jim Smith as Assistant Manager, and Peter Storrie from West Ham came in too to run the administration, and armed with the Crouch money and some financial support from the Chairman, Harry ruthlessly transformed the squad both in the close season and then as the season progressed. According to Tony Pulis, who had worked with him at Bournemouth, Harry had an encyclopaedic knowledge of footballers in England, and described him being quizzed about them from a reference book and not making a mistake. Well, maybe so, but in the desert that was

145

Wilderness football it was not too difficult to identify, for example, the best young defensive prospect around, and Pompey promptly signed Matt Taylor from Luton. Such was the low fee involved compared with his own valuation that Joe Kinnear, the Luton Manager, compared Harry with Dick Turpin. Significant too was the signing of Shaka Hislop, formerly the West Ham goalkeeper, and a gifted and authoritative one, on a free transfer. This showed that Pompey were not kidding, and that Harry had pulling power. So did the signing, again on a free transfer, of Arjan De Zeeuw, a formidable central defender, whose defensive talents I had noted when he was at Barnsley. Another central defender, Hayden Foxe, who had been at West Ham, was also recruited, and, earlier, another former Hammer, Svetoslav Todorov, had been signed as a striker. The most extraordinary signing, though, was that of Paul Merson to run the midfield. Though 34, Merson, once of Arsenal and England, was a winner, the antithesis of the likes of Panopoulos. Players kept coming and going throughout the season. Sometimes they were old timers like Steve Stone from Aston Villa and Tim Sherwood from Spurs, and others included the immensely promising striker, Ayegbeni Yakubu. Gianluca Festa from Middlesbrough proved to be an impressive loan signing in defence. The team was always a work in progress, and it was interesting how existing players like Nigel Quashie and Linvoy Primus raised their game in better company.

THE 2002-2003 SEASON: BACK FROM THE DEAD

The record book showed that no Portsmouth team had achieved anything in any season in the league if they failed to win at least six of their first twelve games, and lost more than four times. So, a good start to the 2002-2003 season was imperative, and, to my surprise and delight, such as start was made and in some style. The opening home game against Notts Forest was won 2-0, and I was present at Bramall Lane for the away game at Sheffield United three days later on 13 August 2002. Pompey drew 1-1, and but for Deon Burton defying the laws of physics by missing an excellent chance near the end a vital win would have been secured. Portsmouth's performance was a revelation to me. Sheffield took the lead thanks to a misjudgement by Taylor in the twelfth minute. Far from the shrugging of the shoulders, could not care less attitude that I had come to be used to from Pompey players over most of the previous half century, Taylor was distraught. Taking the lead in lifting his spirits was Hislop the goalkeeper. Later on, when Merson overran the ball and thus wasted a good chance, his irritation with himself was palpable. The contrast with the indifference that so many others had displayed in the past was stark. Merson played his part in a beautifully worked equaliser, scored by Burton. I was very pleased with Portsmouth's display, and, to her amusement, I bubbled with enthusiasm when my wife collected me, much as one would do a stray dog, at Leeds railway station. I resolved to go to the Crystal Palace away game on the Saturday, but news that my mother was ill meant that I had to go to the Isle of Wight instead. There, I heard the dread news that Palace were 2-0 up. Seeing my dismay, my long suffering wife said to me that it was only half time, and that if I had been right about Pompey being a radically different outfit on the evidence of the Sheffield game then they would turn it around. If not, then they were still rubbish. Harry later remarked about the marvellous display of support the team got when they came out for the second half. Whether or not this backing made any difference, Portsmouth went on to win 3-2, with Foxe and Crowe twice being the unlikely scorers. A week later, Watford were swept aside 3-0 at Fratton Park, and then it was off to the familiar gloomy surroundings of Grimsby, where ten minutes from time Burchill got the only goal. So, that was two away wins and we were not even into September. Brighton (4-2), Millwall (1-0), and Bradford City (3-0) were all beaten at Fratton Park, and there was a 3-1 win at Gillingham to celebrate too, before on 21 September 2002, in their tenth fixture, Pompey tasted defeat for the first time by a single goal at Norwich. For those like me, obsessed by history and statistics, the twelfth game at Rotherham on 5 October 2002 had to be won. It was a tough game, with Rotherham doing well to pull a goal back in the second half when reduced to ten men. In the last minute, a ferocious drive from Lee seemed destined for the top corner but

Hislop clawed the ball clear. Thus, Pompey won 3-2, meaning that they had won ten, drawn one, and lost one of their first dozen fixtures, which added up to the best start to a season that Portsmouth had ever made.

At Rotherham Station, I favoured my fellow Pompey supporters with the view that 31 points from the opening 12 games was an excellent basis for a promotion drive, probably even finishing in first place. I anticipated some falling away on our part to finish with something like 92 points - an average of two points out of three from the forty six game programme. In fact, Portsmouth did better than that, and needed to because Leicester ended up with 92 points when finishing second. Most people had tipped Derby and especially Ipswich to go straight back up after being relegated from the Premiership, but I always thought in terms of Leicester, because of what it would be kind to call their functional style of play, which I believed to be well suited to this level of football. Indeed, on 2 November 2002, Leicester won at Fratton Park 2-0 in farcical conditions more suited to water polo than football. That the game was not postponed, as every commentator thought it should have been, was said to have been explained by the referee on the grounds that he dreaded facing Micky Adams, the Leicester Manager, afterwards if he had done this, though quite why he should feel this way, given that Adams was hardly King Kong, remained a mystery. One virtue of this Portsmouth team was its ability to recover from setbacks, as was displayed after the Norwich defeat, when Pompey won four and drew one of their next five games. After the Leicester defeat, Pompey did not lose another game until 13 January 2003, when we were beaten 2-1 at Fratton Park by Sheffield United, though it has to be said that one win and five draws in December was hardly commanding form. Looking back from the halfway mark, I picked out the 3-0 victory at Burnley on 26 October 2002, which was marked by the debut of Steve Stone, and an excellent opening goal by Quashie. Another fine away win was that achieved at Pride Park on 9 November 2002, when Derby were beaten 2-1, despite being given a goal lead by means of a dubious penalty. Pompey's winning goal was beautifully worked out of defence, with a long pass from Quashie finding Taylor tearing down the left to provide the perfect cross for Burchill to head home. At the end, the 4,000 Pompey supporters were kept behind by the police, whom they serenaded by singing time after time 'We are going up,' and, of course, we were well on our way to escaping from the Wilderness.

With 53 League points in the bag at the halfway stage, Pompey were plainly promotion material, and there was an added bonus in the form of a Third Round F. A. Cup game at Manchester United on 4 January 2003, which had the virtue of getting rid of the Cup commitment at a profit of £1M. The whole business was light hearted, with the numerous Portsmouth fans enjoying a day out that did not matter, and Alex Ferguson joking that he feared for his drinks bill with his old friends Harry and Jim Smith coming to Old Trafford. Pompey played well, and but for a bad miss by Quashie we might have done much better than lose 4-1. That United were given no less than two penalties, one awarded after just five minutes, was remarked upon. It was the Nationwide League programme that mattered, of course, and, after a run of one win (an impressive victory at Notts Forest) in eight games, Pompey came back to form with a 3-0 win over Grimsby (with Yakubu scoring) and then on 8 February 2003 Derby were on the receiving end of a 6-2 drubbing (Yakubu scoring twice). This mattered to me because I remembered, even if nobody else did among the Fratton Park faithful, that Derby had beaten Pompey 6-2 many years ago (on 29 October 1960, in fact), and, at last, revenge had been taken. A 1-1 draw at Leicester made sure that our only serious rivals made up no ground on us, and the results were both chipped out when necessary (1-0 at home against Gillingham and Wolves, for example), and there were stunning displays at Coventry (4-0) and at Millwall (5-0), or, so, in the latter case, we were told. Portsmouth supporters were banned from The Den because of our record of past violence. One Pompey fan known to one and all as Basher somehow contrived to get in, but, otherwise we had to rely on the media accounts of the game, which were full of praise. Yakubu scored twice. Portsmouth contrived to lose 2-1 at Wimbledon three days later, despite providing 75 per cent of the crowd; and there was a controversial home defeat at the hands of Sheffield Wednesday also by 2-1 on 12 April 2003, which temporarily cost Pompey top place in the table for the first time since August. With five games to go, Leicester were ahead, but they only won one of those games, and Portsmouth won four of their last five fixtures to finish six points clear at the top, and with a far superior goal difference.

So, in the 2002-2003 season, Pompey won the Nationwide First Division title with 98 points. It was the first time that Portsmouth had won the second level title in the Club's history. It was not difficult to imagine Pompey having a home record of the order of 17 wins, 3 draws, and 3 defeats, with 52 goals scored and 22 conceded. What was scarcely credible was an away record of 12 wins, 8 draws, and 3 defeats, with 45 goals scored and 23 conceded. By the time that the last match of the season was played at Bradford City on 4 May 2003, the title was already won. Valley Parade had been the scene of several dire displays by Portsmouth teams in the recent past, but this time Merson and Sherwood led the way with an exhibition of what was certainly at this level exhilarating football. Todorov took his total for the season to 26 goals with a hat trick, with Festa and Stone getting the other goals in a 5-0 victory. Pompey needed three more goals to reach the century mark, but Quashie wasted several opportunities, and with everybody including me singing 'feed the Yak and he will score,' Yakubu ran clear and instead of breaking the net with his shot as we predicted he nearly demolished what (presumably to please the sponsors) was called the Symphony Stand. The Pompey Chimes were belted out endlessly, and at the end of the game Merson ran around the ground to be applauded by the Bradford fans with a generosity of spirit that surprised the Portsmouth faithful, whose own behaviour after being crushed in a home game in that manner might well have been very different in tone. So, ended a season in which Pompey had won promotion by playing some of the best football that I had ever seen at this level. Fulham may well have had a better team in the 2000-2001 season with 101 points, and Reading had obtained the formidable total of 106 points in the 2005-2006 season, and, of course, many of the teams of the distant past in the Old Second Division had been impressive, but

Pompey had secured promotion in some style and we looked forward to the Premiership without fear.

THE 2003-2004 SEASON: YAKUBU AND SURVIVAL

With Harry in charge, it was not surprising that it was a much changed team from that which had won promotion that faced Aston Villa at Fratton Park in what was - to please the Sky TV schedulers - literally the first match of the 2003-2004 Premiership season. One involuntary absentee was Todorov, who had been badly injured in a close season training accident, but he was soon covered by the loan signing of Jason Roberts, and Harry had already signed the Spurs and England veteran striker, Teddy Sheringham to add experience alongside the talented but raw Yakubu. In defence, from Vitesse Arnhem, Harry had signed Dejan Stefanovic, an imposing and gifted central defender to play alongside De Zeeuw. In midfield, Amdy Faye was signed from Auxerre in a transfer deal that eventually led to the behaviour of those involved on the Pompey side interesting the Inland Revenue. Allegedly, and presumably to exclude rivals who wished to sign the player, at one stage an apparently bewildered Faye was said to have been secreted away in Harry's house with only Redknapp's dogs for company. Anyway, Faye was recruited to the midfield to eventually play alongside the Russian international Alexei Smertin, loaned from Chelsea, and also Patrik Berger, a Czech international, who had shown himself to be talented, if indolent, when at Liverpool. An experienced Croation international called Boris Zivkovic filled in at full back, at least for the first half of the season. So, what passed for the squad was a bit of a mess, but, with the core of the promoted team still there, (minus, of course, Merson, who was deemed by Harry not to be a Premiership player any more) few Pompey supporters thought that we would return to the Wilderness immediately. The pundits tended to think otherwise. Jimmy Hill made a few desultory remarks in a Sky programme about Pompey's distinguished past, which did not seem to register with the other journalists in the discussion, who were younger or trying to seem so. The general opinion was that promoted teams went straight down, which was true, for instance, in the 1997-98 season, but it would have been more accurate to say that such clubs cannot often expect a long life in the Premiership. Leicester seemed to be the promoted team that most pundits thought would survive, on the basis that they had the Walkers Stadium and Pompey only had the small Fratton Park. This affected revenue streams, of course, and, inevitably, Portsmouth had no long term future without a large, modern stadium; but (a) Pompey had a backer of a kind in Mandaric and Leicester did not, and (b) grounds do not play each other. One pundit, Andy Townsend maintained that Pompey would go down because they played kick and rush football. This observation infuriated Harry, and not surprisingly so. Pompey went to some lengths to play proper football, and what was remarkable about the promotion season was that Harry had made no concessions on this front and Pompey had still done the business. Townsend had got it completely wrong. Pompey would continue to try to play decent stuff, but the question was at Premiership level did they have the players to do this effectively? I thought that of the promoted teams Pompey would just about survive, and that Leicester and Wolves would go down, possibly accompanied by Leeds United, who had only narrowly avoided relegation the season before.

A good start was essential, and Portsmouth lost none of their first five games. The opening game against Aston Villa on 16 August 2003 was won 2-1, with Sheringham and Berger scoring. Needless anxiety was caused by Villa being awarded a penalty when Barry tripped over his own feet. Sadly, inept refereeing decisons were to be a contnuing and disappointing feature of Premiership football. In this case, though Villa scored, Pompey still won. Portsmouth then drew 1-1 at Manchester City, having looked like winning by means of a Yakubu goal until a late City equaliser resulted from a free kick that television evidence indicated should not have been awarded. Then came a midweek 4-0 home victory over Bolton at Fratton Park. Stone scored and then Sheringham got a hat trick. When the going got a bit rougher later, Harry was to emphasise that nobody else had scored four times against Bolton. Those who bothered to check would find that Manchester City defeated Bolton 6-2, but nobody seemed to mind. So, it was on to Wolves, where Pompey drew 0-

152

0, with Berger missing a simple headed opportunity. Then, on 13 September 2003, came the away game at Arsenal. I had used to go to Highbury regularly in my London days, but it had come to look a shadow of its former imposing self. I expected Arsenal to be imposing too, but Pompey ran the match in the early stages. Yakubu gave the Arsenal defence a hard time throughout, and should have scored in the first half when clean through. Sheringham did give Pompey the lead from a shrewd pull back from Stone, but the game then turned against Pompey following Berger having to withdraw because of injury. He was badly missed in midfield, but Pompey might well have won but for another bizarre refereeing decison. Arsenal were getting nowhere, and so Pires decided to take a dive in the penalty area, wrapping his foot around Stefanovich's leg so blatantly that several Pompey supporters around me laughed at Pires's antics. I had been around too long not to distrust officials, and, sure enough, the referee made a fool of himself by giving Arsenal a penalty. Making Thierry Henry take it twice did not right the wrong. Henry scored, and Arsenal went on to get a 1-1 draw that they deserved on the overall balance of play, but which they would not have got if it had not been for what for years afterwards was known as 'the Pires dive,' and without the non-penalty that Arsenal team would not have been the Invincibles.

Whether or not, as the chant went, 'Premiership refs are having a laugh,' Portsmouth were in third place after the Highbury point, we all knew that this could not last, even if we did not expect three consecutive defeats, especially the losses at home to Blackburn and Charlton, both by 2-1. The 2-0 defeat at Birmingham on 27 September 2003 was also hard to take, given that Pompey dominated possession and played what football was on offer. What television evidence showed was a legitimate goal by Yakubu was disallowed, which behaviour on the part of the officials now surprised nobody. The goals were beginning to dry up. My Spurs friends had told me to expect nothing much from Sheringham past the end of September, and, sure enough, Sheringham was to score 9 goals in 32 Premiership appearances, with the sixth coming on 4 October 2003. That said, though, a fortnight after that, Portsmouth contrived to beat Liverpool 1-0 at

Fratton Park, with Berger scoring an early winning goal against his former club, and in the opinion of the sourer of the visitors discarding his usual lethargy especially for the occasion. A couple of 3-0 defeats then followed at Newcastle and Manchester United, both of them thoroughly deserved, though I could have done without Shearer's well executed dive for the penalty. Apart from Shearer and the goalkeeper, Shay Given, Newcastle seemed ordinary enough. Those who made it up from the South coast at great expense were less than pleased with the view, perched up in one of the corners, with what one comedian called a great view of Norway, but I could see the game well enough to appreciate that Pompey were probably flattered by being eleventh in the table. Nevertheless, that is where Portsmouth stayed following a remarkable 6-1 victory over Leeds United at Fratton Park on 8 October 2003. Leeds arrived for the match in disarray, having lost four matches in a row, and with the Manager, Peter Reid seemingly in dispute with several of the players, above all Mark Viduka, who refused to play. According to the travelling fans, those Leeds players who did take the field also declined to play, with the honourable exception of Alan Smith. The Pompey goalscorers were Gary O'Neil (2), Stefanovich, Foxe, Berger, and Yakubu, with only Smith bothering to make the effort to reply. The result was received with disbelief in Leeds. 'Pompey have quite a good team,' I suggested as an explanation, to earn the reply from my wife, 'Maybe, but not that good.' Indeed, Portsmouth only won five fixtures all told in the first half of the season, and, after the Leeds result, the only other Premiership game won was a 2-0 Boxing Day victory over Spurs, and that was marred by Sherwood breaking his leg. As so often in the past, the main problem was Pompey's away form, with no Premiership goal being scored away from Fratton Park between that Sheringham netted at Highbury in mid- September and Yakubu's goal in a 2-1 defeat at Aston Villa in early January. Indeed, a 0-0 draw in an awful game at Middlesbrough on 6 December 2003 was the only away point secured during that run. What was a wretched game was made worse by being held in the splendid setting of the Riverside Stadium, which was in stark contrast to the gruesome Ayresome Park of the past and the dire

154

Fratton Park of the present. Three days earlier, Portsmouth's progress in the Carling (League) Cup was brought to a halt with a 2-0 defeat at Southampton. On 21 December 2003, the Saints prevailed again at the St Mary's Stadium, winning 3-0 in a Premiership game. 'Christmas has been cancelled,' Harry declared, though we all thought that he would be overruled by his wife.

The second half of the season proved to be a lot better for Portsmouth. It even included a couple of away wins, and an F. A. Cup run. This run began with a 2-1 win against Blackpool at Fratton Park on 3 January 2004, with Yakubu scoring the winner in the last minute. In the Fourth Round on 24 January 2004, Matt Taylor got both goals for Pompey in another 2-1 home win, this time at the expense of Scunthorpe. The Fifth Round game was away to Liverpool on 14 February 2004. Few gave Pompey a hope, and those that did had to contend with Michael Owen scoring for the the home team in the second minute. The pessimists were wrong for once, given that the outcome was a draw, thanks to Taylor scoring with thirteen minutes to go, and, earlier, Hislop giving an impressive display of goalkeeping. The replay at Fratton Park on 22 February 2004 was televised, and even the commentators observed that the referee seemed determined to give Liverpool a penalty. Primus was judged to have handled in the penalty box, although it was the white hand of Baros that committed the offence. The linesman intervened to save what should have been the referee's embarassment, but soon the man was at it again with another dubious penalty award. Hislop was said to have a poor record in saving penalties, but this time he saved a tame shot from Owen. With about twenty minutes to go, Smertin, excellent in both Liverpool games, got a pass through to Yakubu, who set up Richard Hughes, and he drove the ball home for what proved to be the winner. So, it was on to the Sixth Round, and a home tie with Arsenal. Pompey could feel aggrieved about being cheated at Highbury, but this time they had to be grateful that Arsenal effectively called the game off when 5-0 up after 50 minutes. Sheringham got a last minute consolation goal. The Pompey fans sang, 'Can we play you every week?' and when Henry was substituted he was given a standing ovation to his amazement and that of his Manager. Henry responded by saying that he hoped that Pompey would stay up, and so we did, though it needed a late run of good results to do the trick. The reality was that of the first nine Premiership games of 2004, Portsmouth won just one (4-2 against Manchester City at home), drew two (home to Wolves 0-0, and Newcastle 1-1), and lost the rest. Pompey were second to last in the table when Southampton were the visitors on 21 March 2004. Following a fine move involving Smertin (the man of the match) and Stone, Yakubu scored with twenty or so minutes to go, and, though Kevin Phillips hit the post in the last minute, 1-0 to Pompey it was. In the last ten games, including that defeat of the Saints, Portsmouth won 6, drew 3, and lost once - yes, of course - to Leicester. Pompey finally won an away game when they defeated Blackburn 2-1 on 27 March 2004. Sheringham scored with a clever free kick, and Yakubu got the winner with a marvellous right foot drive. An away draw at Charlton was followed by a 3-1 home win over Birmingham, and then, on 17 April 2004, a Steve Stone goal gave Pompey a home victory over Manchester United. This win took Pompey to sixteenth position, and delighted my Leeds friends. They were less pleased eight days later when Portsmouth won 2-1 at Elland Road. Faye and Smertin ran the midfield. An excellent pass from Faye sent Stone down the right wing in the ninth minute, and he delivered an accurate cross for Yakubu to head home. Quite why Michael Duberry, his marker, just stood there and watched Yakubu execute a perfect header only he could say. Pompey controlled the game easily enough, and whould have gone farther ahead before half time but for an appalling miss by De Zueew. Six minutes after the interval, Robinson could only knock a Taylor corner up in the air, and Lua Lua headed home. There were still about forty minutes to go, of course, and the general opinion among the Pompey faithful - whose mood had not been sweetened by a very long and very early journey - was that the score was really 2-1 and not 2-0 because with Uriah Rennie around some sort of refereeing blunder was inevitable. With seven minutes left, it was a linesman who made the mistake, not the much maligned Rennie, who was persuaded by this official that Duberry had been fouled by Primus when it was the other way around. Ian Harte scored from the spot, and Pompey were hanging on. Hislop thwarted Barmby when the latter looked like getting an undeserved equalizer, and, suddenly, it was all over, and Pompey were fourteenth, and we were safe, and Harry and Jim Smith and the players were heroes of the hour. It was important, if only to me, that Pompey did not now just call it quits for the season. A late equalizer restricted Pompey to a 1-1 home draw with Fulham, and there was the exactly the same result when Arsenal were the visitors on 4 May 2004, with Yakubu being the scorer in both fixtures. Sherwood had boasted on television that Arsenal would not win twice that season at Fratton Park, though they did manage a draw. At the end, Henry donned a Pompey shirt to salute the Fratton End, who roared their approval. Four days later, we tried to pretend that relegated Leicester completing a double over us did not matter.

Then, in the last week of the season, came a crisis in the form of a dispute between Harry and the Chairman. As ever with Portsmouth, the rumour mill was going full pelt. Some said that Mandaric, who seemed to need to be loved by the Pompey fans, was jealous of Harry's popularity with them. Then again, the dispute was said to be about what 'Bald Eagle' Smith actually did for his money. Further than this, the pair were said to differ about whether or not to retain the services of Sheringham, who had seemed half dead to me long before the end of the season. They differed too about whether or not to sign Martin Keown, a once impressive player for Arsenal who, by this stage, needed to be nursed along by Manager Wenger so that he could get to the number of league appearances that would give him another title medal. Harry was said to think otherwise. Anyway, whatever the dispute was about, it came to be resolved for the present, and everybody celebrated when Pompey beat Middlesbrough 5-1 in the last home match of the season. Sheringham got a farewell goal, but the star of the show was Yakubu, who scored four times. This took Yakubu to 16 goals in the Premiership (eleven in the final ten games), plus 3 Cup goals. According to Harry, he had bet the Yak £10,000 of his own money that he would not score 20 goals in the season, and he said that if he had known how close he was to winning the bet he would have had him substituted. Everybody laughed, as, of course, everybody did laugh with Arthur Daley. We were well pleased by Portsmouth finishing thirteenth in the Premiership with 45 points, especially as Pompey had only won 2 away games, and only scored a dozen goals on their travels. All told, Pompey scored 47 goals and conceded 54. No less than 34 of Portsmouth's points were secured at Fratton Park, where Pompey won 10, drew 4, and lost 5 of their fixtures, scoring 35 goals and only conceding a goal a game. So, the intimate or, if one prefers, hostile atmosphere of Fratton Park had paid off, at least this time, but what future there was for us with an average attendance of 20,054 crammed into this little ground had to be in the back of our minds.

THE 2004-2005 SEASON: THE TROUBLE WITH HARRY

Consolidation was the watchword as Portsmouth prepared for their second season in the Premiership, and there were no more than routine summer signings to offset the departures, the most notable of which was Sheringham. There was no sign of Keown among the newcomers, who included Jamie Ashdown (a goalkeeper from Reading), Andy Griffin (a back from Newcastle), David Unsworth (a defender with one England cap from Everton), Ricardo Fuller (a Jamaican international striker from Preston), and Diomansy Kamara (a Senegal international striker from Modena). An Unsworth penalty earned Pompey an opening day home draw on 14 August 2004 with Birmingham, and a goalkeeping error by the normally assured Hislop meant that Pompey lost 2-1 at Charlton a week later. When he came out for the next home game with Fulham, the Pompey crowd, well aware of Hislop's many fine performances for Portsmouth in previous games, gave the goalkeeper a standing ovation. Pompey won the Fulham home game 4-3, and defeated Crystal Palace 3-1, also at home, the following Saturday. Yakubu got a hat trick in the Fulham game, and Harry went on and on about a magical pass for one of the goals that had emanated from Eyal Berkovic, a recruit from Manchester City and one of his favourites. The rest of us noted that the failure of Berkovic to track back ensured that

Bocanegras was unmarked for Fulham's final goal. An insipid display followed at Blackburn where, with Berkovic this time more or less invisible, Rovers won 1-0. When the Blackburn goalkeeper, Freidel, brought down Fuller near the end, all the Portsmouth fans rose as one to demand a penalty for an obvious foul, and, of course, some sort of reward for their part in providing what little atmosphere there was at Ewood Park that day. The young referee, Mark Clattenburg, failed to make the correct decision. This could not have been because of fear of the home crowd, which had seemed to have taken a vow of silence. Once again, those given to cynicism among the Pompey supporters had found their bleak view of the world to be justified, though, undeterred, the rest of the Portsmouth fans dominated the remainder of the game by singing continually 'Clattenburg's a wanker.' However tuneful, it seemed unlikely that this melodic display helped Pompey's cause in any way. A 1-0 home defeat by Everton was followed by a 2-2 draw at Norwich, after Pompey had led twice. A Yakubu goal then gave Pompey a 1-0 win over Spurs on 18 October 2004, but the following Saturday saw another lead thrown away when Pompey got a 1-1 draw at Middlesbrough. Portsmouth went up to ninth place on 30 October 2004 when Pompey surprisingly defeated Manchester United again at Fratton Park, this time by 2-0, Unsworth (penalty) and Yakubu scoring. Three straight defeats followed at the hands of Aston Villa (3-0 away), Southampton (2-1 away), and Manchester City (3-1 at home). Pompey were now twelfth.

Worse was to come. Mandaric and Harry had fallen out again. Though Pompey were barely established in the top flight, Milan seemed to think that it was about time that we moved on to what he always referred to as 'the next stage.' Well, fair enough, we all thought, as if what we thought mattered, and, eager as football fans always tend to be when it comes to spending other people's money, talk soon surfaced about turning Fratton Park around and doubling the size of it to render Portsmouth Football Club into a financially viable top flight club with a multiplicity of income streams. An alternative site at Hilsea was also identified, as was one at Horsea Island, a disused naval base. Pompey would also have to acquire a modern training ground, instead of renting a very basic one that, according to Harry, had facilities comparable with those on the Hackney Marshes, possibly being worse. Then again, better players would have to be signed, always assuming that they would tolerate the training facilities. If the term meant anything substantive, meeting these objectives was what 'the next stage' involved. Now, compared with most of those who had run Portsmouth Football Club in the past, who could have gone head to head with Scrooge and won easily, thus far Milan Mandaric had been financially generous in the backing he had given. That said, though, the sums expended had not been of an order that were needed to translate Pompey into a major club again. Most Pompey fans I knew assumed that Milan was a billionaire, though one whose money was almost all tied up in some way. Well, if so, it seemed to me that money of the order that 'the next stage' by definition required was not going to be magically untied now. Anyway, *The Sunday Times* Rich List did not name Mandaric as one of the 70 or so billionaires living in this country, and, indeed, that List for 2012 showed him to be in at number 740, being worth £107M. It always seemed to me that the compilation of this List probably owed much to guesswork, but what did seem clear was that in terms of disposable wealth Milan did not have the means to fulfil either his dream or our fantasies. So, it did not come as a surprise when Milan announced that 'the next stage' was not going to involve heavy expenditure. The way forward was structure - which was nonsense, of course - and he brought in Vilimir Zajec as Director of Football over Harry's head. Milan implied that Zajec had been the biggest thing to hit football in Yugoslavia since the invention of the ball. Whether or not Zajec had been a great player in his day was, though, irrelevant because Zajec knew nothing about Premiership football, and it did not help that he could not or would not speak English. Indeed, Zajec cultivated a strange image, as if taking part in a movie about the wartime French Resistance. He always appeared in a black beret, and maintained silence, as if unwilling to divulge anything to, say, the Gestapo, let alone the English media. Unwilling to replicate the role that Rix had been reduced to when he himself had been Director of Football, Harry resigned in a dramatic manner, making his way down Frogmore Road to the Main Entrance of Fratton Park past worshipping fans, some in tears. 'You're not going to go down the road [to Southampton] are you?' went the cry - and Harry said no. I took more seriously the comment of his wife, Sandra Redknapp that Harry would not be able to stay out of work for long – and where else was there to go at short notice than Southampton? That we all knew the name of Harry's wife was testimony to his gift for self publicity.

Eventually, a chaotic press conference was arranged, which purported to show that Milan and Harry were parting on a friendly basis. Meanwhile, for the hard core fans like me, it was off to the gloom of Bolton on 27 November 2004. There, it became evident to me that the majority of the Pompey fans were behind Harry, and the talismanic John Portsmouth Football Club Westwood confirmed this in conversation with Paddy Thomas, the Chairman of the Central Branch of the Supporters Club, and, less importantly, myself. As usual, my line pleased few people, though I am proud to say that Bogart as Philip Marlowe could not have done better. I argued that we had to stick by Milan. Alright, he did not seem to have the money to take us much farther, but he was the best placed man to find a very rich successor when at last he worked out that he could not consummate his stated love for Pompey in the form of serious success. Harry had no such contacts, no such money, and no such love. Further than this, it would be for the best if Harry did go to Southampton, and for two reasons. One was he would be a continuing focus of discontent at Pompey if he just sat there in his Sandbanks mansion in Poole as A King Over The Water, a sort of Bonnie Prince Harry. Secondly, Harry could not possibly succeed at Southampton, and, once more, for two reasons. The Saints had been members of the top flight since 1978 and for a club of that size that was a very long time, which meant that they were overdue for relegation. The likes of Matt Le Tissier were no longer there to bale them out. Then again, the Saints had a Chairman in Rupert Lowe with no real money and plenty of attitude who was certain to antagonize Harry. So, it was in our interests that Harry went to Southampton, and, inevitably, failed. Then, when the Zajec experiment had also inevitably failed, we could have him back. The general opinion was that if Harry went to Southampton, then we did not want him back. I had lost most of my audience as usual. Anyway, Harry foolishly did go to Southampton, thus becoming Judas especially to those who had loved him, and with Mandaric now becoming the hero ouce more. Personally, I thought the pair of them were made for each other, but even I was amused by the tales of how Harry was soon hating things at Southampton. Whether or not Rupert Lowe really did greet him in the 'Morning, Redknapp' manner, or whether Lowe really did try to rally the troops before a game in the dressing room until Harry stopped this practice nobody really knew, but they were such good stories that many believed that Harry had circulated them himself.

Though Harry had left Pompey in twelfth position with 14 points (all but one obtained at home), as I saw things, the overriding problem for Portsmouth was not what the Saints did - because they were going to be relegated anyway - but to somehow survive as a Premiership club themselves with Zajec in charge. Things did not go too badly at first. Pompey actually won at Bolton 1-0. De Zeeuw scored from a corner. He also deserved praise for not retaliating when Bolton's Diouf spat in his face, given that under football's bizarre rules those who retaliate are more often than not punished more harshly than the offender. Ashdown played very well in goal, for once. Then on 4 December 2004, Pompey came from behind to beat West Brom 3-2, with Lua Lua heading in a late winner from a Berkovic free kick. On the following Saturday, Pompey came from behind again, this time at Newcastle to draw 1-1, thanks to a deflected Stone shot that wrong footed Shay Given. Three days later, Pompey once more came from behind to get a 1-1 draw at Liverpool, with Lua Lua scoring in the last minute. Then came a 1-0 home defeat at the hands of Arsenal. Despite having fouled Yakubu, who was left lying on the ground, Sol Campbell was allowed by the referee to progress and he scored a soft goal from some distance. A Primus goal ensured the Pompey won 1-0 at Crystal Palace on Boxing Day, to leave Portsmouth in ninth place with 23 points at the halfway stage. There were, though, rumours of disaffection among the players, with Amdy Faye leading the way with a transfer request. Faye was said to be missing Harry (and also, presumably, the dogs), and eventually moved on to Newcastle. Faye had never looked as effective once his former midfield partner Smertin had gone back to Chelsea, and so his departure did not explain why Pompey's form deteriorated so badly that only 5 points were obtained from the next dozen matches, with a sour Fourth Round F. A. Cup defeat at Southampton thrown in for good measure. Some strange transfer deals weakened the team. Zajec insisted on needlessly signing another goalkeeper. Though very tall, Kostas Chalkias seemed to have special difficulty in dealing with the ball in the air. The explanation we were offered was that footballs in Greece were different, which was supposed to excuse Chalkias's ineptitude. 'Champion goalkeeper? Champion of a kebab house' was Harry's later verdict, and Chalkias had to be sidelined after just 5 games. Another Greek called Skopolitis was added to the midfield, but he looked out of his depth. There was more to Pompey's dramatic decline in form, though, than the recruitment of a couple of mediocrities, and in early April, with relegation really a threat, the Chairman brought forward a previously announced appointment, and Alain Perrin from Marseilles became the Team Manager. The idea seemed to be that replacing an imitation Frenchman with a real one would stop the rot, though the inept Zajec still seemed to be in overall charge. There were eight games to go, and Pompey won just two of them, though this proved to be enough to survive. Charlton were beaten 4-2 at Fratton Park on 9 April 2004 - but the result that really mattered, because it effectively sent Southampton down, was the 4-1 home win over the Saints on 24 April 2004. All the goals came in the first half, and Southampton were torn apart in much the same manner as Pompey had been at The Dell in 1960. It was pace that did the trick, according to Harry, having in mind the speed of Yakubu and Lua Lua, with the latter scoring twice. With chants of 'Harry, Harry, what's the score?' ringing in his ears as well as that of 'Judas,' there was a very strange moment at the end of the game when Harry seemed to go out of his way to acknowledge Mandaric. As will be imagined, the delight among the Portsmouth faithful that Pompey had 'sent the Scummers down' respected no limits, especially those related to sanity, given that the song concerned was still being sung throughout the the game at Manchester City the following Saturday.   This served to distract the singers, and, it seemed, most of the rest of us who were deafened by their efforts, from the reality that the flattering 2-0 defeat that Pompey suffered that day indicated that relegation for ourselves was being merely postponed, unless we could recruit several better players sooner rather than later. A 1-1 home draw with Bolton followed, before in the last game of the season Pompey lost 2-0 at West Brom accompanied by the Scummers song once more, with rejoicing at the final whistle that West Brom's victory was supposed to have ensured that the Saints were relegated.   My own cold blooded view before the event was that (a) the arithmetic demonstrated that Southampton would go down anyway because they would lose their last day game against Manchester United, as, indeed, they did; and that (b) Portsmouth's games wherever they were or whoever they were against were there to be won and not conceded. Pompey finished the season in sixteenth place with 39 points, having won 10, drawn 9 and lost half of their fixtures, scoring only 43 goals (Yakubu 12) and conceding 59.   Pompey had contrived to lose 7 home games and the away total of 11 points was poor. Pompey continued to get devoted support from its 20,072 crowd, but the prospects were bleak.

THE 2005-2006 SEASON: HARRY RETURNS

That Zajec had vanished from the scene was about the only good news of the summer of 2005 from a Portsmouth point of view.   Alain 'Reggie' Perrin was later to comment that he had little say in the transfer dealings that took place, which was just as well for his reputation.   Yakubu had been discontented for some time, believing that Pompey had lost direction since Harry had left. If one of the bigger clubs had come in for Yakubu with a huge fee, then transferring him might have made some sense, always assuming a suitable replacement could have been recruited. Transferring Yakubu to Middlesbrough, a similar sort of club, for £7.5M (well below the current market rate for a 22 year old striker with 35 goals in 81 appearances) was pathetic behaviour. This was matched by the recruitment of Dobray Dario Silva, the supposed replacement, who was to score twice in 13 appearances. Chalkias was retained, presumably as a statue, but Hislop was effectively thrown out. Under Harry, Portsmouth was a good place to play football, Hislop was later to say, but no longer. Another goalkeeper was signed in the shape of Sandar Westervald. He was to play just six times. De Zueew was thrown out too, being replaced by Andy O'Brien, a Newcastle central defender whose limitations were no secret. Brian Priske, a Danish international right back proved to be a useful signing, which could not be said of a left back, Gregory Vignal, who was to play just 14 games. In place of the departed Berkovic in midfield came a Colombian international called John Viafara, who was also to make 14 appearances. The signing of the winger Lauren Robert from Newcastle underlined the stupidity of the behaviour of those conducting what it would be kind to call a transfer policy. At best, the self indulgent Robert was an icing on the cake type of player. There was no cake.

For me, it was just a question of waiting for Harry to return, hoping that he would come back before it was too late. Since my attitude towards Harry had always been one of amiable cynicism, my line surprised many people, but my reasoning was, of course, based on the supposition that Harry would not return without the promise of serious money to spend, and this, of course, was the only way forward. The majority of Pompey fans had initially loved Harry, but now felt betrayed and hated him, and many of them scratched around to detect virtues in the regime run by 'Reggie' Perrin. Unlike in Harry's day, training was said to be serious. For a start, Harry's critics said, Perrin was actually there and not at the races. However earnest the 'Reggie' regime was supposed to be, Portsmouth's results were poor from the outset. On 13 August 2005, Portsmouth lost the opening home game to Spurs by 2-0, and by the end of August Pompey had just one point from four games, a 1-1 home draw with Aston Villa. After the usual defeats at West Brom and Manchester City, few of us expected much from the trip to Goodison Park, and, sure enough, Pompey showed no sign of scoring from their own efforts. On the hour, however, Duncan and Disorderly Ferguson headed into his own net to give Pompey a 1-0 victory over Everton. Was this the turning point? Since Ferguson could not come to our aid on a regular basis, this seemed unlikely, and none of the next five games were won. There were a couple of home draws with Birmingham and Newcastle respectively, an away draw at Middlesbrough, and a home defeat at the hands of Charlton and an away loss at Bolton. Those of us who had made the journey to Bolton had the doubtful pleasure of being informed by those who had watched the game on television that Davies was offside when he headed the ball back for Nolan to score the winner. We could not possibly see this as we were located behind the goal. That made the trip all the more worthwhile, of course, as, indeed, did the fact that Yakubu got the equalizer for Middlesbrough in the 1-1 draw at the Riverside on 15 October 2005. Yakubu declined to celebrate, or, for that matter to thank the wretched Skopolitis (who, for no good reason, was supposed to be marking him) for just standing there and watching him head the corner concerned past Ashdown. Nobody was looking forward to the Sunderland trip a fortnight later, and Pompey were 1-0 down at half time, thanks to a penalty. Sunderland were devoid of confidence, however, and Pompey suddenly cut loose and eventually won 4-1. One of Matt Taylor's two goals was a spectacular shot from the halfway line that sailed over the home goalkeeper, Kelvin Davis, who was left looking as though he was stargazing. This was the turning point again, according to the perennial optimists, but Pompey then lost four games in a row without scoring, and, in the midst of this run, 'Reggie' Perrin was dismissed. A players' delegation led by Stefanovic had gone to see the Chairman and told him that things could not go on as they were.

Rumours of Harry's return to Fratton Park had been circulating for some time before the Stefanovic episode. Incensed, and in his role as self appointed spokesman for the masses, John P.F.C. Westwood went to see Milan Mandaric to protest about Harry coming back as Manager. By becoming a fan and not keeping his distance, Mandaric had invited this form of discourse, but the Chairman stuck to his guns, and Harry was back. Never short of an opinion apparently, Stefanovic told Harry on his return that the current team was rubbish, and that coming back to Fratton Park was evidence that Harry had gone mad. This was one of the more generous interpretations of Harry's behaviour on offer at the time. Whether or not Harry was off his castors, the facts were that Pompey were in the relegation zone with just two wins and ten points from sixteen games. More immediately, Pompey were off to White Hart Lane on 12 December 2005 to see if defeat in a row number five could be averted. With four minutes to go, an unlikely draw seemed possible before the award of a classic 'homer' penalty gave the Spurs an opportunity to take the lead, and, by the end it was a 3-1 defeat. Next up, it was West Bromwich at Fratton Park. Could Portsmouth register their first home win of the season? After all, there were still eight days to go before Christmas. Todorov scored and Pompey won 1-0. During the television interview afterwards, Harry's mobile phone went off. Quick as a flash, he commented: 'That's Sandra checking up where I am.' On Boxing Day, a Gary O'Neil goal earned Pompey a 1-1 home draw with West Ham, and another goal from the same player gave Pompey a 1-0 win over Fulham in another home game on New Year's Eve. In between, Harry had fielded a weakened team at Arsenal, who, fortunately for Pompey, rested on a 4-0 interval lead. Then came the January 2006 transfer window, and if Harry had returned to Pompey without cast iron assurances that he could spend freely in that window then he really was crazy. The money came from somebody called Sacha Gaydemak, who eventually wished to take over the ownership of Pompey from Milan Mandaric, and in the meantime was willing to fund, or, at least to guarantee the funding of, the much needed reconstruction of the squad to try to ensure that relegation was avoided. So, Harry was able to be active in the market even by his standards. Dean Kiely from Charlton was brought in to solve the goalkeeping problem, and Noe Paromot was hired from Spurs as cover for the central defence. Other Spurs imports were Pedro Mendes and Sean Davis to shore up the midfield, together with Andres D'Alessandro from Wolfsburg on loan. Up front, Benjamin Mwaruwari, a Zimbabwe international striker, was recruited from Auxerre. He became known as Benjani, and the subject of an admiring song, but actually scoring was not one of his strengths. Though nobody played the Sky football politics game of make believe better than Harry, he also knew that, contrary to that channel's party line, the lower half of the Premiership was not up to much, and with these signings he would be able to just about rescue Pompey and send down three even worse teams. For some time in the early part of 2006, many thought that Harry had got it wrong. Portsmouth took just one point from their first eight games of the year, and that from a late equalizer in the home game against Bolton on 1 February 2006. Pompey lost the other seven games, including a well deserved 5-0 defeat at Birmingham, a fellow relegation struggler. The Fratton Park crowd remained enthusiastic, of course, and when asked by a Sky reporter what he was thinking in the second half with Manchester United on the way to a 3-1 victory, Ruud Van Nistelrooy remarked that the noise was so loud that he could not think. That said though, the harsh reality remained a month to the day afterwards, on 11 March 2006 in fact, that Pompey had just ten games left and they were second to bottom with just the one point from the Bolton match to their name since the Christmas period. Manchester City were the opponents, and, when City equalized with eight minutes to go, all looked lost. Pedro Mendes had earlier scored an excellent goal, and, as if in a fairy tale, scored a magnificent winning goal in the last minute. 'We are staying up' sang the Fratton End, and, obviously, so we were. A week later, it was West Ham away. The Hammers were on their way to the F.A. Cup Final, and seemed distracted. Pompey were 3-0 up at half time, and Mendes had scored a fine goal once more. The final result was West Ham 2 Portsmouth 4, and on 1 April 2006 Pompey won 3-1 at Fulham. A week later, in a strange game in which Bellamy seemed to be playing Portsmouth on his own most of the time, Pompey drew 2-2 at home against Blackburn. On 12 April 2006, again at home, Pompey were trailing to a Henry goal against Arsenal when Lua Lua got an equalizer, and, contrary to promises he had made to Harry to cut out a form of goal celebration that had injured him previously, Lua Lua did his celebration act once again and, of course, injured himself. Easter Saturday meant the visit of Middlesbrough, and a goal from

O'Neil ensured a 1-0 victory and that Pompey moved up to seventeenth place and, thus, out of the relegation zone. On Easter Monday, it was off to the Valley, and a good goal from the gifted D'Alessandro meant that Pompey went ahead, but, to their credit, Charlton rallied, scored twice, and so Pompey needed two wins from three games to stay up. Since the last game of the season was against Liverpool, effectively this meant winning the other two games. I had booked a holiday in Italy, and I found it difficult to find out the score in the home game against Sunderland. Eventually, I learnt that Pompey had made hard work of winning 2-1, with Taylor deciding the match with a late penalty. On returning to England on the Saturday evening following the Wigan away game on 29 April 2006, again I had difficulty finding out the score. Once we got to the hotel room, I switched on the television and there was Harry singing the praises of the Managers of West Brom and Birmingham. So, it seemed obvious that these clubs had been relegated together with Sunderland. Luckily, I had no way of knowing that Pompey had been 1-0 down at Wigan, but in the second half an equaliser had come from Benjani, scoring for the first time on his fifteenth appearance in a Portsmouth shirt, and Taylor got the winner from the penalty spot. As tends to happen with unfashionable clubs, the penalties in the Sunderland and Wigan games were the only ones that Portsmouth were awarded all season in the Premiership. Pompey duly lost the last match of the season to Liverpool, but we were safe. Over the season as a whole, Portsmouth finished sevebteenth, winning 10 games, drawing 8, and losing 20 of their Premiership fixtures, thus gaining 38 points, and they scored 37 goals and conceded 62. For once, Pompey won as many games away as they did at home, five in each case. The season had been saved in those last ten games with six wins and twenty points gained, and with Pompey scoring only one goal less in those games than in all the others put together.

THE 2006-2007 SEASON: TOP HALF FINISH

The summer of 2006 proved eventful, with Harry travelling out to Israel to meet Arkady Gaydemak, the father of

169

the new owner of Portsmouth. Nobody thought that the trip was a social one, and in the discussions Harry was said to have learnt of the transfer budget he was to work with, and this was believed to be very generous. Quite why the Gaydemak family should be interested in Portsmouth remained a mystery, as did the form which their financial support would take. It was unlikely to be a Sugar Daddy form of investment, and if it was all to be done by loans how committed were the assumed guarantors going to be? What happened if they pulled the plug? What safeguards did the Premier League have in place if this happened? One guessed that the answer would be none at all. Of the Pompey supporters who expressed concern, the most perceptive and informed of them was my great friend and fellow Professor, Jim Riordan. Since Jim had 'crisis of capitalism' political views, not everybody gave him a hearing, but what was obvious anyway was that it was Arkady Gaydemak who had the real money, which he was said to have made through being an international arms dealer, and he was involved in the diamonds trade too. We learnt that, though Russian, he had located himself in Israel, because that country did not have an extradition treaty with France. This mattered because he was effectively on the run from the French judicial system, having been sentenced to three years in prison *in absentia* for money laundering and tax evasion. Though Hitler, Stalin, and Chairman Mao, though possibly not Pol Pot, could have passed the Fit and Proper Persons Test that the Premier League applied to prospective owners, Arkady Gaydemak could not do so. This was because if he set foot in England he would be shipped off to France, since the U.K. did have an extradition treaty with that country. His son, Sacha Gaydemak was a conventional businessman, and so he passed the Test, though he did not remotely have money of the order needed to run a Premier League club. So, to go through the familiar litany, Pompey needed five or six years of further heavy expenditure in which to build, say, a new 40,000 capacity ground with all the accompanying income streams and the training ground and all the rest, together with somehow sustaining a Premiership squad worthy of the name at the same time. It never seemed likely to me that the Gaydemaks would be around long enough to see something like this through, though, of course, they might be able to sell the Club to other people who could and would do so. As for myself, my attitude was that it was the responsibility of the Premier League authorities to vet prospective football club owners and then to regulate their behaviour, and if they did not do this job properly – which they never showed any sign of doing - there was nothing I could do about it. I was just a fan. I would just have to wait upon events.

Soon after Harry's trip to see Gaydemak Senior, I was down in Portsmouth, and, in gorgeous sunshine I met up with some of my greatest Pompey friends. They were full of talk of Harry meeting up with such as Sol Campbell and David James, players of a level Pompey had not had in their ranks for half a century. My amazement that Campbell actually signed was shared by Arsene Wenger, who had released him from his contract at Arsenal on the understanding that Campbell would go abroad. Wenger drily remarked that the last time he checked Portsmouth was in England. Anyway, Campbell signed, and, soon afterwards, so did James, and so did another England international, Glen Johnson, on loan from Chelsea, who had started out with Harry at West Ham. Nico Kranjcar, a Croation international, was recruited from Hadjuk Split for the midfield at a cost of £3.5M, which accounted for most of Pompey's outlay in terms of transfer fees. Kranjcar proved to be the gifted but idle type that Harry liked for reasons lost on many of the rest of us. Up front, Middlesbrough turned down a £15M bid for Yakubu, one more piece of evidence that selling him in the first place had been foolish, and Harry spent most tof the summer pursuing Jermain Defoe of Spurs, but without success. So, Harry was stuck, and Pompey eventually settled for signing the former Arsenal striker, Nwankwo Kanu, who was supposed to be thirty. Kanu had done little when at West Brom, but the idea seemed to be that the sea air and sunshine of Portsmouth allied to the demonic atmosphere of Fratton Park would mean that Kanu would flourish once more. Another veteran striker, Andy Cole, was signed too, this time from Manchester City. The squad now seemed to me to be strong enough to enable Pompey to finish in the top half of the table. I feared that Pompey would be short of goals again, but this would offset by a defence that in front of the most gifted of the contemporary England goalkeepers in James was going to read at least at first Johnson, Campbell, Primus, and Stefanovic. Linvoy Primus had confounded Harry who had written him off years before, and he proceeded to have the best season of his career alongside Campbell in central defence. Injury also ensured that this was also to be effectively Primus's last season.

After five games, Portsmouth were top of the Premiership with 13 points and no goals conceded. The fixture computer was kind to Pompey, as, indeed, it had been last summer, with only Chelsea away on 21 October 2006 involving Pompey playing one of the then Big Four. That said, though, few Portsmouth fans could have looked forward to the opening home game on 19 August 2006 with much optimism, given that Pompey had not defeated Blackburn Rovers at Fratton Park since 1990, and only one point had been secured against these opponents in the previous three meetings. Pompey promptly won 3-0, with Kanu scoring twice and Todorov once. The Blackburn Manager said afterwards that the visistors had been swept aside. Four days later, Portsmouth did well to get a 0-0 draw at Manchester City, a game that will be mainly remembered for a disgraceful foul on Pedro Mendes by the City defender Ben Thatcher, which, for reasons known only to himself, the referee failed to punish severely. The authorities did act later to discipline Thatcher. To Pompey's credit, they did not allow this unsavoury incident to deflect them from securing a draw. Then, at the end of August came a spectacular 4-0 win at Middlesbrough, with Kanu scoring twice, and Benjani and Todorov once each. 'Afterwards, we were sitting at the airport, waiting for the baggage to come, when suddenly [Kanu] couldn't get up,' Harry was to recall, 'His body had given up. We had to lift him into a wheelchair, and wheel him out of the airport. He had to leave his car there too, but what a player he was, what a signing.' On 9 September 2006, Wigan were defeated by a brilliant Benjani goal, and a late Lua Lua goal then ensured a victory at Charlton. Pompey were top of the Premiership, but the unbeaten run came to an end with a 1-0 home defeat at the hands of Bolton, entirely underserved in the opinion of Bolton friends of mine, but still in the record book. An away defeat then followed at Tottenham by 2-1. As it was a midweek game, I had to watch this on television, noting that the opening goal for Spurs followed from an obvious foul on Johnson. Everybody, aside from the officials, recognised that Zakora later dived to get a penalty that, once converted, gave Spurs a 2-0 lead, and, thus, victory. Through Kanu, Pompey got the only legitimate goal of the game, but it made no difference to the outcome. Kanu scored again in a 2-0 home win against West Ham in the next game, with Cole getting the second goal. An away defeat at Chelsea followed, and then came an impressive display and a 3-1 home win over Reading. Then, in early November, it was off to Old Trafford, only to find that Campbell and Johnson were ruled out by illness and injury respectively. Pompey were 2-0 down within a quarter of an hour. On television later it was susggested that Rooney won a penalty in the third minute. I was perfectly placed at Old Trafford to see that Rooney dived, and, thus, cheated, to fool the referee. Saha scored, and Ronaldo got a second from a dubious free kick. I have received endless praise from armchair types for actually going to the games when I can, but this sort of crass behaviour on the part of officials acts as a deterrent to attending. With a weakened team, Pompey might well have lost 3-0 anyway, but the manner of the defeat was distasteful. A Cole equalizer earned a 1-1 home draw with Fulham on 11 November 2006, and, a week later, relegation certainties Watford were beaten 2-1 at Fratton Park, with Kanu and Lua Lua (with a scrappy penalty) scoring, and Portsmouth were in third place in the Premiership table. A 1-0 defeat at Newcastle was followed by a 0-0 draw at Liverpool, which pleased me immensely, and which proved to be the first of six games in which Pompey were unbeaten. Two Taylor goals secured a home draw with Aston Villa, and, in the Everton home game on 9 December 2006, Taylor matched his long range goal at Sunderland with a magnificent shot to get the opening goal in a 2-0 win, the first victory over Everton at Fratton Park for just over 49 years. On 16 December 2006, Taylor scored a superb goal just after the interval to give Pompey a 2-0 lead against Arsenal at the Emirates, on what was my first visit to that stadium. A storming performance from Adeboyar was at the heart of Arsenal's rally to earn them a 2-2 draw. A week later, it was Pompey's turn to rally in their home game with Sheffield United, when a 1-0 half time deficit was turned into a 3-1 victory. That win took Pompey to the halfway stage of the season in sixth place with 32 points and only 17 goals conceded in 19 games.

With a defensive record like that, I was delighted with the way things were going, and the second half of the season started off well with a 2-1 win at West Ham on Boxing Day 2006, with Primus scoring twice. There then followed, though, six games without a win in the Premiership, and Portsmouth's involvement in the F. A. Cup proved to be brief. A last minute goal from Kanu ensured that Pompey got past the Third Round at the expense of Wigan by 2-1, but then in the Fourth Round it was Manchester United away again and, though Pompey held out for a long time, a couple of goals from Rooney outdid one very late goal from Kanu. The poor run in the Premiership began with a 3-2 defeat at Bolton in a rainstorm. Taylor put Pompey ahead in the second minute, but, not long after the hour mark, Bolton had gone into a 3-1 lead, and Nicholas Anelka was running riot. The heads were dropping in the Pompey ranks, and it was interesting to see Campbell berating the players for their attitude. Cole got a superlatively worked goal near the end, but it was too late to make any difference. A 1-1 draw with Spurs on New Year's Day 2007 was followed by a similar result at Sheffield United, with the Pompey equalizer from O'Neil owing much to a piece of luck. Harry plainly thought that he needed a specialist left back, but the poor display of Djimi Traore at Bramall Lane demonstrated that his recruitment from Liverpool had been a mistake. The signing of Lauren from Arsenal to cover at right back proved a better move, though only in the short run. A home defeat at the hands of Charlton by 1-0 on 20 January 2007 went down badly, as did a 0-0 home draw with Middlesbrough. There was also a single goal defeat at Wigan to endure before Pompey seemed to get back on track with a 2-1 home win against Manchester City, with Pedro Mendes scoring early on and Kanu getting the other goal.   However, Pompey lost badly at Blackburn 3-0, and at home to Chelsea 2-0, before draws at Reading and Fulham respectively. Then, entirely unexpectedly, came a 2-1 home victory over Manchester United on Easter Saturday with Taylor scoring once more before Rio Ferdinand added a ridiculous own goal. Entirely unexpected too was a 4-2 Easter Monday defeat at Watford, and Portsmouth really needed three wins from their last five Premiership games to qualify for European football the next season. Pompey did defeat Newcastle and Liverpool in home games both by a 2-1 margin, and drew at Aston Villa 0-0 but lost at Everton by 3-0. So, the home match on the final day of the season with Arsenal would decide matters. This ended up as a 0-0 draw, with Pompey having what television replays showed to be a legitimate goal being ruled out. The referee concerned did not have the benefit of such replays, and, as so often, one had to wonder if the Pompey fans helped their cause by spending the rest of the game serenading the official with an improvised song consisting of the words 'Graham Poll, Arsehole.' So, Pompey did not qualify for Europe, finishing in ninth place in the Premiership with 54 points, having won 14 games, drawn 12, and lost 12, scoring 45 and conceding 42. The goals against column was the most impressive outcome since the Golden Age, though, of course, there were four fewer fixtures to contend with. No doubt the majority of the Fratton crowd were disappointed that European football had been denied to Pompey, but my attitude was that Portsmouth did not have the resources for such a campaign *and* a further advance up the Premiership table. Twenty two points from the second half of the Premiership programme, and no away wins in that period, meant that the progress shown in the early part of the season had not been maintained, but there seemed good cause to be pleased enough with the best top flight placing that Portsmouth had achieved since the distant 1954-55 season.

THE 2007-2008 SEASON: WINNING THE F.A. CUP

For other Portsmouth supporters, the summer of 2007 was a time of looking forward to the new season with optimism, but for myself major surgery for cancer and its effects dominated my life for several weeks. While recuperating, I made the mistake of watching the European Under 21 tournament on television, which was very boring. Easily the worst of the England players was the striker, David Nugent from Preston, and to my alarm Harry was later to sign him for an initial fee of £4.5M. The annual pursuit of Defoe had failed again, and it seemed to me that Harry panicked, not least because Kanu took his time about agreeing another contract. Such behaviour did not stop Kanu from telling John Utaka, another Nigerian international striker, that Portsmouth was 'a great place to come,' and Utaka was signed from Rennes for £7M. For the midfield, and for the same sum, Harry signed Sulley Muntari, a combative and skilled Ghana international from Udinese; and also Papa Bouba Diop from Fulham, a gifted Senegal international, whose poor injury record did not tally with his formidable physique. For the defence, Harry eventually managed to persuade Glen Johnson to sign for Pompey on a permanent basis, with the fee being £4M. Harry also recruited Hermann Hreidarsson, an Icelandic international left back on a free transfer, and Sylvain Distin, a central defender from Manchester City, on the same basis. After five seasons with City, Distin had become convinced that they were going nowhere, though one had to wonder what Harry said to convince this talented defender that Pompey would be any different. So, it was a much strengthened squad that set off to compete for the Barclays Asia Trophy, one of those tournaments that the bigger clubs seem to go in for, while at the same time complaining about fixture congestion. The big club in this case was Liverpool, and Portsmouth duly played them in the final in the Hong Kong Stadium, and, following a 0-0 draw, won the Trophy on penalties. There were jubilant scenes afterwards, and much talk among the Pompey faithful about the 2007-2008 season being one to remember. They were right.

With the then Big Four all having to be played in the first six Premiership games, it seemed imperative that Portsmouth should start off with a win at promoted Derby on 11 August 2007, but those friends who went all told me that my enforced absence was fortunate because poor defensive work meant that Pompey had to be satisfied with a 2-2 draw. Four days later, the opponents were Manchester United at Fratton Park. It seemed unlikely that Pompey would repeat earlier home wins over United, and, given that Campbell was absent, the most that we could hope for was a draw, and that, indeed, was the outcome. A header from Benjani earned Pompey a 1-1 draw in a game in which Muntari got himself sent off, as did Ronaldo for United. For the home game against Bolton on 18 August 2007, with Campbell still injured along with others, Portsmouth had to field a makeshift defence comprising four left footed players. Pompey won 3-1, with Utaka scoring a fine goal. Next up was Chelsea away, and a 1-0 defeat that those able to afford the ridiculous admission prices told me was undeserved. Arsenal away came next in the Premiership, and Pompey lost 3-1 at The Emirates. The general opinion among the faithful was that we played poorly, even managing to allow Arsenal to increase their lead to 3-0 after Senderos had been sent off. Kanu got a consolation goal. Then, on 15 September 2007, Pompey drew 0-0 at home to Liverpool, with Kanu missing a penalty. The difficult six game opening sequence was now over, and Pompey had averaged only a point a match, and they were fifteenth. Given the opposition, I was not too dismayed. The most that Portsmouth could expect to do in terms of the Premiership was to finish somewhere between fifth and tenth, and to do that we had to win at places like Blackburn, which was the next game on the list. Once Kanu had put Pompey ahead, the defence made sure it stayed at 1-0. The Blackburn Manager, Mark Hughes, was admiring of Portsmouth's performance, finding it hard to believe that the very physical Blackburn team had been outmuscled, as he put it. Harry was convinced that 'we have a powerful team and I have a back four who I wouldn't swap for any other in the country.' Events proved this assessment to be a shrewd one in general terms, but the Reading home game on six days later on 29 September witnessed Pompey conceding four goals. Fortunately, the overall score was 7-4, with Benjani getting a hat trick, and, besides an own goal, Hreidarsson and Kranjcar and Muntari (penalty) also scored. This was headline stuff, of course, and that's what entertainment's all about sentiments were everywhere to be heard. Weighed down by history and scepticism, I would have preferred 3-0. Scoring seven times in a game was all very well, but such feats were only too often followed by goal droughts, almost as if you had used up all your luck at once. Sure enough, Pompey did not score another Premiership goal at Fratton Park in 2007.   In date order, the results were West Ham 0-0 (with Benjani missing a last minute penalty); Manchester City 0-0; Everton 0-0; Spurs 0-1; Arsenal 0-0; Middlesbrough 0-1.

Against that, until the victory at Ewood Park, Pompey had not won an away game in 2007, and the Blackburn result proved to be the first of no less than six successive away wins in Premiership games. This was the best away run Pompey had ever managed in the top flight. There were 2-0 wins at Fulham and Wigan in October, and then came Newcastle on 3 November 2007, the date of my return to the fray. I have always liked Newcastle as a city, second only to Leeds in the North of England in my opinion, but it had come to have the air of a place that was going nowhere. They could remake *Get Carter* from more than thirty years before without much difficulty. On the way up to the ground, as ever, I bowed before the statue of Jackie Milburn. All the local males seemed to be dressed in black and white shirts, and, of course, they all went off to different parts of the ground. I faced the long climb up to where the Pompey supporters were perched.   On previous occasions, my masochistic fitness programme had made climbing the many rows of steps straightforward enough, but this time I was just pleased to make it to the top, and, thence, to my seat. I hardly cheered up my friends by informing them that Portsmouth had not won at St James's Park for 58 years, and they did not cheer me up at all by reminding me that Newcastle were unbeaten at home in the current season. The nature of the early exchanges made it hard to see why this was the case, and Pompey scored from their first attack. In the eighth minute, a corner was cleared from the Newcastle penalty area, and from fully 30 yards left back Pamarot hammered the ball into the top corner. In the ninth minute, a through ball from Diop split the home defence, and Benjani held off Capaca, his marker, and drove the ball past Harper. In the eleventh minute, Benjani flicked the ball on, and indecision in the home defence enabled Utaka to take the ball on, round Harper, and make the score 3-0. Newcastle reduced the deficit in the sixteenth minute when, after Michael Owen had

178

failed to score from a straightforward opportunity, the ball rebounded into the net off Campbell. Not long after this, the referee failed to award Pompey an obvious penalty when Rozehnal blatantly handled in the box, and he continued to favour the home side to such an extent that Harry remonstrated with him. Of course, what worried Harry and the Pompey fans was that Newcastle would somehow get a second goal and then it would be game on. That said, Pompey held out and had a 3-1 lead at half time. The defence had played particularly well, and James had made a couple of fine saves look deceptively easy. What I wanted from Pompey in the second half was for them to kill the game off, inviting Newcastle to come on and then punishing them on the break. The Newcastle fans were using the occasion to berate their Manager, Sam Allardyce, whom they believed was importing into St James's Park the rubbish football he had favoured when running Bolton. Like those of Tottenham, the Newcastle supporters seemed to want United to play in an attractive and attacking style with, it seemed, the results a secondary consideration. That particular afternoon, it made no difference what they wanted, with Campbell and Distin at the centre of the defence dominating the opposition, and Johnson being a revelation at right back. Pompey contained Newcastle with some ease, and in the seventy first minute the three goal lead was restored. Barton fouled Kranjcar, who from a difficult angle slammed the free kick past Harper to make the score 4-1. Despite the antagonism to them shown by their embittered supporters, Newcastle kept coming forward, and James made another fine save, this time from Martins. All told, though, Pompey kept possession very well, and played out time. When the final whistle sounded, the Pompey supporters were understandably exultant. As for myself, I did wonder at one stage if I had died, and gone to Heaven (an unlikely destination, I concede), or dreamt the whole thing up. It seemed to me that half the Newcastle fans had walked out, and so I was by the photo booth meeting place on Newcastle station well before the promised time. My wife and my daughter told me that the score had been relayed to the customers in the shops, and they were in a state of shock. I have made so many mistakes in my life that I

179

have lost count, but one thing I did get right for once was making the effort to go to Newcastle that November day and see a display the Portsmouth *Sports Mail* well described as superb. It was by a long way the best away performance I had seen a Pompey team give for more than half a century.

That Saturday we learnt without surprise that what Portsmouth *News* on 25 April 2007 had described as 'Pompey's Dream - Incredible Plan for a £600M Harbourside Ground' had come to nothing. This time, the local politicians had hardly begun to wind themselves up, and various headcases had merely started to argue that the scheme would disfigure Gosport and just about everywhere else within a hundred mile radius, when the Royal Navy pulled the plug by saying that Portsmouth Harbour could not be narrowed in any way because two aircraft carriers would be based there and they would need to get in and out. There were those who either never believed that these vessels would ever see the light of day, or that, even if they did, it would be impossible to staff them without denuding the rest of the Navy of personnel, but it made no difference. 'The Hard is history,' *The News* proclaimed on 3 November 2007, 'The Club have now switched their 36,000 stadium dream from The Hard further up Portsmouth Harbour to [Horsea] Island close to Port Solent.' How long it would take this new ground to be built was unclear, and an unwanted reminder of the difficulties of the planning permission process came in early 2008 when Fareham Council took the opportunity to play the fool by turning down Pompey's proposal for a 50 acres training ground at Titchfield, even though the development involved no change of land use. An alternative site for a training ground was later found in Gosport, which seemed viable, always assuming the money was available to complete the scheme. Rather more important than plans for new grounds in various locations that many thought would never be built anyway were the rumours that the Gaydemaks wanted to sell Portsmouth Football Club, presumably in advance of the completion of any or all of these ventures.

On the football field, in stark contrast with so many past seasons, things continued to go well. 'I expect Portsmouth to be

180

the one club fighting to break into the top four,' Alan Shearer had said on a radio programme, 'I thought so before the season started.' This seemed Shearer fantasy to me, despite Pompey literally being fourth in the Premiership after the Newcastle victory. That said, though, Pompey did win their next two away games, beginning with a 2-0 victory at Birmingham on 24 November 2007. The goalkeeper should have saved Muntari's opening goal, but I am unsure that any goalkeeper could have stopped Kranjcar's free kick for the second goal. On the long walk back to Birmingham city centre from the ground in the incessant rain, I found it difficult to believe the utterly professional display that I had just witnessed, and a fortnight later Pompey were even more authoritative in another away victory, this time at the expense of Aston Villa by 3-1. Muntari scored twice, and one of his goals, driving through the middle like a tank, was superlative. A 4-1 defeat at Liverpool, an actual Big Four club, brought the away run to an end. The Arsenal home draw on Boxing Day 2007 took the season to the halfway stage, and Portsmouth were in seventh place with 31 points, two points more than a year before at this stage, and two places lower, and, surely, to the amazement of almost everybody, the lion's share of the points had come from the away fixtures. The New Year period witnessed rumours that Harry was going to replace the fallen Allardyce as the Manager at Newcastle. It was a done deal according to the newspapers. Harry was going to commute by private jet. There were supposed sightings of Harry at an airport, the name of which kept changing. There were pictures of Harry walking his dogs (whom we learnt were called Rosie and Buster) near his home in Dorset, though these did not seem to prove anything, except that, like many owners, Harry was getting to look uncannily like his dogs. Since the life expectancy of Newcastle Managers since Jim Smith took the job in December 1988 had been 25 months, I could not see Harry taking the risk, or Sandra tolerating a move to the North East, and Harry chose to stay at Pompey. As would be expected, Harry was active in the January 2008 transfer window. Gary O'Neil had been transferred to Middlesbrough in the previous window, and before this one shut Matt Taylor was transferred to Bolton and Benjani to Manchester City. That City got their way over the fee in the case of Banjani, driving it down to the level they wanted, seemed to me to bear out the rumours that the Gaydemaks wanted out, and this feeling persisted even when Harry was able to sign Lassana Diarra, a midfield player from Arsenal, and, at long last, Jermain Defoe, who professed himself to be surprised how many good players there were at Pompey. Diarra showed no such taste for diplomatic comment, making it clear that he expected to move on sooner rather than later to a bigger and better club. Harry pointed out that players who kissed the badge were not necessarily more loyal than the brutally frank Diarra. With the departure of Bejani, who signed off by scoring a hat trick in a 3-1 home win over Derby, Harry brought in Milan Baros, a Czech international striker, who failed to score in the 12 games that he played for Portsmouth. The same could not be said of Defoe, who scored 8 times in the dozen games that he played, all of these goals being recorded in February and March, and all but one at Everton scored at home. The goal that Defoe scored against Aston Villa on 15 March 2008 helped Pompey to a 2-0 win that gave them their first ever double over Villa. I may have been the only Pompey fan who cared about this, and possibly too the only one who was soon to be glad that Defoe was Cup tied, given that I was unconvinced that he could play as the lone striker which was what I hoped would be Pompey's Cup winning formation demanded. As it was, the loss of vital players to the African Cup of Nations affected Portsmouth's results in the early part of 2008, but Pompey still hovered around the seventh, eighth, and ninth positions in the table. Portsmouth were still unable to beat Chelsea even at home, drawing 1-1 on 2 February 2008. The decisions from the referee were so favourable to Chelsea in the opinion of the Pompey faithful that they sang to him 'Chelsea rent boy.' A week later, Diarra's winning goal at the Reebok Stadium was offside according to my Bolton friends. I did not doubt their word, but this 1-0 win for Pompey also owed much to the best display of goalkeeping that I have ever seen. James was in unbeatable form. Portsmouth had earlier also won at Reading 2-0, and they were to win 1-0 at West Ham on 8 April 2008, as the result of a stunning goal by Kranjcar. All told away from home, Pompey registered nine wins, the best tally since the 1949-50 season at this level. There were also nine away defeats, together with that opening day draw. In the end, Pompey got more home points than they gained on their travels by a margin of just one. Overall, Pompey got 57 points, having won 16, drawn 9, and lost 13 of their Premiership games, scoring 48 goals and conceding 40, the best defensive return since the 1949-50 season. Pompey finished eighth in the Premiership, their best placing since the 1954-55 season, which should have pleased the Fratton faithful, though there loud complaints from some fans when Pompey coasted through their last four fixtures, losing the lot. 'They've got short memories,' Harry remarked, and he could have said not much sense, given that by May 2008 winning the F. A. Cup was the priority.

Several people later told me that, from the outset, I had predicted that Portsmouth would win the F. A. Cup in 2008. What I actually said was that sooner or later a club from outside the then Big Four would win the trophy, simply on the law of averages. Since 1991, in fact, only Everton in 1995 had brought this off. So, by 2008, a further success for another club from the middle class of the Premiership, or, for that matter, Everton again, was a possibility, or, alternatively, it might take a bit longer. What Pompey had to do was to be opposite the right spot on the roulette wheel when the opportunity occurred. So, luck had to be on our side, and, sure enough, the opponents in the Third, Fourth, and Fifth Rounds came from the Coca Cola Championship, the ridiculous name given at the time to the second level of English football. That said, though, Pompey made hard work of beating Ipswich away in the Third Round on 5 January 2008. Ipswich were unbeaten at home and made a game of it despite their midfield player, Trotter, being sent off in the first half. Pompey eventually won 1-0, with Nugent scoring. The Fourth Round game on 26 January 2008 was against Plymouth at Fratton Park. Pompey eventually won 2-1, and, to judge from sour comments relayed to me from the ranks of their supporters, Plymouth were unlucky to lose. 'James keeps Pompey's hopes afloat' ran the headline in *The Independent*, who observed that 'James made a string of saves in the second half as

Portsmouth hung on to a lead that they scarcely deserved, but Portsmouth remain many people's dark horses to win the Cup outright.' Harry commented: 'We've got a chance, but the Big Four are still there, that's the problem. You wouldn't bet against them, but I think when everybody's back from the African Nations, we'll be strong and capable of giving anyone a game.' The reporter thought that the then recent signing of Diarra 'offers the most evidence that Portsmouth are able to take on more illustrious rivals. The French interational ... was easily their most accomplished oufield performer. His goal [in the thirty fourth minute] got Portsmouth back into the game after they had fallen behind to Chris Clark's fifth minute deflected strike ... Portsmouth got their winner on the stroke of half time after Plymouth failed to clear a Johnson cross. The ball fell to Nico Kranjcar, who slotted the ball past McCormick [the visiting goalkeeper]. The second half was just about survival for Portsmouth.' Paul Sturrock, the Plymouth Manager, told *The Daily Telegraph* that 'it was just the finishing and their goalkeeper that made the difference in the end,' with the reporter concerned adding: 'and the small matter of Diarra.' According to the Pompey defender, Glen Johnson, '[Diarra] is like a young Claude Makelele with pace.' So it proved, and in passing we can note that the Plymouth goal was the only one that Pompey conceded in their 2008 Cup run. The Fifth Round draw paired Portmouth with Preston away on 17 February 2008. 'Preston Wrong End' was the headline on the cover of the football section of *The Times* the next day. 'James Stands Tall And Saves The Day For Redknapp's Men' was the headline of the report of the game itself. Pompey won 1-0, but the reporter believed that 'Preston should have been out of sight by the time [that] Portsmouth claimed an undeserved winning goal ... with virtually the last kick of the game. But in James [Preston] came up against a brick wall ... Simon Whaley may have most reason to curse James, who saved the Preston midfield player's sixtieth minute penalty ... James appeared to be on a personal crusade to keep the scores level ... The longer such heroics went on, the longer it looked like not being Preston's day, and, when Portsmouth won a corner in the third and final minute of stoppage time, the locals could have been forgiven for fearing the worse ... Nico Kranjcar's corner should have been cleared by Paul McKenna, but the Preston midfield player misjudged a header, and after the ball rebounded off Hreidarasson, [Darren] Carter seemed bamboozled by the melee around him and thrashed the ball into his own goal.' So, 'Portsmouth [had] the last laugh,' and the reporter concluded that 'with luck like this their name may well be on the trophy this season.'

'When [the] draw [for the Sixth Round of the F. A. Cup] came out, I was playing golf with Jamie [Redknapp], some Old Etonian, and Alistair Campbell,' Harry later recalled for the benefit of *The Independent*, 'Peter Storrie was describing the draw on the phone. When he went "Manchester United ... Portsmouth," I threw my eight iron further than the ball.' If this was not just one of Harry's stories, his reaction was forgivable. This was the third time since Harry became the Manager that Pompey had been drawn away to Manchester United in the Cup, the two earlier meetings having been lost. Pompey had not won at Old Trafford since the autumn of 1957, and a matter of weeks before the Sixth Round game, United had outclassed Portsmouth in a Premiership game, in effect declaring when 2-0 ahead. Further than this, United had beaten Arsenal 4-0 in the Fifth Round. One of my friends, an Old Trafford season ticket holder, pointed out that United had a vital Champions League game with Lyon three days before meeting Pompey, and that contest would tax them to the limit. While noting this, and also praying that the referee would do his job for once in a game between a Big Four team and outfit like Pompey, I fell back yet again on my favourite football maxim, which was that on any particular day any professional team could beat any other professional team. In my mind, I was back at the Highbury semi-final of 1949 yet again. Surely, Portsmouth's wait for some more silverware had to end sometime? Well, maybe so, but United were not worried, and, indeed, *The Observer* on 9 March 2008, reported that 'Portsmouth had offered to bring tickets for a possible replay up to Manchester, but United said not to bother.' This form of arrogance was unjustified, and two days after the Sixth Round game on 8 March 2008, we learnt that in the dressing room before the match, Harry had delivered a speech to the Pompey team that sounded like a cross between *Henry V* and Jack Palance's famous challenge to Alan Ladd in *Shane*. According to *The Guardian*, Harry had declared: 'I keep telling the newspapers how good you are. I keep saying I've got the best goalkeeper [James] in the country, two centre halves [Campbell and Distin] I wouldn't swap for anybody, a right back [Johnson] who should be playmg for England, that there's no better midfield player anywhere than Diarra and that Kanu's a magician. Well, get out there and prove it will you?'

'When we stood on the pitch we weren't scared of the task in front of us,' David James told *The Observer*, 'Early doors, Nico [Kranjcar] had a shot - last time we came to Old Trafford I don't think we had a shot on target the whole game. For most of the afternoon we had it under control, and most importantly we kept Ronaldo quiet.' James continued: 'You do the right things and you get the results. Some might say that we rode our luck, with two chances off the line, a free header from Vidic, and the one [from Evra] I tipped on to the post - it was all action. But there was nothing scrappy about our performance, it was sheer hard graft.' James thought that the turning point was [Distin's] clearance off the line [from Carrick]. Had they gone 1-0 up then, it would have been game over for us. It was mayhem in there for a bit, but everyone did their job ... With that chance gone, I could sense their fans getting nervous. Meanwhile, our fans were getting into the spirit of things. They sang throughout the game, top drawer. When Milan [Baros, the substitute striker] came on he had a huge impact, chasing balls and causing problems. I don't think that United expected that. The goal settled it, and there was a huge sense of relief from our back line.' James confessed that 'I actually miskicked the ball to set up Milan for the penalty shout. I wanted to put it over the top, but in the end I sliced it and [Baros] turned a bad ball into a blinder. Nico's ball too was a blinder ... When United left the pitch they had their heads down. Part of you can't help feeling bad for your England team mates. Then again you think: sod it.' To fill in some of the blanks of James's account, there were other turning points. In the seventh minute, a superb pass from Rooney sent Ronaldo

186

clear of Hreidarsson. As he tore into the penalty area, Distin moved across, stood his ground, and Ronaldo fell over, and plainly did so to get a penalty kick. Most of the commentators thought that the referee [Martin Atkinson] should have given in to Ronaldo, but he rightly refused to do so. For, to have done so would have been to reduce football to something like ballroom dancing. Was Distin supposed to have stood aside, as in the pasa doble? Another turning point in the first half was when, in the words of a writer in *The Independent on Sunday*, 'Tevez and Rooney found themselves two against one on the break and really should have scored. Somehow Campbell and James foiled Rooney, and, with the keeper out of his goal, Johnson headed off the line from the Argentinian.' As United failed time after time to take advantage of their dominace of possession, the same reporter believed that 'there was a cruel inevitablity about what happened next. Kranjcar and substitute Milan Baros broke [away in the seventy seventh minute]; the latter was felled by Kuszczak, who came on at half time after [the United goalkeeper] Van der Sar sustained a groin injury. [When Kuszczak was sent off] Rio Ferdinand took over in goal, but could not deny Muntari from the spot.' My own version of events was that, unlike Kuszczak, I had no belief that Baros would have scored anyway, and so there was no point in bringing him down. Once Muntari was assigned the kick, I knew that he would score and exactly where the ball would be hammered. After Pompey's 1-0 win, Distin told *The Daily Telegraph* that though Portsmouth expected to win the F. A. Cup, 'just because you beat United it doesn't mean you are guaranteed to beat anyone else.' Of course, but with the weekend over, none of the then Big Four were left in the competition. Manchester United had put Arsenal out in the previous round, and now United were out of the Cup too. Barnsley had disposed of Liverpool at Anfield in the Fifth Round, and, incredibly, followed this up by defeating Chelsea at Oakwell in the Sixth Round. More predictably, West Bromwich disposed of Bristol Rovers, but few surely expected Cardiff City's win at Middlesbrough. So, Portsmouth were the only Premiership team left in the F. A. Cup, and suddenly we were the favourites to win the trophy. Pompey certainly now had a team that merited that confidence, and the shrewdest assessment of it came was not that advanced by any of us in the Pompey ranks but by Daniel Taylor of *The Guardian*, writing about the victory at Old Trafford. He remarked on '[the] show of appreciation from the Stretford End as the scrum of back slapping, high fiving Portmouth players made their way to the tunnel ... It was a stirring sight, and, as James, Diarra, Campbell, and the rest of Portsmouth's heroes waved back, something else became apparent: none of the players in blue and white was holding a souvenir red shirt. For once nobody had rushed to Ronaldo or Rooney at the final whistle. The best souvenirs from an F. A. Cup run are medals, and Harry Redknapp's players were not at Old Trafford to admire the view, soak in the atmosphere, and go through the usual small club routine of hunting out keepsakes. It was only a small thing, but it spoke volumes about this obdurate Portsmouth side.'

As one of the staff at Wembley Stadium searched my bag after I had gone through the turnstiles for the Semi-Final game with West Bromwich on 5 April 2008, he looked up at my worried face, and informed me that with the luck that Pompey had enjoyed in defeating Manchester United it was obvious that Portsmouth's name was on the F. A. Cup, so relax and enjoy it. Memories of 1949 were still in my mind, and nobody with much sense would rule out another upset, but it did seem to me that Pompey's win at Old Trafford had at last exorcised the ghost of the F. A. Cup defeat at the hands of Newcastle in 1952. So, my prediction was that in 2008 Pompey would win the Semi-Final 1-0, and then the Cup Final itself by the same margin. '[Portsmouth] did not play well [in the Semi Final],' Glenn Moore of *The Independent* later wrote, recording that Harry had admitted that '[Pompey] have not played well at any stage of their Cup run. But Portsmouth never looked like being beaten. Redknapp spoke afterwards of playing 4-4-2 instead of his favoured 4-5-1 so as not to appear negative, but it did look as if Portsmouth's game plan involved defending deep to suffocate West Brom's free scoring attack in the safe knowledge that the Championship club's notoriously porous defence would eventually leave a hole. Redknapp's reputation may be built on attractive football [and] on indulging flair players ... but the reality is that he builds the tricksters' platform first.   Look at Saturday's defence ... The back four have played more than 1700 matches between them, including 131 internationals. They have pace in Johnson and Distin and are physically imposing with an average height of 6ft 2ins.   Not many teams are going to beat that quartet in the air. Nor are they easy to get behind. So you have to play through them. Albion tried. They dominated first half possession with Greening pulling the strings, [but] only once, when a flowing move ended in Gera worrying James from the edge of the box, did they threaten.   From less possession, Portsmouth had looked more dangerous, and, early in the second half [in the fifty fourth minute, in fact] Baros turned Albrechtsen and, though Keily saved his shot, Kanu tapped it in.' It seemed to me that Kanu put more energy into his celebration than he did into anything else he did in the game, and the reason that he was in the place that he was for the rebound from Keily was because he could not keep up with the play. The goal came as a relief to the Pompey loyalists who, in the first half, had seemed to fear that a golden opportunity to win the F. A. Cup in the absence of any Premiership rivals was in danger of being thrown away. Diarra had outshone both Scoles and Hargreaves in the United game, but early on in this match he had given Kevin Phillips, among others, too much freedom. Words from Hreidarsson and others ensured that he got down to business, and Portsmouth's containment strategy functioned more coherently after that. That said, though, the Pompey loyalists were worried, and my sons told me that they had never seen these fans being reduced to silence before. Get to half time 0-0 and if there was anything to sort out Harry would do it was my line. Once Kanu scored, the game was effectively over. For West Bromwich, Koren had a shot that hit the top of the bar, but James had it covered, and the wonderfully named Ishmael Miller missed a half chance, and that was just about it. With little for the media to comment upon, Harry gave a master class afterwards in filling up their reports with stories and jokes.   Martin Samuel, then of *The Times*, plainly thought that there was more to Harry than the Arthur Daley routine. 'The familiar line is that Redknapp is treated generously by the Press and public because he is good company and a lovable rogue,' Samuel wrote, 'but that analysis is as shallow as the suggestion that his teams are solely about acumen in the transfer market and the throwing together of disparate elements in the hope that it will work.' The West Bromwich Manager, Tony Mowbray, knew why his team had lost, and there was nothing random about it: 'Portsmouth have built their team on strong defence. They are sixth in the Premier League on the back of defensive organisation.' When I got back home, everybody told me what an awful game it had been on television, but I did not care. I just wanted Pompey to win, and, within the rules, I did not care how this was done. Several people asked me what I thought about the New Wembley Stadium, and my reply was that it was not as imposing as the Stade de France in Paris. Again, I did not care. What I cared about was that, having seen Pompey lose on no less than 84 different grounds, I had no wish for the New Wembley to be number 85. I had set my heart on Pompey winning the Cup for the second time in my life, and this time in my presence.

It proved to be a long six weeks to have to wait for the Cup Final, since it was not to be played until 17 May 2008. The opponents were another second level club in Cardiff, who had defeated Barnsley in the other Semi-Final. Remembering how Leeds had failed to raise their game in the 1973 Cup Final after being in poor form beforehand and had lost, I would have preferred Pompey to have had a better finishing run in the Premiership, but I still thought that the odds were heavily in Portsmouth's favour. When picking up on my accent, a Cardiff fan asked me on the Tube on the way to the Final how I thought the game would go, I replied that I expected that Pompey would play very defensively, get one goal somehow, and then close the game down. That was what happened. Sure enough, Harry selected a 4-5-1 formation to do the business. In goal it was James, and the back four was Johnson, Campbell, Distin, and Hreidarsson. The midfield was Utaka (Nugent 65), Muntari, Mendes (Diop 78), Diarra, and Krancjar. Alone up front was Kanu, until replaced by Baros three minutes from time. Cardiff took the game to Portsmouth early on, and, with Pompey's central midfield being less than commanding at that stage,

Ledley and Parry attacked at speed, and James had to move sharply to cut out Parry. After that, the five man midfield got a grip on Cardiff's four, and gradually Pompey asserted themselves, though it was an individual piece of sublime skill from Kanu that made the first opening in the twenty second minute. Kanu turned central defender Loovens, and fooled goalkeeper Enckelman, and, faced with an open goal, he steered the ball against a post and wide. It was a dreadful miss. In the thirty seventh minute, Utaka outwitted Capaldi and crossed to the near post. Enckelman tried but failed to catch the ball, and, as it ran loose, Kanu steered the ball into the net. For some reason, the referee, Mike Dean, took what seemed to be an eternity to signal a goal. Not long before half time, Dean was well placed to disallow what would have been an equaliser for Cardiff for handball by Loovens. The second half witnessed Cardiff being forced to resort to high balls that were gobbled up by Pompey's tall defence. '[Portsmouth] did what Redknapp's teams tend to do; they got hold of the ball in midfield and they passed it. Sometimes aggressively and sometimes conservatively, but always with a respect for possession and an awareness that this was how the Cup would be won.' So wrote Patrick Collins of *The Mail on Sunday*, adding that 'Mendes, Diarra, and Muntari organised that midfield with pleasing efficiency and set Cardiff a long afternoon chasing shadows. It was scarcely spectacular but it gave [their] earnestly striving [opponents] the kind of problems to which they had no answer.' Referee Dean somehow found four minutes of added time, but Cardiff never looked like piercing a defence that only let in one goal in the six ties needed to win the trophy. That Pompey only scored seven times in those six contests tells you largely what you needed to know about the methods used by the ruthless Redknapp.

'It was the best we [had] played in weeks,' David James told *The Observer*, 'At the whistle it hit me. I hadn't dared look at the clock before then. I didn't want to tbe distracted by the countdown. It's then that you think of the run in. The build up to [the Final] had been immense. No matter what people say about scrappy 1-0 wins, there were so many twists and turns en route to the Final - own goals, penalty saves, clearances off the line. The whole thing was entertaining, dazzling.' Like several other writers, Duncan Castles of *The Observer* went in for sentiment: 'The Pompey Chimes rang out as the F. A. Cup was liberated from the big boys and returned to an old south coast home. Seven years the grand old trophy spent at Fratton Park as football waited out the Second World War ... It was refreshing ... that Portsmouth v Cardiff guaranteed a first victory for a team outside the top tier's fearsome four since 1995.' Roy Collins of *The Sunday Telegraph* commented that 'the [2008 Final] was not a classic ... though compared to the dreadful fare served up by Manchester United and Chelsea last year ... it was a feast of football. Portsmouth had waited 69 years to win another F. A. Cup, which, frankly, is about how old their hero Kanu looked.' Well, maybe so, but, as Sol Campbell, Pompey's captain, collected the trophy, and the team ran to us in celebration, I cared only about the fact of victory.

CHAPTER 7: THE POMPEY CHIMES AND TIMES

So, a year after I had been pronounced ready for the graveyard, and several decades after those running Portsmouth Football Club had embarked on a series of suicide attempts with doubtless more to come in the future, I was walking away from the New Wembley Stadium and down Wembley Way in triumph with my Pompey flag donated to me by the sponsors. I was well aware that not only for the first time in my long life as a Pompey supporter Portsmouth had won every game I had seen them play in a football season; but also that the last of those victories in the 2007-2008 season had meant that Pompey had won the F.A. Cup and, thus, the fourth major honour in their history.

That Portsmouth had not won a serious trophy for 58 years, or, for that matter, won the F. A. Cup itself for no less than 69 years was unimpressive, and not just at first sight - but the harsh reality of the history of English football is ruthlessly emphasised by the fact that even now only 23 clubs have won the F. A. Cup and have also been English Champions. With the dates on which the clubs concerned first entered the Football League in brackets, these clubs are in alphabetical order: Arsenal (1893), Aston Villa (1888), Blackburn Rovers (1888), Burnley (1888), Chelsea (1905), Derby County (1888), Everton (1888), Huddersfield Town (1910), Ipswich Town (1938), Leeds United (1905 as Leeds City), Liverpool (1893), Manchester City (1892), Manchester United (1892), Sheffield United (1892), Sheffield Wednesday (1892), Sunderland (1890), Tottenham Hotspur (1908), West Bromwich Albion (1888), Wolverhampton Wanderers (1888). As for the dates on which these clubs attained the distinction of having been both English Champions and F. A. Cup holders during their history, then in alphabetical order the following picture emerges: Arsenal (1931), Aston Villa (1894), Blackburn (1912), Burnley (1921), Chelsea (1970), Derby County (1972), Everton (1906), Huddersfield Town (1924), Ipswich Town (1978), Leeds United (1972), Liverpool (1965),

Manchester City (1937), Manchester United (1909), Newcastle United (1910), Nottingham Forest (1978), Portsmouth (1949), Preston North End (1889), Sheffield United (1899), Sheffield Wednesday (1903), Sunderland (1937), Tottenham Hotspur (1961), West Bromwich Albion (1920), Wolverhampton Wanderers (1954).

The twelve founder members of the Football League were all drawn from the North of England and the Midlands, and this was true of the oldest clubs too. One can see the expanding the Football League in a dramatic manner shortly after the Fisrt World War gave that League more of a national character than before, but the establishment of a Second Division in 1892 had meant that clubs likely to achieve very much were already within the fold, especially once Spurs had become a member from 1908 onwards. Football had become so well established in the major centres of population in the North of England well before the First World War that there was little scope for newcomers to make their mark, and, sure enough, none of original members of the Third Division (North) ever went on to win a major honour, and this was true of later additions to that Division too. The South of England always seemed likely to be more promising territory, but those who expected clubs in the South outside London and several within its boundaries to achieve very much were to be disappointed. What may well have encouraged an optimistic outlook was that Spurs had won the F. A. Cup in 1901, and Southampton had been beaten finalists in 1900 and 1902, when members of the Southern League. Turning the First Division of that League into what eventually became the Third Division (South), though, did not greatly disturb the established clubs, except, of course, when the clubs admitted later inflicted the Cup upsets that delight the mass media and those people who love the underdog as a matter of principle. Of the latecomers, though, it will not take us very long to list the clubs other than Portsmouth who have achieved anything. Charlton won the F. A. Cup in 1947. Norwich City won the League Cup in 1985, having also won that trophy in 1962 when it could not seriously be considered to have ranked as a major honour. Queens Park Rangers and Swindon Town won the League Cup in 1967 and

1969 respectively, and in some style. Southampton won the F. A. Cup in 1976, and, thus, their only major honour. Oxford United, elected to the Football League in 1962, won the League Cup in 1986, before being relegated from the Football League in 2006 and returning four years later. Wimbledon, elected to the Football League in 1977, won the F. A. Cup in 1988, before going out of business in that form in 2004. Ipswich Town, elected to the Third Division (South) in 1938, proceeded to become the English Champions in 1962, F. A. Cup winners in 1978, and winners of the E. U. F. A. Cup in 1981.

The best of the rest, meaning the clubs who entered the English Football League at Third Division level after the First World War, has to be Portsmouth, because Pompey have in their history won back to back titles in the 1940s and F. A. Cup successes in 1939 and 2008. Even now, only fourteen clubs have been English Champions more times than Pompey, and none of them have a shorter League history. It is still the case that Pompey have won the title as many times as an important club like Spurs, and that an admirable club like West Ham have never won the title at all. So, there is every cause for Pompey supporters to be proud of what Portsmouth Football Club has achieved. I feel this pride myself, and it has helped to sustain me as as a Pompey fan with a record of loyalty going back all the way to the first season after the Second World War. In many ways it was fitting that my father and the other ultra loyalists of my distant youth had enjoyed Portsmouth's best days. Though they were long since dead, I thought of them all as I made my way back home on Cup Final day 2008. I hoped that I had been a good enough supporter over the years to presume to be their representative at New Wembley that day, much as I had been on other days at Barnsley, Burnley, Carlisle, Scunthorpe, and Tranmere and at the Railway End at Stockport, and at countless other best forgotten locations where Pompey have played in their time and in my presence. How those veterans of the past would have loved Cup Final day 2008, but, then, how they would have hated the long and tedious years waiting for more glory when those owning Portsmouth Football Club ran it in such an uninspiring and tawdry manner that for a lot of the time Pompey were not much more than Swindon by the Sea, or Watford with attitude.

The brutal reality is that Ordinary Joe clubs have to seize the time. What this meant was 17 May 2008 was Pompey's day in the sun, in the same way as it had been for Southampton on Cup Final day 1976, or for Coventry in 1987, or for Wimbledon in 1988, when those clubs won that trophy. These clubs then proceeded to win nothing that mattered. My delight at the winning of Portsmouth's fourth major honour was not accompanied by any belief that some sort of Golden Age would follow, unless, that is, the Gaydemak regime or some immensely rich successor transformed Pompey's financial base in a manner indicative of a secure and prosperous long term future. There was no sign of this, and this was crucial. Once the Premier League had really established itself, the sums of money needed to achieve any form of serious success came to be massive compared with the past. There would sometimes be exceptions to this rule, and Portsmouth in 2008 had been one of them in winning the F. A. Cup, but the brutal reality was that immense wealth had come to dominate the higher reaches of English football. Gale force renderings of the Pompey Chimes were not going to alter that reality: the predicament of Ordinary Joe clubs like Portsmouth has become unenviable. What happened to Pompey when the Gaydemak regime folded is for another book, but nobody who has lived the Portsmouth story, or, for that matter, who has read this book, would be at all surprised to learn that the ownership of Portsmouth Football Club was then taken on by a succession of strange individuals who had no serious money at all, but who still somehow passed the ownership tests that the inept football authorities administered. This was certainly an achievement for one of those supposed owners, since it eventually became clear that he had never existed anyway.

Responsibility without power, the prerogative of the mug throughout the ages – that is the lot of the football fan. Should they choose, such supporters can survey the world of football with well merited cynicism, unsurprised by the twists of fate that seem to conspire to make their lives a misery not just during the

196

ninety minutes with or without extra time and penalty shoot outs, but also in harsh retrospect. Sadly, real football fans cannot keep their emotional distance for very long, however wise that detachment would be in principle. In practice, they will always be back for more. This is because football is an addiction, a form of illness, and, for people like me, there is no known cure. I have been told many times, and rightly so, that in my personal life I am an enviably happy man, and, to state the obvious, that means that I have been very lucky. Supporting Portsmouth this side of the 1955-56 season has proved to be the only part of my life that has not worked out, but nobody forced me to adhere to this commitment, and that I have done so is solely my responsibility. So, I have no regrets. Whatever happens in the future, nobody can sensibly deny that Portsmouth have made a contribution to English football in producing one indisputably great team, and the winning of four major honours is impressive in relation to clubs of comparable standing. That said, though, the City of Portsmouth, with its proud history and its war memorials covered it seems endlessly with the names of the dead, has deserved better than the fools who have so often run the football club that bears its name. The Pompey supporters have deserved better too, but then all football fans think that. As for myself, I will continue to support Portsmouth Football Club until its death or my own. In my case, exasperation at yet another Pompey defeat and its manner would seem to be the most likely cause of, say, a heart attack, which, of course, would be a suitably ironic way for a fitness fanatic to go. If so, it would not surprise me if I dropped down dying in a disagreeable setting, such as the men's lavatories at the away end at somewhere like Blackburn or Bury. If this proves to be my fate, I hope that I will have the presence of mind to make my last words 'Tell my wife that I will always love her.' Like most football widows, though, she would probably bet serious money on those last words being 'Play Up Pompey.'

Printed in Great Britain
by Amazon